Momentum
Explained

Martin J. Pring on Technical Analysis Series

Momentum Explained, Volume I
How to Select Stocks Using Technical Analysis
Candlesticks Explained
Technician's Guide to Day and Swing Trading
Breaking the Black Box

Momentum Explained

Volume II

Martin J. Pring

McGraw-Hill
New York   Chicago   San Francisco
Lisbon   London   Madrid   Mexico City   Milan
New Delhi   San Juan   Seoul   Singapore
Sydney   Toronto

Library of Congress Cataloging-in-Publication Data

Pring, Martin J.
    Momentum explained, vol. 2 / by Martin J. Pring.
        p.   cm.
    ISBN 0-07-139859-7
    1. Investment analysis. I. Title.

  HG4529 .P7478 2002
  332.63'2042—dc21   2002003845

McGraw-Hill

A Division of The McGraw·Hill Companies

1 2 3 4 5 6 7 8 9 0   AGM/AGM   0 8 7 6 5 4 3 2

p/n 0-07-139859-7
part of ISBN: 0-07-138403-0

The sponsoring editor for this book was Stephen Isaacs and the production supervisor was Clare Stanley. It was set in New Baskerville by MacAllister Publishing Services, LLC.

Printed and bound by Quebecor/Martinsburg

This publication is designed to provide accurate and authoritative information in regard to the subject matter covered. It is sold with the understanding that neither the author nor the publisher is engaged in rendering legal, accounting, or other professional service. If legal advice or other expert assistance is required, the services of a competent professional person should be sought.

—From a Declaration of Principles jointly adopted
by a Committee of the American Bar
Association and a Committee of Publishers

McGraw-Hill books are available at special quantity discounts to use as premiums and sales promotions, or for use in corporate training programs. For more information, please write to the Director of Special Sales, Professional Publishing, McGraw-Hill, Two Penn Plaza, New York, NY 10121-2298. Or contact your local bookstore.

 This book is printed on recycled, acid-free paper containing a minimum of 50% recycled de-inked fiber.

To my beloved wife, Lisa

Contents

Acknowledgments		ix
Preface		xi
1.	Linear Regression Lines	1
2.	Linear Regression Indicator	4
3.	R-Square	10
4.	Linear Regression Slope	18
5.	Volume Rate of Change	29
6.	Volume Oscillator	42
7.	The Chaikan Money Flow Indicator	56
8.	The Demand Index	70
9.	The Chande Momentum Oscillator	86
10.	The Relative Momentum Index	97
11.	The Dynamic Momentum Index	110
12.	The Klinger Oscillator	121
13.	The Herrick Payoff Index	127
14.	The TRIX Index	141

15.	Aroon	151
16.	Qstick	157
17.	The Relative Volatility Index	163
18.	The Inertia Indicator	167
19.	The Directional Movement System	171
20.	Interpreting the ADX and the Directional Indicators	181
21.	Extremes in the ADX	193
22.	The Commodity Selection Index	203
23.	The Parabolic Indicator	207
24.	Price Projection Bands	225
25.	Price Projection Oscillator	232
	Appendix A	242
	Appendix B	256
	Quiz Answers	266
	Index	275
	Installation Instructions	289

Acknowledgments

The year 2002 will see the publication of eight of my books by McGraw-Hill. Six of these form part of the Martin J. Pring on Technical Analysis Series, a series of multi-media CD-ROM/workbook tutorials. None of this would have been possible without the help of several key people.

In particular I would like to thank Jimmie Sigsway, my wonderful mother-in-law, whose support of our busy family allowed both me and my wife, Lisa, to allocated sufficient time to work on this project.

Without a doubt, a might thanks goes to Jeff Howard of Interactive Software Design, who has, as usual, pulled out all the stops and done a superb job creating the installation program and multimedia programming for the CD-ROM tutorial contained at the back of this book.

I would also like to thank many of our subscribers, workshop attendees, and purchasers of our CD-ROMs, whose kind and constructive comments have greatly encouraged me to expand the "Pring library."

Above all, a special thanks goes to my wife, Lisa, who, despite multiple pressures from major domestic construction work, minding the kids (including me), cooking the meals, and maintaining our Web site at pring.com, was still able to deliver the artwork for this book on time.

Preface

This book forms part of the series *Martin J. Pring on Technical Analysis.* Like all the others in the series, its main value lies in the CD-ROM enclosed in the back cover. This little disk contains a complete multi-media presentation of the subject matter contained in the workbook.

Years ago I published videos on technical analysis, but the CD_ROM format is far superior. Not only does each chapter play as a continuous presentation but also the need to fast forward or rewind is eliminated. Instead, the user can click on any subject matter in the contents and move instantly there. This format also allows for an interactive quiz, so the user can quickly move through multiple choice questions or chart examples, all of which are scored at the end. In this way, you can easily discover any area that needs brushing up. The only title in the series that does not contain a quiz is *How to Select Stocks Using Technical Analysis.*

The series itself is designed to expand on several of the subjects covered in the fourth edition of *Technical Analysis Explained.* Each of the book/CD-ROM combinations takes the reader into greater depth on the individual subjects. Diagrams and theoretical concepts are explained and then adapted to practical marketplace examples. It is normal in presentations of this nature to indicate the strong points of any indicator or concept, but these presentations also advise you of any known weaknesses of pitfalls they may have.

Technical analysis is the art of identifying trend reversals at a relatively early stage and riding on that trend until the weight of the evidence shows or proves that the trend has reversed. The objective of this series is to present a substantial amount of that evidence in the form of indicators and concepts, so that readers of the workbooks and viewers of the CD-ROMs will be in a stronger position to identify such trend reversals. Please take note of the fact that technical analysis deals in probabilities, *never* certainties. Armed with the information in this series, the probabilities should now move heavily in your favor.

With that in mind, good luck and good charting!

Martin J. Pring
Sarasota, Florida

Momentum
Explained

1
Linear Regression Lines

Introduction

In recent years, some of the more mathematically inclined technical analysts have started to apply several well-known statistical techniques to the markets with the objective of trying to identify price trend reversals at a relatively early stage. One of these is linear regression. Indeed, linear regression forms the basis of several of these relatively new indicators. This section of the book explains some of these finer points, but to begin, I would like to briefly discuss the application of a simple linear regression line.

Technicians have worked for decades with the technique of smoothing data with various types of moving averages. The idea is to simply smooth the data to iron out random fluctuations. In this way, it is possible to gain a better understanding of the underlying trend. The linear regression line is another technique for obtaining this same objective.

Linear Regression

The linear regression line, just like a moving average, is based on the trend of a security's price over a given timespan. The trend is determined by calculating a linear regression, using the mathematical technique of least squares fit. To individuals not well versed in mathematics like myself, that sounds a bit intimidating, but in reality it is not.

1

Essentially, this technique fits a trendline to the chart's data by minimizing the distance between the data points and the linear regression trendline. In effect, the line is drawn through the middle of the data, as shown in Chart 1-1. I have made a comparison between a linear regression line and a moving average, but as you can see, in many respects a linear regression line is really a statistically derived trendline. In a way, the linear regression line is a kind of equilibrium point for the prices included in its calculation. Consequently, the line acts as a rubber leash. If prices fluctuate too much from the line, they may be expected to be pulled back toward it before flying off in the other direction. In Chart 1-2, for instance, the linear regression line is bounded by two parallel lines that act as constraints on upward and downward price movements.

Chart 1-1   McDonald's and a linear regression line. (Source: *pring.com*)

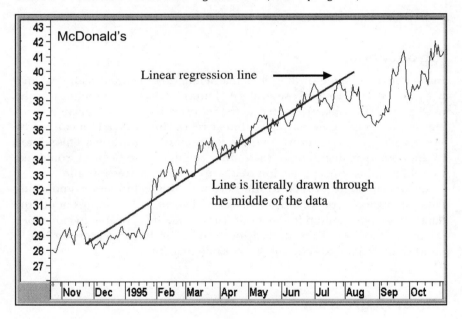

Chart 1-2 McDonald's and parallel linear regression lines. (Source: *pring.com*)

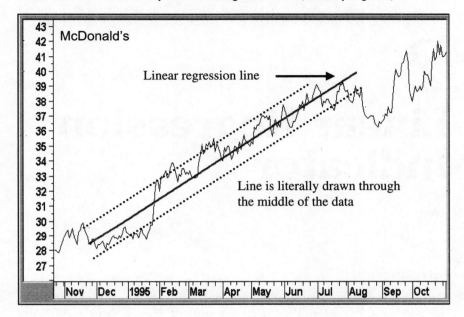

Linear regression lines are not particularly useful in their own right, but several very useful indicators have been derived from this basic calculation. They are the subject of this first few chapters of the book. Chapter 2 will begin this discussion with an explanation of the linear regression indicator.

2
Linear Regression Indicator

Introduction

The linear regression indicator plots the last point of a linear regression line, but it does so continuously. Charts 2-1 and 2-2 feature three solid linear regression trendlines. Each has a length of two calendar months, which roughly corresponds with 40 trading periods. The smoother line is a 40-period linear regression indicator, which intersects the ends of each trendline. In a sense, the regression indicator is like a kind of moving average. The longer the timespan, the slower it is to turn because it connects endpoints of linear regression trendlines that are much longer. This means that linear regression indicators based on longer lines (or timeframes) experience fewer whipsaws. If the timespan is short, the line gives more timely buy-or-sell signals but many commensurately more false signals.

Interpretation

The interpretation of linear regression indicators is similar to that of moving averages. The linear regression indicator, though, has two advantages. First, the regression method does not experience as much of a delay. This is because it is calculated by fitting the line to the data points, rather than by averaging them. In effect, the linear regression indicator is more responsive to price changes.

In Chart 2-3, the moving average has been plotted as a solid line and the linear regression indicator as a dashed one. Both have a 30-day timespan.

Chart 2-1 American Century 2020 Fund and a linear regression indicator. (Source: *pring.com*)

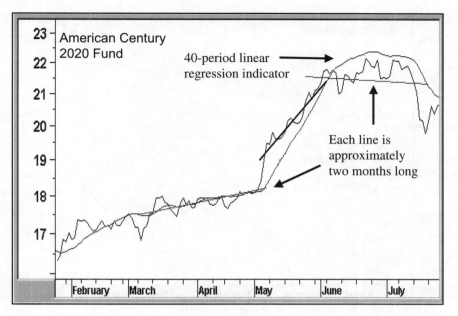

Chart 2-2 American Century 2020 Fund and a linear regression indicator. (Source: *pring.com*)

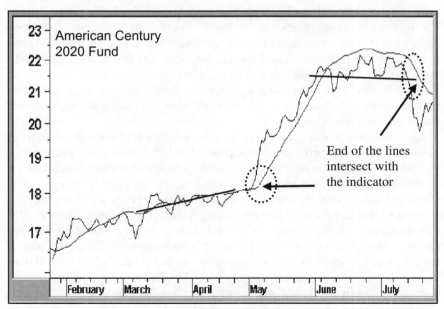

Chart 2-3 S & P Composite comparing an MA to a linear-regression indicator. (Source: *pring.com*)

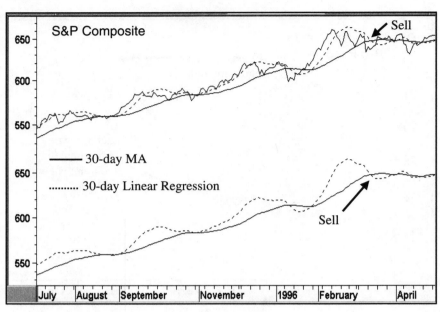

You can see how the regression line turns ahead of the simple average in every instance. Both have been plotted separately in the lower panel, where the leading characteristics of the linear regression indicator are more apparent. It is also possible to create an indicator based on the interrelationship between the two. The idea is to buy when the linear regression indicator crosses above or below the moving average, as in February 1996 in Chart 2-3. This is by no means a perfect indicator, but you might want to take some trouble researching it through your charting software's system tester optimization feature.

A second aspect of the linear regression indicator is that it is a rough forecast of the next period's price but plotted today (Chart 2-4). This occurs because the regression indicator is a statistical extension of the data included in the calculation. Only when the price itself changes direction for a couple of periods does the indicator reverse direction. However, since it is still moving in the direction of the prevailing trend, the regression line is able to experience a crossover more quickly than a simple, even exponential, moving average using the same timespan. This is shown in Chart 2-5, where the initial crossover of the linear regression indicator takes place several days prior to that of the 30-day moving average (MA). Also note how the regression line extends its upward trajectory well after the price peak.

Chart 2-4 S & P Composite comparing an MA to a linear regression indicator. (Source: *pring.com*)

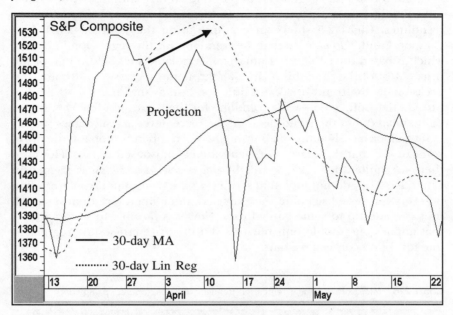

Chart 2-5 American Century 2020 Fund and linear regression trendline analysis. (Source: *pring.com*)

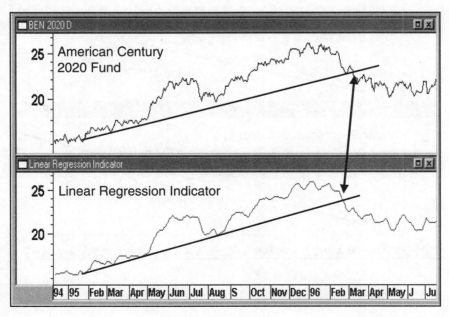

Since the regression indicator is a very responsive type of moving average, one very useful approach is to plot one average with a relatively short-term timespan in a separate window and use it as a basis for constructing trendlines. Chart 2-5 shows an example using the Benham 2020 Zero Coupon Fund. You can see that the trendline for the regression indicator, which is based on a 15-period timespan, is violated well before that of the price. Most of the time this technique favors the regression indicator, but occasionally the trend break is a little too fast, as shown in Chart 2-6 featuring Microsoft. See how the trendline for the regression line is only partially violated, but the trend break in the price never actually takes place.

If you look closely at the relationship between this indicator and the price, you can see that there are some fairly timely buy-or-sell signals. However, there are quite a few what we might call *inconvenient whipsaws* flagged in Chart 2-7. They do not look that serious on the chart, but if you are acting on every buy-or-sell signal in the expected, disciplined way, then such failures can add up to some costly losses. Now it is possible to set up a filter that implies one should only buy or sell if the price crosses the regression line for 2 or 3 consecutive days.

Chart 2-6   Microsoft and linear regression trendline analysis. (Source: *pring.com*)

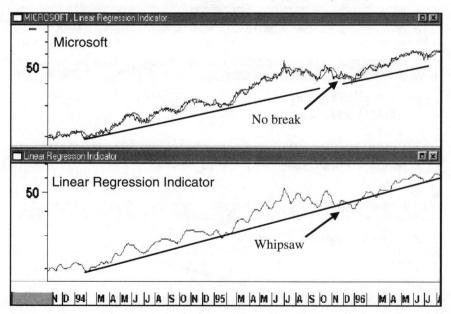

Chart 2-7 Microsoft and linear-regression trendline analysis. (Source: *pring.com*)

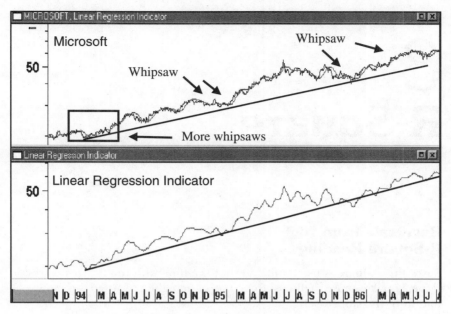

As an alternative, I tested for several combinations of timespan and filtering mechanisms based on a percentage crossover. In other words, the rule might be "buy when the price crosses 1 percent above the linear regression indicator, sell when it falls 1.5 percent below," and so forth. This was not a scientifically based test because I only used five or six securities, each with about 4 years of history. What I did find with this initial test was that crossovers of the 20- and 35-day timespans usually offered a profitable result when combined with a 1.5-percent filter for buy signals and a 2-percent filter for sell signals. In other words, when the close rallied 1.5 percent above the regression line, it qualified as a buy signal, and when it fell 2 percent below the line, it was a sell signal. What did surprise me about all the tests was that there was a very high persistence to create profits, whatever the combination of timespan and filtering. I am sure this was partly due to the fact that more than half of my sample consisted of stocks in a bull market, but even those that lost money on a buy-hold approach had a surprisingly small amount of losses in my test. The range of periods tested was 10 to 65 days.

3
R-Square

Reversals from High R-Square Readings

Since the r-square is used quite a lot of the time with the linear regression slope, it makes sense to discuss this concept first, then proceed with an explanation of the slope itself.

Moving averages offer us the basic ingredient for many other indicators, so, too, does the regression technique. One example is the r-square indicator. The objective of r-square is to show the *strength* of a move, as opposed to its *direction*. The direction, can be derived from overbought-or-oversold readings in the momentum indicators. There are also some methods for determining direction from the regression approach, as we shall later learn. Essentially, the r-square calculation tries to display the amount of a price trend that can be expressed purely as a trend factor and that part which is explained as random noise. *The higher the reading, the greater is the trend factor and the lower the random noise.* Also, the longer the time span from which the r-square is calculated, the lower the r-square value needed to determine if a trend is statistically significant. One of the things about rising and falling trends is that once they start to lose momentum, the price either consolidates or reverses. Since the r-square indicator can provide some useful information on when a trend is starting to lose momentum, it is possible to use peaks in this indicator as a signal that a trading range is about to start or that the trend itself is close to a reversal. Chart 3-1 features a 35-day

Chart 3-1 The FTSE Index and a 35-day r-square. (Source: *pring.com*)

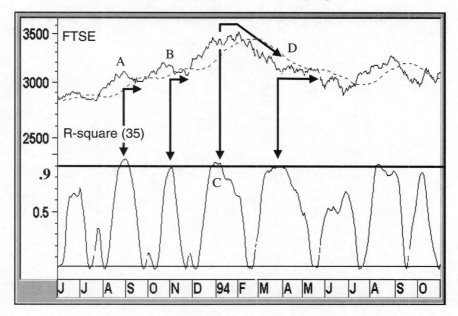

r-square indicator. The arrows against the price indicate when it reverses direction from above its 0.9 overbought zone. The first one (A) signaled a temporary interruption of the strong uptrend that at B just touched the overbought line, but the result was similar. Finally, the overbought reversal at C signaled a loss of upside momentum quite close to the final peak. This indicator is not directionally biased, so it does not differentiate between an up- or downtrend. At point D, the overbought reversal developed after a strong downtrend, and it was followed by a sideways trend or a consolidation of losses.

Reversals from Low R-square Readings

The r-square can also be used to help determine when a trading range market is about to give way to a trending one. In Chart 3-2 the solid and dashed arrows indicate when the r-square indicator first touches the oversold, or I should say *trendless*, level. The concept revolves around the idea that if a market has been in a trading range and the r-square reverses direction to the

Chart 3-2   The FTSE Index and a 35-day r-square. (Source: *pring.com*)

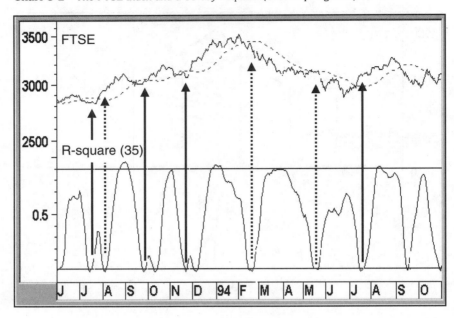

upside from a low reading, this should indicate a trending market. I have drawn the arrows at those points where it is obvious that the r-square has bottomed. Quite often, this occurs as the price is breaking out from a consolidation, so two pieces of evidence of a potential trending market are given. Chart 3-3 shows some classic examples: first, at the February 1994 top, and second, at the resumption of the downtrend in March 1994. The three examples between July and September in Chart 3-4 did not offer such obvious chart points, although the moving-average crossovers did trigger signals that the consolidation period was over. In this case, the average is a 25-day simple average that has been advanced by seven periods. In situations where a signal is triggered well after the price has reached its turning point, such as that in Chart 3-5, it is as well to move on to another situation. This example is shown with the benefit of hindsight, but what would we have done in the actual market place? After all, we did not know at the time how long the r-square was going to remain in the trendless zone. The answer lies in looking at the other indicators to see what they are doing. One should never buy and sell on r-square alone. In most of the examples shown in Chart 3-3, the price gave some good trend-reversal signals. However, it is as well to check out some momentum indicators to add additional weight to any trend-reversal possibilities.

Chart 3-3 The FTSE Index and a 35-day r-square. (Source: *pring.com*)

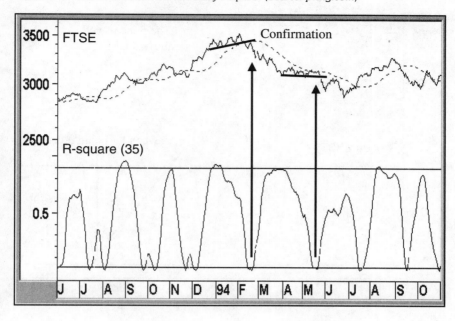

Chart 3-4 The FTSE Index and a 35-day r-square. (Source: *pring.com*)

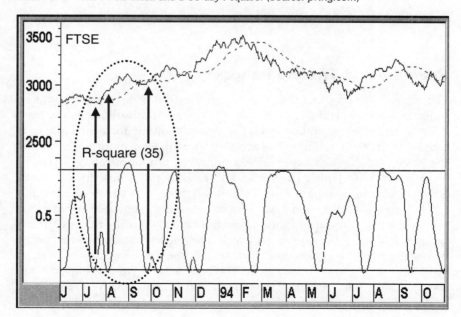

Chart 3-5 The FTSE Index and a 35-day r-square. (Source: *pring.com*)

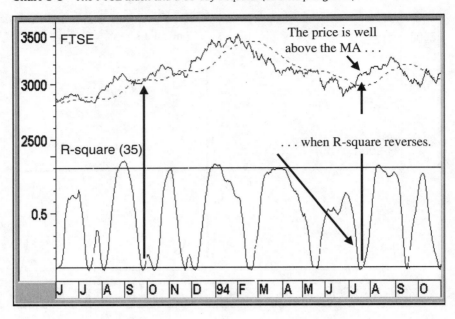

R-square and Trading Ranges

Sometimes, the very fact that the r-square indicator does form a trading range can be especially useful. In Chart 3-6 we see it consolidate in the over-bought region for several periods. The violation of the horizontal line indicated that the period of trending was over. The top formation suggested that the price was about to experience a period of non-uptrending, that is, a change in the prevailing (up)trend This could imply a new downtrend or a period of trading-range activity. Chart 3-7 shows that the price action in the box following this signal was indeed a trading range. Shortly after we see another price pattern in the r-square (Chart 3-8), only this time it is a bottom. In effect, the r-square indicator is telling us that a trending market is now the most likely outcome. In this case, the three-week consolidation was followed by a two-week downtrend (Chart 3-9). Again, it is important to use these signals in combination with other indicators, which can then help to determine the direction of the new trend.

Chart 3-6 The Philadelphia Gold and Silver Share Index, FTSE Index, and a 35-day r-square. (Source: *pring.com*)

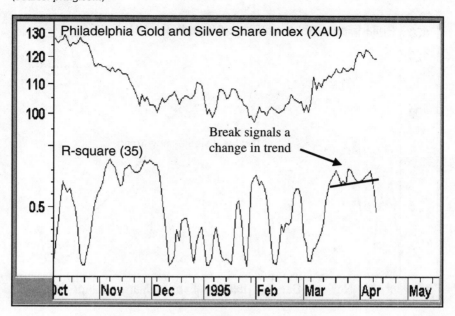

Chart 3-7 The Philadelphia Gold and Silver Share Index, FTSE Index, and a 35-day r-square. (Source: *pring.com*)

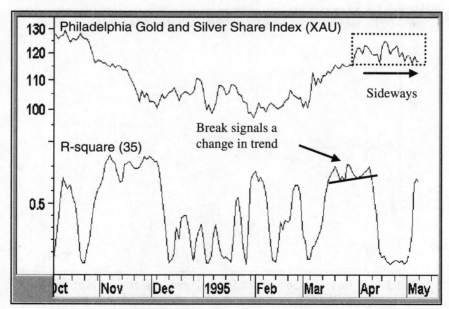

Chart 3-8   The Philadelphia Gold and Silver Share Index, FTSE Index, and a 35-day r-square. (Source: *pring.com*)

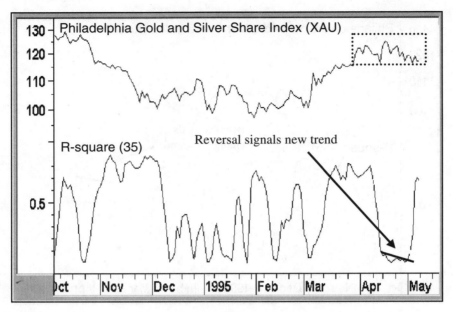

Chart 3-9   The Philadelphia Gold and Silver Share Index, FTSE Index, and a 35-day r-square. (Source: *pring.com*)

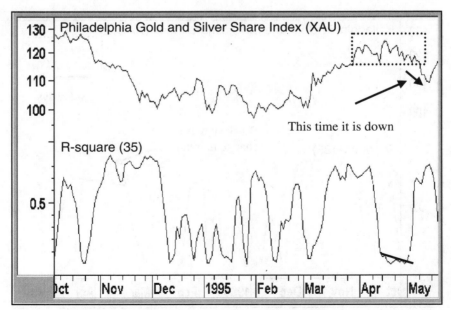

Chart 3-10 The FTSE Index and a 35-day r-square. (Source: *pring.com*)

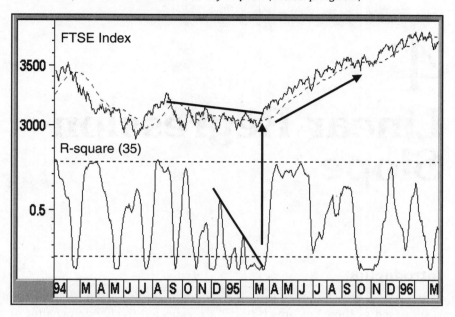

Finally, Chart 3-10 shows an r-square indicator that experiences a smaller-and-smaller trading range. When it finally breaks out on the upside and is confirmed by the price, a very strong trending move results. In Chapter 4 we will learn how the r-square can be used in conjunction with the next linear regression indicator to be covered, and that is the linear regression slope.

4
Linear Regression Slope

Introduction

The *linear regression slope* is a variation on the linear regression indicator. It is supposed to show how much prices are expected to change per unit of time, otherwise known as *rise over run*. Just think of the linear slope as a momentum indicator derived from the linear regression indicator. The dashed line in the upper panel in Chart 4-1 of General Motors, features a 14-day linear regression indicator. The lower panel displays a 14-day linear slope. Chart 4-2 shows a variation by moving the linear regression indicator to the lower panel. It is evident that the fluctuations of both series are very similar. As with all momentum indicators, the linear slope has a tendency to lead the linear regression indicator itself. An example is shown at A.

We can even take it a little further. In Chart 4-3 the three series have been separated. Note how all three trendlines were all violated at around the same time, thereby offering a very strong buy signal. Remember, the more indicators pointing in the same direction, the greater the probability that the signal will be valid, and the greater the chances that a good trending move will follow. That was certainly true of the rally that followed this triple upside breakout. Then, in October it was possible to reverse the procedure with the construction of three more trendlines. Again a worthwhile trend followed.

Chart 4-1   General Motors and a 14 linear regression slope. (Source: *pring.com*)

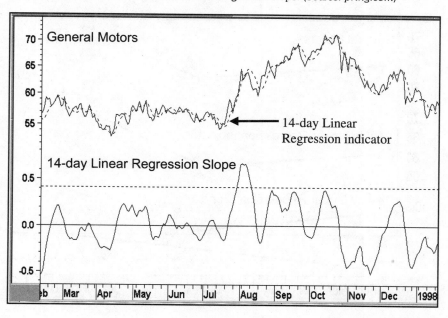

Chart 4-2   General Motors and a 14 linear regression slope. (Source: *pring.com*)

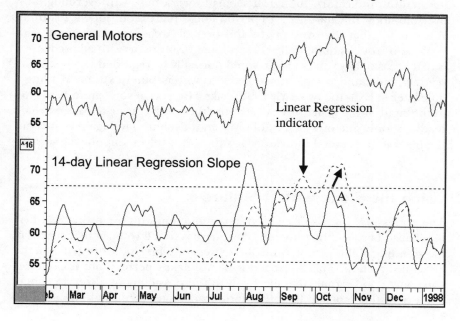

Chart 4-3   General Motors and two linear regression indicators. (Source: *pring.com*)

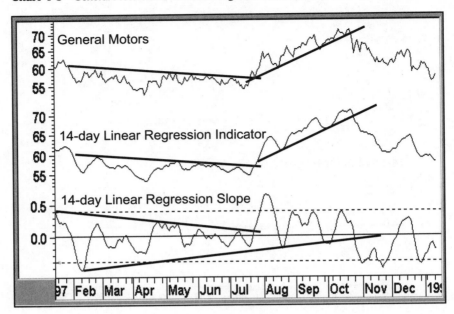

The interpretation of the linear regression slope is very similar to other momentum indicators, though it seems to work best with overbought-or-oversold lines. In Chart 4-4 a 14-period linear regression slope is featured. You can see that the overbought and oversold readings correspond with peaks and troughs quite well. The problem with this, as with all oscillators, is that occasionally you get what would normally be regarded as an extreme reading, indicating a top, only to be faced with another extreme reading a little later, such as the two early 1992 peaks. However, if you continue to look to the right of the chart you can see that there is a cluster of four extreme readings, only one of which is followed by a decline. This again points out the need to use several indicators at a time, not relying on one alone.

Using the Slope with R-Square

The regression slope is often used in conjunction with the r-square indicator. This is because the function of r-square is to tell you whether a market has trending ability or not, while the regression slope indicator tells you the general direction. This approach is by no means perfect, but it can offer you some good signals that alert you to the possibility of a trend change. You would then consult the other indicators to get confirmation.

Chart 4-4   General Motors and a 14 linear regression slope. (Source: *pring.com*)

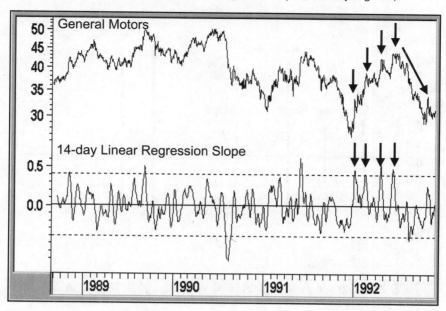

Chart 4-5 features a 45-day regression slope and a 45-day r-square. It is then a good idea to look for those periods when the slope is either overbought or oversold and where the r-square indicator is also at an extreme high. If the slope is overbought and starting to decline, this tells you that the trend is about to reverse to the downside. Confirmation of this is given by the r-square also reaching an extreme, because this indicates that the trend is weakening.

Chart 4-5 features 45-day timespans on both indicators. The thick vertical arrows indicate where both series are rolling over from an overbought level. As a general rule, this type of timespan when used in conjunction with these indicators, appears to work reasonably well. The dashed arrow represents a bottoming signal, since the slope indicator was deeply oversold when the r-square was at an extreme. However, the slope indicator got to oversold during September 1992, but there was no extreme reading in the r-square. That is why the arrow is represented in a half signal or dashed format.

Chart 4-6 shows a 45-day period for the slope and a 30-day one for the r-square. Once again we are considering that the r-square indicates whether a security price is trending or not, while the slope tells you the direction of the trend and when it is overextended.

Chart 4-5   Ford, a linear regression slope, and an r-square. (Source: *pring.com*)

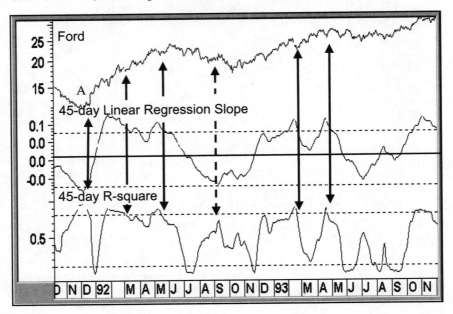

Chart 4-6   CRB Composite, a linear regression slope, and an r-square. (Source: *pring.com*)

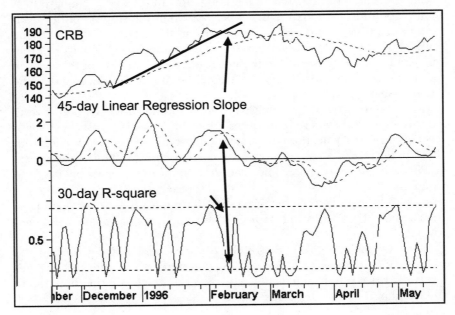

This means that you should look for an extreme in the slope that has begun to reverse and then for a high and reversal reading in the r-square. Remember, a high reading in the r-square indicates that the price trend has a high trending quotient and a low random noise factor. When r-square reverses, then it is telling us that the trend is also dissipating. This can mean either that an actual reversal or a sideways trend is about to start.

The arrows flag when the r-square has retreated from an overextended reading, and this is confirmed by the slope crossing its 10-day linear regression indicator. You can see that the price also violated its trendline. In this particular instance, the new trend was sideways rather than a downward one. See how the price moves in a slightly declining trading range in this area. Then, the r-square breaks out from a base. Remember, low r-square readings mean that there is no discernible trend, so a rally in r-square offers the probability that a new trend is beginning. The combination of the sell signal in the linear regression slope at this point, and the price trend break here, indicated that this new trend was most likely going to be negative.

In March 1996, charting r-square peaks and the slope gives a buy signal from an oversold condition (Chart 4-7). This should have indicated a rally. A small one did materialize, but it was never possible to construct a meaningful trendline for the price. Actually, what happened was a trading range between March and April. Then in late April, the r-square violates a down-

Chart 4-7 CRB Composite, a linear regression slope, and an r-square. (Source: *pring.com*)

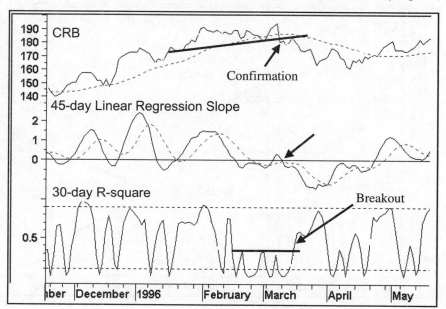

trend (Chart 4-8), indicating a trending market; the slope diverges positively with the price and gives a buy signal, and finally the price violates a good downtrend signalling that a new trend has begun. Notice that the price also violates its moving average at the same time the trendline is violated. This provides additional evidence that the tend has reversed.

One of the important points to note about this particular combination of indicators is that you have to hunt down specific situations, possibly using the other indicators, such as the smoothed RSI, as a filter. This is because the r-square does not give such clear-cut signals as many of the smoother series.

Linear Slope and Long-Term Momentum

There is no reason why the linear regression slope cannot be employed to monitor long-term, or primary, trends in momentum. That is precisely what Chart 4-9 tries to do. The trend's status is determined by the relationship of a 400-day linear slope to its 100-day simple moving average. If the indicator is above its average, and the price is above its 100-day moving average, the trend is regarded as bullish and the price is represented as a thin line. If the slope is positive but the price is below its 100-day MA, this downgrades

Chart 4-8   CRB Composite, a linear regression slope, and an r-square. (Source: *pring.com*)

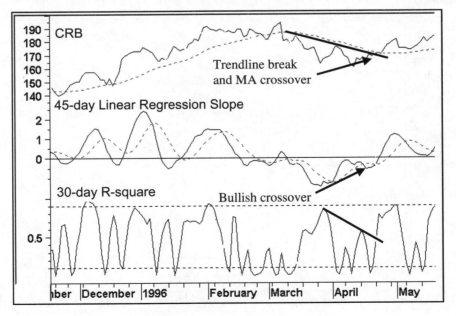

Chart 4-9   TSE Oil and Gas Index and a linear regression slope indicator. (Source: *pring.com*)

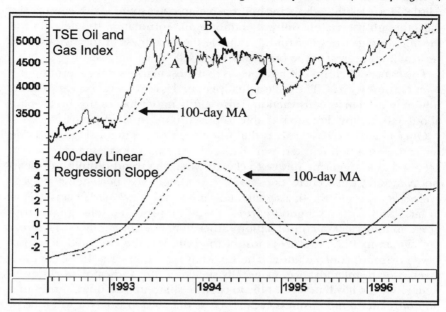

the trend to neutral and the price plot is displayed in gray. A neutral trend is also called for when the price is above the 100-day moving average but the indicator is below its average, and a bearish trend occurs when both the price and the slope are below their moving averages and so is reflected by a thick line.

The price moving averages have been introduced as a fail-safe for those periods when the price moves too quickly for the slow-moving slope indicator to catch.

The neutral trend sometimes serves as an early warning that the primary trend is about to reverse, since the system will sometimes move into a neutral trend just prior to going bullish or bearish. A great deal will depend on the degree to which the slope is overbought or oversold. The more overextended it is, the greater the possibility that a neutral trend signal will begin a new primary trend.

In this example of the TSE Oil and Gas Index, the neutral trend preceded a bearish one in late 1993. But if you look at the position of the slope, you can see why: it was very overextended. A little later on, the trend moves back to neutral again. However, there was little chance of a reversal in the primary trend because the slope was still very overextended.

Chart 4-10 again plots a 400-day linear regression slope together with its 100-day moving average. The moving average has also been shifted to the right by 20 periods. This means that crossovers by the regression slope are delayed a little. However, this advancing approach eliminates some of the whipsaw signals, though it certainly will not eliminate all. Fortunately, the delay in the moving average does not unduly impede the timeliness of the signals. The vertical lines represent the buy (thick) and sell (thin) signals.

The concept behind this indicator is that most markets revolve around the 4-year business cycle. The cycle actually is a bit less than 4 years. The 400-day timespan used in its construction is also a little under half of the 4-year span, about 940 trading days, so it is able to pick up the 4-year rhythms.

Once again, the basic rule is that when the slope is in a rising trend, the security is in a bull market, and vice versa. The moving-average crossovers are used as a triggering device to classify when the trend is bullish or bearish. Naturally, the security does not always oblige by experiencing a 4-year cycle. For example, the first signal totally misses the 1987 market crash. That in late 1988 captures a good part of the rally and then a sell signal is triggered in mid 1990. A consolidation rather than a decline follows. The next buy signal, in 1992, captures most of the rally and the late-1993 sell is followed by more consolidation. The final buy signal, in early 1995, captures a very worthwhile advance. Generally speaking, this indicator works quite well. However, it will never be able to capture sharp up-and-down moves that do not relate to the business cycle, such as the 1987 crash. Nor will it be of

Chart 4-10 ASE Oil and Gas Index and a linear regression slope indicator. (Source: *pring.com*)

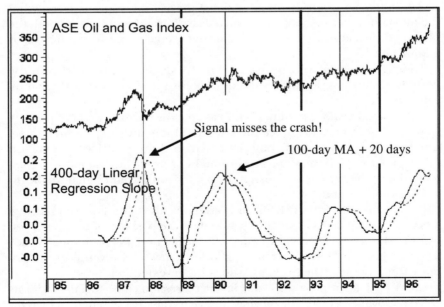

much help in strong trending markets, such as the Japanese bull market of the 1980s or the bull market in the United States that began in 1990. One way in which it can be effectively used is to look for periods when it is at an extreme overbought or oversold level because at that point, the risk of a major reversal is that much higher. In 1987, for example, the indicator was clearly overextended, so it should not have been surprising that a sharp correction of some kind would develop. In a situation such as that, where the slope is overextended, be on the lookout for negative divergences in your short-term indicators that can be confirmed with a good trendline break in the price. Quite often, when the slope is overextended and starting to flatten, the next short-term decline can act as the first trigger in a kind of domino effect.

Linear Slope and Weekly Data

When I first converted the 400-day timespan to the weekly format, I found that the indicator did not experience the nice swings that are apparent on the daily chart. Consequently, I decided to expand the timespan out to 104-weeks, or 2-years, and to use a 26-week, or 6-month, moving average (Chart 4-11). The triggering average for the price is 26-weeks.

Chart 4-11 ASE Oil and Gas Index and a linear regression slope indicator. (Source: *pring.com*)

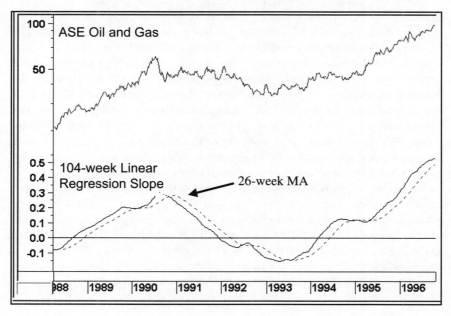

Chart 4-12 American Electric Power and two linear regression slope indicators. (Source: *pring.com*)

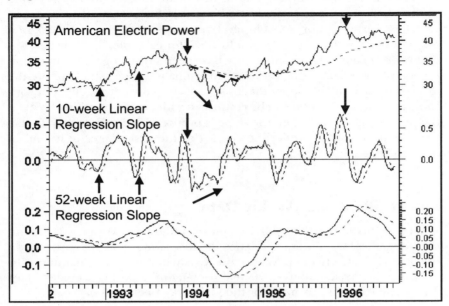

The same bullish, bearish, and neutral trends are highlighted, and the principles of interpretation are the same as with the daily linear slope.

Chart 4-12 features a 10- and 52-week linear slope on the same chart. The 52-week series attempts to reflect the 4-year cycle and, therefore, serves as a proxy for the long-term trend. The effect is very similar to the 400-day series considered previously. The moving average is a 5-period one for the 10-week series and a 10-week one for the 52-week slope. The average plotted against the price is a 65-week Exponential Moving Average (EMA). The 10-week series is used to time short-term trends and the 52-week indicator to identify the direction and maturity of the long-term, or primary, trend. The 10-week slope can also be interpreted with positive and negative divergences, though these are rare relative to other oscillators.

Moving-average crossovers by the 10-week series can be used to time intermediate rallies and reactions. Some of these are highlighted with the upward- and downward-sloping arrows. A positive divergence develops right at the bottom of the 1994 decline, and this is confirmed then by the price breaking above the dashed trendline in the early summer of 1994. Later on the 52-week series crosses above its moving average and this is confirmed by the price completing a reverse head-and-shoulders pattern.

5
Volume Rate of Change

The Basics

The basic principles of volume interpretation are covered in our Introduction to *Technical Analysis CD-ROM Workbook Tutorial,* so it is assumed that you are already aware that it is normal for volume to go in the direction of the prevailing trend, that is, expanding on rallies and contracting on declines. It is also assumed that volume in an uptrend will usually lead price. In these next few sessions, we will be dealing with momentum indicators that are derived from volume alone or a combination of price and volume.

Normally, volume is displayed as a histogram underneath the price, as in Chart 5-1. A quick glance at any chart often reveals a noticeable increase in the size of the volume bars that are associated with breakouts, selling climaxes, and so forth. This is all well and good, but occasionally there are subtle shifts in the level of volume that are not easily detectable by this method. By massaging the volume data with an ROC calculation, it is possible to observe some new insights into the dynamics of volume interpretation. This is very important, since most of the indicators we deal with are a statistical variation on the price. However, an oscillator based purely on volume can give us a totally independent view of what is happening under the surface.

Chart 5-2 shows a 10-day ROC of volume, together with a regular volume histogram. As the price is breaking above the trendline in August, we do not get much of an impression that volume is expanding if we just look at the histogram. However, the ROC shows a definite jump over a period of several days, thereby confirming the breakout.

Chart 5-3 shows the opposite set of circumstances, where the ROC rallies sharply prior to the breakout. But when the breakout materializes, the ROC

Chart 5-1 DuPont 1999–2000 and a volume histogram. (Source: *pring.com*)

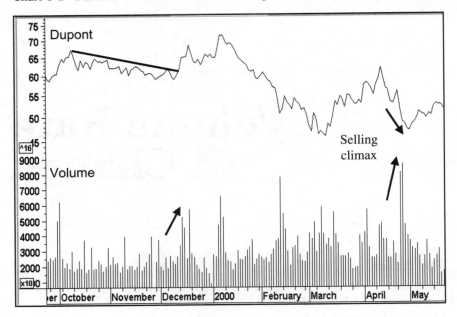

Chart 5-2 Briggs and Stratton volume histogram versus volume ROC. (Source: *pring.com*)

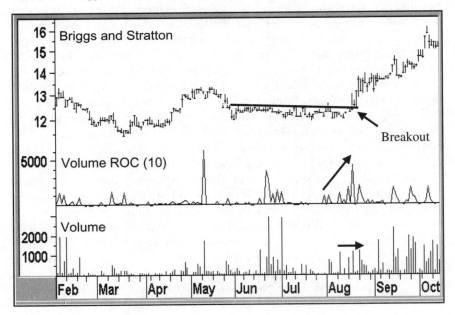

Chart 5-3 Briggs and Stratton volume histogram versus volume ROC. (Source: *pring.com*)

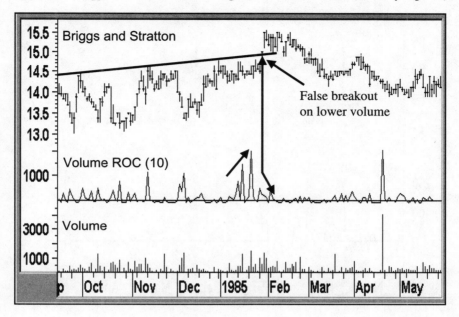

is at a much lower level. The volume histogram, alternately, shows that activity expanded a little on the breakout. However, this study shows us that it is the volume rate of change that is relatively more important, since the breakout proved to be a false one.

Sometimes, short-term trades can take advantage of overbought readings, since they often flag near-term turning points. For instance, the small arrows in Chart 5-4 of Abbott Labs show small selling climaxes by the upward-pointing arrows and rally turning points by the downward-pointing ones.

Divergences are sometimes flagged with this indicator. Look at the series of declining volume momentum peaks, as flagged by the two dashed arrows and the slightly rising peaks in the price in Chart 5-5. This pointed out potential weakness, and, sure enough, the price did experience a decline. Also, note how it is possible to construct a trendline joining a series of declining peaks in volume. When the line is violated, it indicates that the downtrend in volume momentum has terminated and that we should expect a change. In this case, prices started to rally along with volume. This characteristic is flagged by the two diverging dashed arrows.

Chart 5-4   Abbott Labs and a 10-day volume ROC. (Source: *pring.com*)

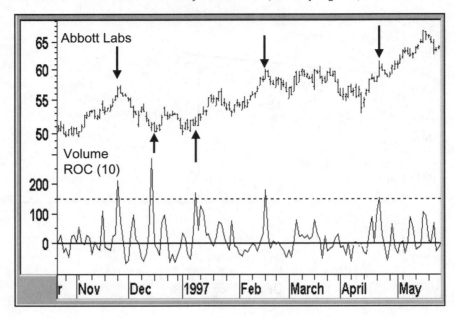

Chart 5-5   Abbott Labs and a 10-day volume ROC. (Source: *pring.com*)

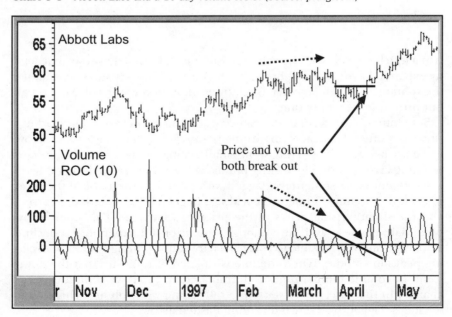

Smoothing the Volume ROC

I prefer to run a moving average through a volume rate of change indicator because it smoothes out the jagged nature of the raw data. Chart 5-6 shows a 3-day simple moving average of a 15-day ROC of volume. I have drawn in an overbought line and flagged those periods when the indicator moves meaningfully above the overbought line. This does not happen very often (about once a year, in fact). However, you can see from the arrows that in the vast majority of cases, we are being warned that something petty important is happening with the price. It all depends on the previous trend. If it is down, then the arrows indicate a selling climax. If it follows a rally, then this is usually a top of some kind. Alternately, if it is a rally coming off a low, then the signal is bullish, as with the one at the extreme left-hand part of the chart.

The volume ROC in Chart 5-7 is based on a 10-day moving average divided by a 25-day MA. This series is a lot smoother than those we looked at so far. As you can see, it lends itself more readily to price pattern and trendline analysis. First, note that the overbought-or-oversold lines are not drawn on

Chart 5-6 Snap-On and a 3/15 volume ROC. (Source: *pring.com*)

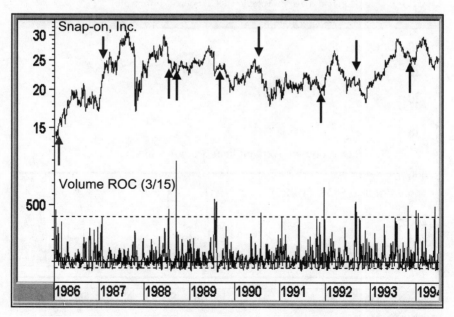

an equidistant basis. This is because the calculation treats the ROC as a percentage. And volume can expand, even on a smoothed basis, by 200 percent or 300 percent quite easily, yet can only fall by 100 percent. This means that downside action is far more limited than upside potential. Later on, we will look at some alternative forms of plotting. At this point, there are two things to note. The first, in Chart 5-8, is a head-and-shoulders top in the volume ROC. The head represented a buying crescendo, so the violation of the neckline was merely a confirmation that the volume trend was down. Since the price was also declining, both were in gear and were not telling us anything significant, except that the technical position was weakening.

Later on, Chart 5-9 shows that both the price and volume violate important downtrend lines. Since both were reversing their direction, they were now in gear on the upside, which was a nice confirmation that the uptrend was healthy. The downtrend line for the oscillator actually represents the neckline of a reverse head-and-shoulders pattern. I did not display the S-H-S letters because the left shoulder was also the right shoulder of the previous upward-sloping head-and-shoulders top. And this would have complicated things.

Chart 5-7   Snap-On and a 10/25 volume ROC. (Source: *pring.com*)

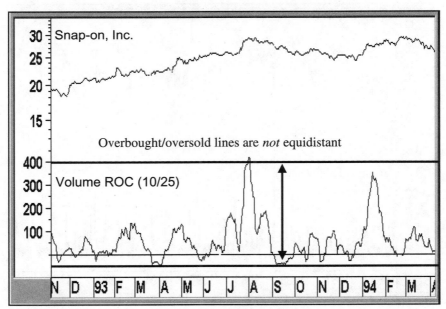

Chart 5-8   Snap-On and a 10/25 volume ROC. (Source: *pring.com*)

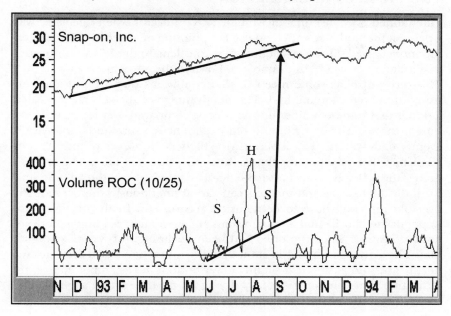

Chart 5-9   Snap-On and a 10/25 volume ROC. (Source: *pring.com*)

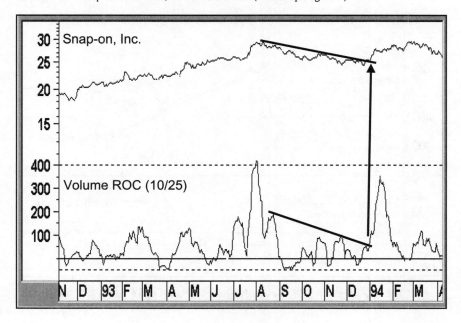

Two Methods of Calculation

I mentioned previously that the volume ROC indicator, when calculated with
a percent method, does not lend itself to pointing out oversold volume conditions very well. One way round this is to calculate the ROC, substituting
a subtraction, instead. An example is shown in the lower area of Chart 5-10.
This series displays some nice oversold conditions that are not apparent
using the percentage method. The disadvantage of the subtraction calculation is that volume momentum cannot be compared over long periods of
time if the security being monitored experiences a substantial increase in
average daily volume. This is because the higher volume will distort the overall picture. For shorter-term charts, the subtraction method is a better technique, though it is important to remember that because the volume level
for individual stocks and markets can vary tremendously, the overbought/
oversold lines will have to be adjusted accordingly. In this instance, the
upper dashed horizontal line represents an overbought reading in both volume indicators. Since the price had been declining, this was a selling climax. The arrows in Chart 5-11 show that the subtraction-based oscillator was
deeply oversold at the next slightly lower bottom in December, hence, the
indication that volume was totally drying up on the second slightly lower

Chart 5-10   Snap-On comparing two 10/25 volume ROC calculations. (Source: *pring.com*)

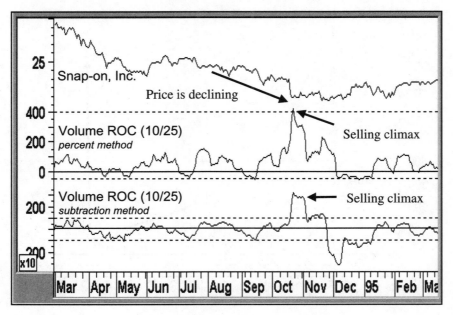

Chart 5-11 Snap-On comparing two 10/25 volume ROC calculations. (Source: *pring.com*)

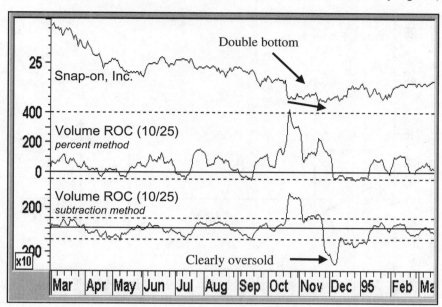

low, a classic double bottom characteristic. While you could see this taking place on the percent chart, it is much more apparent on the subtraction-based series. It is important to note that a high overextended reading in a volume oscillator does not necessarily mean that the price is overbought, merely that volume is overextended. Thus, *a high reading in the volume indicator can mean a top or a bottom,* depending on the previous price action. I will have more to say on that point a little later.

Interpretation

There is an old Wall St. adage that says, "Never short a dull market." Basically, this means dull markets often reflect a sign that selling pressure has almost completely dried up. Chart 5-12, featuring the subtraction-based volume momentum, shows that extreme low readings are a sign that prices may be bottoming. We see two such instances in December and February. Alternately, a market that rallies on low volume may also be considered dull. But in this case, it is usually bearish, since it indicates that prices may be rising but that there is not much enthusiasm for such a trend. When some selling comes out of the woodwork, prices are likely to decline.

Chart 5-12   Wausau Paper Mills and a 10/25 volume ROC. (Source: *pring.com*)

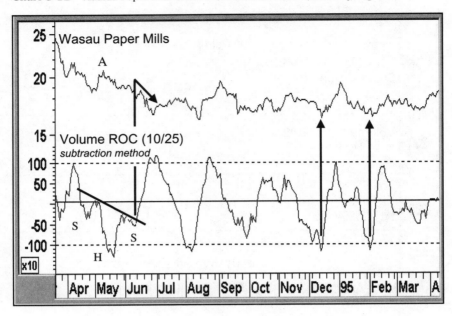

The trough in volume in May 1994 at point A is a good example of this. Also, note how the oscillator traced out a reverse head-and-shoulders pattern. When the breakout (indicating a trend to higher volume) took place, this was associated with the final sell-off in the price. The decline then ended in June with a selling climax (a high-volume ROC reading).

Chart 5-13 features a 15-day MA of volume divided by a 65-day timespan. The price was rising in the November 1983 to March 1984 period. Then it experienced some trading range activity, which ultimately turned out to be the high for the move. About halfway through this process, the volume indicator broke down from a head-and-shoulders top, which indicated that the volume trend was now downward. We then had a situation where the run-up to the final marginal new high was associated with declining volume, a bearish sign, which is flagged by the two diverging dashed arrows. In fact, the situation was even worse than this because the volume ROC was very close to a zero reading during the sessions when the price was recording its high for the move. This indicated that there was virtually no upside volume momentum, an extremely bearish characteristic. Then, as the price began to slip, the volume oscillator started to rally, which is abnormal and bearish behavior.

Volume momentum can also be quite effective using weekly charts. Chart 5-14 of Family Dollar features an 8-week simple moving average of a 13-week

Chart 5-13 Warner-Lambert and a 15/65 volume ROC. (Source: *pring.com*)

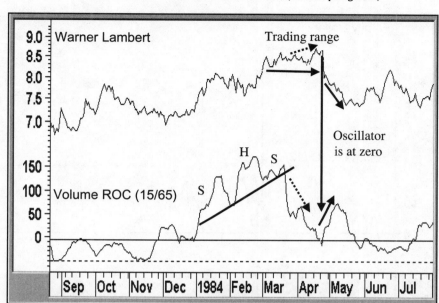

volume ROC using the percent method. Note the very low volume, as the price was moving sideways in the summer of 1987. Then price started to slip and volume expanded, a deadly combination. At the October bottom, we see an overbought volume reading, indicating a selling climax. This is shown in Chart 5-15. Whenever a volume ROC reaches an extreme overbought reading, one of three things usually happens. First, the price reverses on a dime; alternately, it experiences a trading range and then reverses direction; or third, it experiences a trading range and then resumes its trend prior to the overbought reading. In this third case, the price formed a classic bottom. After the selling climax, the volume ROC moves into negative territory, thereby indicating a definite contraction in the level of activity. Then the price breaks out of the trading range on expanding volume (Chart 5-15).

It is often a good idea to wait for the formation of a trading range after an overbought volume reading before taking any action. The next overbought condition in the April/May 1989 period looked like a selling climax and, therefore, a potential buying point (Chart 5-16). However, a trading range did not develop afterward. More to the point, as the price rallied in August of 1989, you can see that the volume oscillator remained well below

Chart 5-14   Family Dollar and a 13/8 volume ROC. (Source: *pring.com*)

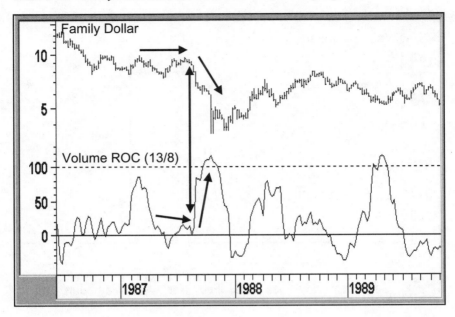

Chart 5-15   Family Dollar and a 13/8 volume ROC. (Source: *pring.com*)

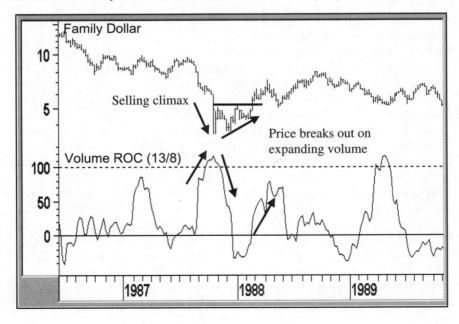

Chart 5-16   Family Dollar and a 13/8 Volume ROC. (Source: *pring.com*)

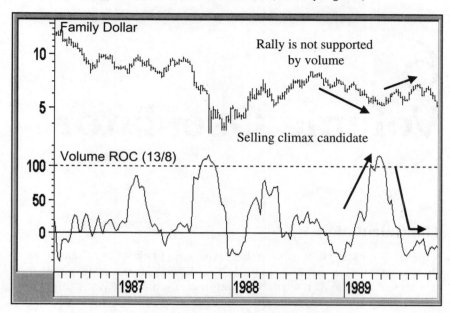

zero. This was certainly not a sign of a market wanting to take off on the upside. In actual fact, this event was followed by a decline to a new marginal low and then some indecisive trading action.

Summary

The rate of change of volume

1. Often gives signs of subtle changes in the level of volume that are not apparent from volume data represented as a histogram.

2. Can be expressed as a percentage or subtraction format.

3. Can be used with overbought/oversold crossovers, trendline analysis and price patterns.

4. Can be followed by declining or rising prices, in the case of overbought readings, depending on the nature of the previous trend.

6
Volume Oscillator

The Calculation

A method of expressing volume that sometimes works better than a rate-of-change calculation involves plotting the difference between two moving averages of volume. It is a trend deviation method in which the calculation substitutes volume for price. This technique also offers a way in which subtle changes in volume levels can be accentuated in a graphic manner.

As Chart 6-1 shows, the process involves the construction of two moving averages, the shorter being divided by the longer. It is also possible to subtract one average from the other, which, in some situations, is superior because it better reflects the contraction of volume in a similar way to that discussed previously for the volume ROC calculation. The upper area shows the volume together with its 10-day moving average. The center area then features this 10-day series together with a 25-day moving average. As you can see, they are continually crossing above and below each other. Finally, the lower area shows the 10-period average divided by the 25-period series. This is the volume oscillator. The equilibrium line represents points where the two moving averages are at identical levels. Chart 6-2 eliminates the top area, where it is evident that movements above and below the horizontal line indicate that the two averages are crossing each other. The solid vertical lines signal upside crossover points and the dashed ones downside crossovers. The timespans of the averages can be varied to reflect short-, intermediate-, and long-term trends. For daily charts, I favor the combination of a 10-day divided by a 25-day simple moving average. This may be too long a span for very short-term traders, who may prefer a 5/20 EMA combination.

Chart 6-1   Calculation of a volume oscillator I. (Source: *pring.com*)

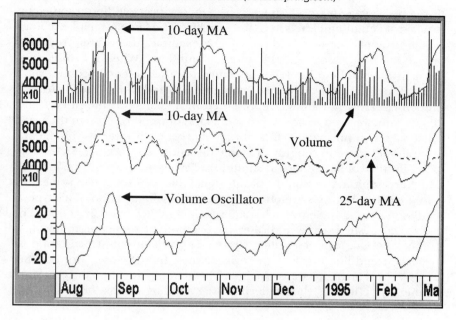

Chart 6-2   Calculation of a volume oscillator II. (Source: *pring.com*)

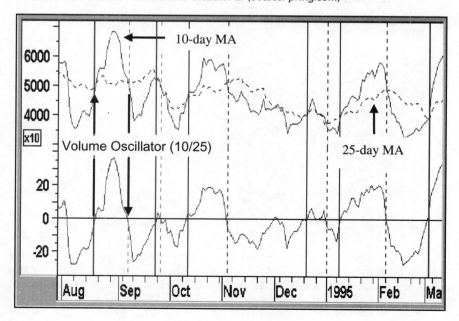

One advantage of the volume oscillator over the volume ROC calculated by the percentage method is that overbought-or-oversold lines can be constructed at equidistant levels from the zero line. The same principles of interpretation apply for both indicators. For example, the volume oscillator reflects overbought-or-oversold volume conditions. When it crosses back through one of these levels on its return toward the equilibrium level, a reversal in the trend of volume momentum is indicated. This is usually, though certainly not always, represented by a change in the price trend. Once again, we need to be alert to some kind of trend reversal in the price, which acts as confirmation. In a normal market environment, volume and price should move in roughly the same direction. For instance, in the case of a rally, the volume oscillator should rise. When it reverses from an overbought condition, this would typically signal that a correction of some kind is in the cards. Bottoms are often signaled by a selling climax. This type of condition existed in September 1996 for General Motors (Chart 6-3). The horizontal dashed arrow indicates an overbought oscillator following a decline, a classic sign of a selling climax. This is later confirmed by a positive downtrend line break by the price. Notice how the oscillator declines as the price is breaking above the line. This is not a cause for concern, since volume, by definition, should decline after a selling climax. It is one of the

Chart 6-3   General Motors and a 10/25 volume oscillator. (Source: *pring.com*)

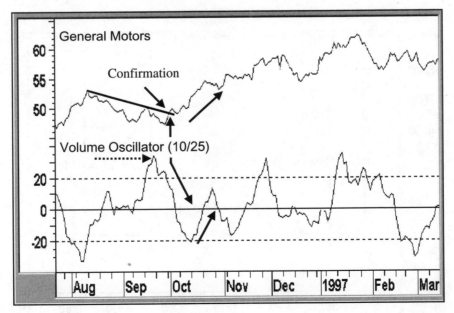

few times when rising prices and falling volume are not bearish. Of course, if prices were to subsequently extend their rise on declining volume, this would be a negative factor. In this instance, though, the volume oscillator quickly moved to an oversold condition and reversed to the upside. The initial oscillator rally was not particularly impressive, since it was unable to move to its overbought level. However, the next one did manage to get there. The price then completed a small top, and a little decline followed (Chart 6-4). Once again, my suggestion is that once you see a reversal in an overbought volume indicator, look for a trading range to develop. Then watch very closely to see which way the price breaks out, since this is usually a reliable signal of the direction of the next short-term trend. In this case, the dashed lines indicate that the price traced out a small rectangle-type formation.

The decline did not last very long, and the volume oscillator and price both traced out a small pattern (Chart 6-5). The joint violation then indicated that the line of least resistance was upward. Once again, the volume oscillator rallied to the overbought level in January 1997. The price then experienced a sideways trading range, finally breaking to the downside. Do not forget that the oscillator was perfectly consistent with a decline in this instance because both price and volume were contracting.

Chart 6-4   General Motors and a 10/25 volume oscillator. (Source: *pring.com*)

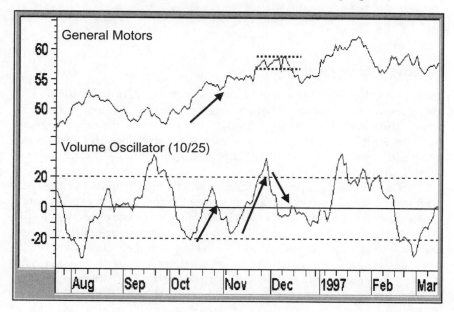

Chart 6-5   General Motors and a 10/25 volume oscillator. (Source: *pring.com*)

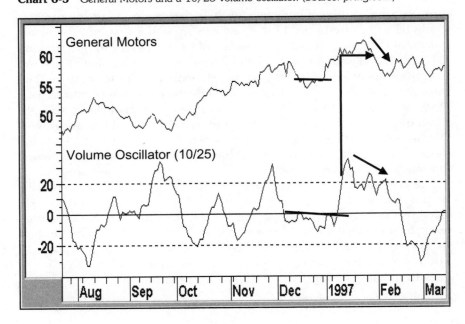

Setting Parameters

Setting parameters for the volume oscillator is crucial. Obviously, the smaller the timespan between the short moving average and the longer one, the greater the volatility. Chart 6-6 compares a one-day moving average against a 200-day series. Since the 200-day average is relatively flat, the result is not much different than displaying volume as a histogram, as is fairly evident by comparing the two lower areas.

Chart 6-7 shows the opposite extreme, where the oscillator is calculated from two moving averages that are very close in time. The curve is definitely smoother, but the turning points often develop in an unrelated way to the price. The key, then, is to use two moving averages that are fairly well separated. My personal preference when working with daily charts is a 10/25-day combination, although I freely admit there may well be a superior setting. Just remember not to look for perfection, but more for compromise. In other words, do not fit the data to make the past work for a specific market, try and find something that works reasonably well most of the time.

Chart 6-6 General Motors and a 1/200 volume oscillator. (Source: *pring.com*)

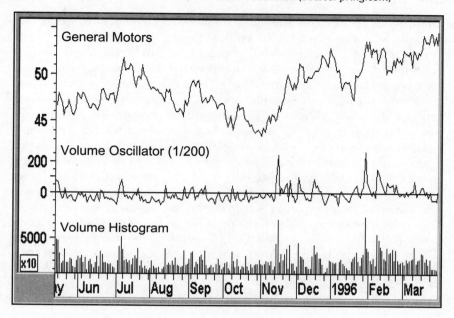

Chart 6-7 General Motors and a 15/20 volume oscillator. (Source: *pring.com*)

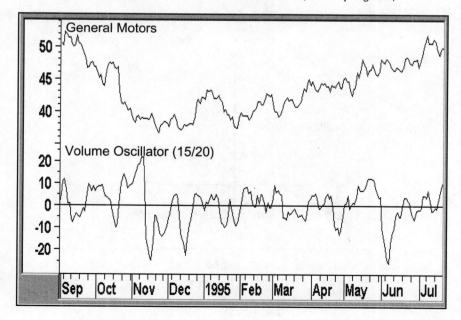

Interpretation

Chart 6-8 of Daimler Chrysler features a 10/25 combination. I find that overbought/oversold readings, trendline breaks, and pattern completions work very well, in the sense that they provide relatively reliable signals that the trend of the volume oscillator has reversed. Once again, though, this does not always translate into a change in the actual price trend. Let me quickly run through this example. Both price and volume were expanding between May and early August, then the price moved sideways in a narrow band, as flagged by the dashed arrows. As is normal in a trading range environment, the level of volume subsided, since the trading range represents a period of evenhandedness between buyers and sellers. Volume reached an oversold level in early August, rallied, and then tested the oversold level later in the month. As it reversed from this low level, it also violated a downtrend line, as the price broke out from the trading range on the upside. Thus volume was expanding on the price breakout, which is a bullish combination. Then the volume oscillator quickly rallied to the overbought zone (Chart 6-9). As it crossed below this upper extreme zone on its way back toward zero, the price completed and broke down from a small double top.

Chart 6-8   Daimler Chrysler and a 10/25 volume oscillator. (Source: *pring.com*)

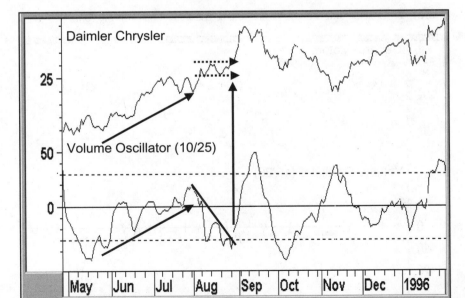

Chart 6-9 Daimler Chrysler and a 10/25 volume oscillator. (Source: *pring.com*)

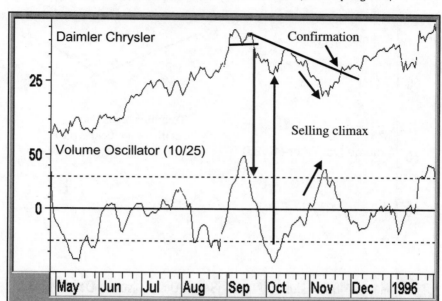

The next oversold condition was followed by a small rally, but there was nothing in the price action that would have confirmed this brief trend change to the upside. Finally, volume expanded to a crescendo in November, and the selling climax was followed by a rally, which was signaled by a price trend break at the end of the month.

The rally itself was not particularly inspiring from a volume momentum point of view, since the oscillator was barely able to rally above zero (Chart 6-10). This would have indicated that the advance was suspect. The actual signal came when the uptrend line was violated in early January. Needless to say, a sharp decline followed. The last event is shown in Chart 6-11, where mid January saw the completion of a small base in the price and a breakout from a somewhat larger base in the volume oscillator.

Obviously, not all combinations of volume oscillator and trendline–price pattern analysis work out this well, but the explanation at least gives you a few pointers to watch out for. There is one final point. If you review all of the trend turning points in the volume oscillator, the overbought/oversold reversals, price patterns and trendline violations, and so on, you will appreciate that they had a very high degree of reliability in signaling a reversal in the prevailing volume momentum trend.

Chart 6-10   Daimler Chrysler and a 10/25 volume oscillator. (Source: *pring.com*)

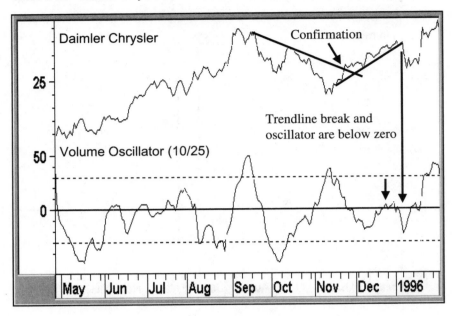

Chart 6-11   Daimler Chrysler and a 10/25 volume oscillator. (Source: *pring.com*)

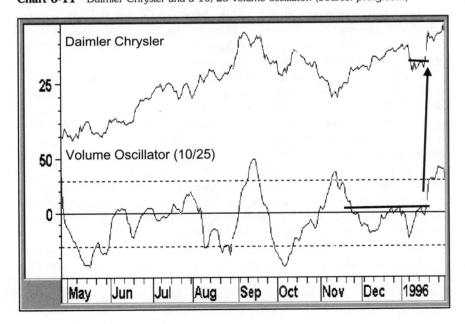

Volume versus Price Oscillators

Combining a volume and price oscillator on the same chart can offer a further dynamic to the analysis. This is because it then becomes easier to spot those situations where things are in gear and those where there are discrepancies. In this respect, it is vital to remember that the two series can move in opposite directions and remain consistent. For example, volume moves to an overbought condition during a selling climax, and the price oscillator falls to an oversold one. Alternately, a rally could see a price oscillator in an overbought position and a volume oscillator declining below zero. This would indicate weakness, since rising prices would be accompanied by declining volume. Chart 6-12, featuring Family Dollar Stores, is based on weekly data. The timeframe for the two oscillators reflect 10- and 25-week trend deviations. The sell-off in early Fall 1994 is associated with a mini–selling climax, as you can see from the overbought reading in the volume oscillator. The price then breaks above a small downtrend line and the positive reading in the price oscillator sets the scene for a rally. Normally, I would have expected a larger rise than the one that took place because the price oscillator was at a fairly subdued level when it began. It would, of course, be normal for the volume oscillator to be declining on the first upward thrust

Chart 6-12 Family Dollar and a price and volume oscillator. (Source: *pring.com*)

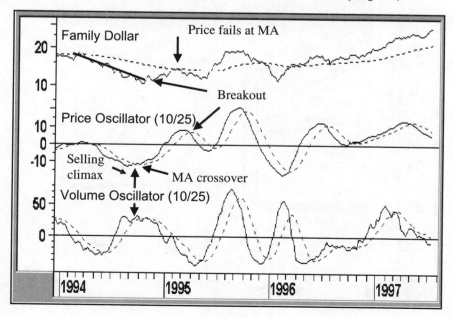

in the price. However, as the declining trend of volume progressed, it would have become apparent that the rally was becoming suspect. The warning sign began to appear when the price was unable to cross above its 65-week EMA in early 1995 and the price oscillator reversed to the downside.

As it turned out, this was to be a test of the low. Then at the second vertical arrow in Chart 6-13, the price stabilizes, the two oscillators reverse to the upside, and the price breaks above the horizontal trendline and the 65-day EMA, a classic buy signal combination.

The rally does not last as long as I would have suspected from such a combination. However, the next event is what I call a *double whammy*. A double whammy develops when a volume oscillator is overbought and a price oscillator oversold. Both indicate that the decline in price is most probably over. You can recognize a double whammy because both series move toward each other: obviously, the closer, the better.

Since volume is a totally independent variable from price, it makes sense to look at some more examples comparing a volume momentum indicator with a price momentum series.

Chart 6-14 shows an example of *churning*. That is a condition wherein, after a good rally, volume expands to very heavy levels, yet there is little response in the price. Such a situation developed for Hecla Mining in early 1996.

Chart 6-13   Family Dollar and a price and volume oscillator. (Source: *pring.com*)

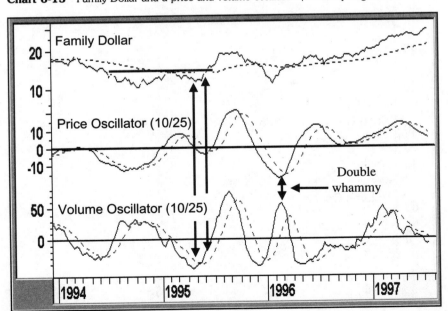

Chart 6-14 Hecla and a price and volume oscillator I. (Source: *pring.com*)

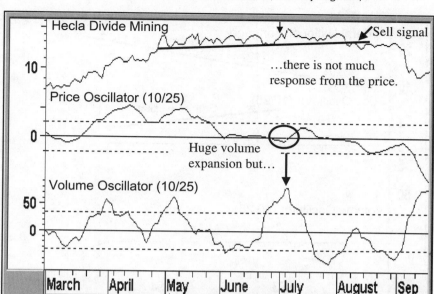

The price rallied to a new recovery high, as the volume oscillator moved up to very overbought. However, at the time of the high (flagged by the vertical arrows), the price oscillator was still marginally below zero. It is true that it eventually rallied again, but this was more of a lagged statistical response, since the actual price was lower at this point. This type of action would have warned that something was definitely very wrong. However, the actual sell signal would have come much later, when the price broke below the slightly upward-sloping trendline.

Federal National Mortgage (Chart 6-15) offers a great example of the interaction between price trends and price and volume oscillators. The chart shows that the price was able to remain above its 65-week EMA and uptrend line between 1992, right up until mid 1994. During this period, the peaks in the price oscillator were in a declining trend, so that by the time the price reached its final peak, the oscillator was barely above zero. This was bad enough, but look at the progress of the weekly volume oscillator. At the time of the final peak, it has actually been below zero for some time. Since the price was not much above its previous high, it could be argued that the stock was in a trading range. This would mean that declining volume reflected a tight balance between buyers and sellers. A break to the upside on expanding volume would, therefore, resolve the dilemma in a bullish way. However, the weaker action of the price oscillator at the second 1994 peak, combined

Chart 6-15 Federal National Mortgage and a price and volume oscillator. (Source: *pring.com*)

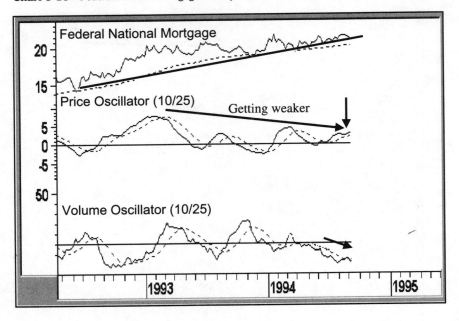

Chart 6-16 Federal National Mortgage and a price and volume oscillator. (Source: *pring.com*)

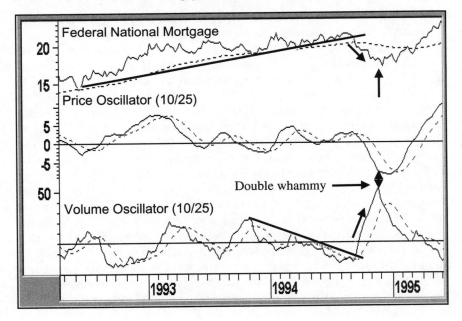

with the contracting volume, argued for a break in the opposite direction. When the break did occur (Chart 6-16), it was to the downside, and volume expanded tremendously. What we end up with is a double whammy effect, as the price and volume oscillators converge on each other for a classic selling climax.

Summary

The volume oscillator

1. Allows us to plot both overbought and oversold zones.

2. Does not always translate into price trend reversals during volume trend reversals.

3. Adds depth to the analysis when combined with the price oscillator.

4. Can be calculated with any combination of timespans, but a good all-round combination is a 10-period divided by a 25-period moving average.

7
The Chaikin Money Flow Indicator

The Concept

The Chaikin money flow indicator (CMF) is based on the principle that rising prices should be accompanied by expanding volume, and vice versa. The formula emphasizes the fact that market strength is usually accompanied by prices closing in the upper half of their daily range with increasing volume. Likewise, market weakness is usually accompanied by prices closing in the lower half of their daily range with increasing volume. This indicator can be calculated with any timespan: the longer the period, the more deliberate the swings. Money flow indicators calculated with a short-term timeframe, such as 10 periods, are, therefore, much more volatile.

When prices consistently close in the upper half of their daily high-low range on increased volume for the period under consideration, the indicator will be positive (that is, above the zero line). Conversely, if prices consistently close in the lower half of their daily high-low range on increased volume, the indicator will be negative (that is, below the zero line).

Divergence Analysis

It is possible to construct overbought- or-oversold lines and use these as buy-and-sell alerts, but the indicator really comes into its own with divergence analysis. In Chart 7-1 of National Semiconductor, we can see some good examples in practice. In early 1994 (point A), the Chaikin was falling

Chart 7-1 National Semiconductor and CMF divergences. (Source: *pring.com*)

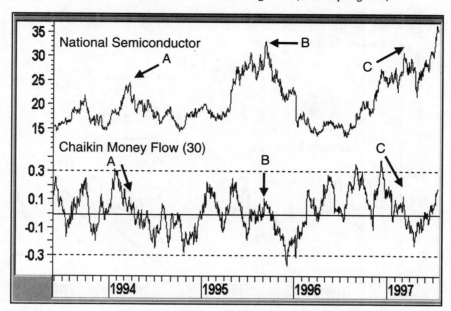

sharply as the price ran up to its final peak, and at the time of the actual high, it was barely above the equilibrium line. This showed that the quality of the last few weeks of the rally left a lot to be desired. In fall 1995 (point B), the divergence was more blatant, since the indicator was barely able to rise above the zero line at a time when the price was making a new high. Both these examples were followed by long downtrends. However, the negative divergence (C) that took place in early 1997 was followed by a quick, but sharp, sell-off.

Positive divergences also work quite well with the Chaikin indicator. Look at the early 1996 bottom in Chart 7-2. See how the price makes a marginal new low, but the oscillator is hardly below zero. This compares to the late-1995 bottom, where it was at an extremely oversold condition. Of course, this is merely a positive momentum characteristic; we still need to witness some kind of trend reversal in price to confirm this event. Divergences are not uncommon in momentum indicators. What sets the money flow indicator apart from the rest is that the divergences are usually far more blatant than, say, for the RSI or ROC. As a result, it can provide clues of probable trend reversals that may not be apparent elsewhere.

Chart 7-3 features a 20-week money flow. The indicator made a very low reading about halfway through the mid-1986 trading range. Then it shot up

Chart 7-2 National Semiconductor and CMF divergences. (Source: *pring.com*)

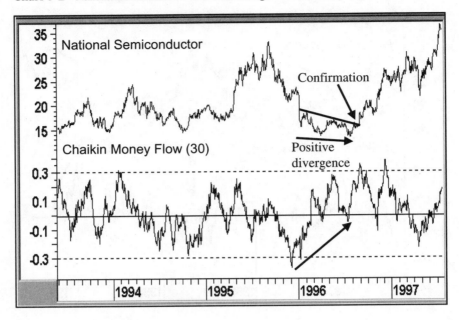

Chart 7-3 Alexander and Baldwin and CMF divergences. (Source: *pring.com*)

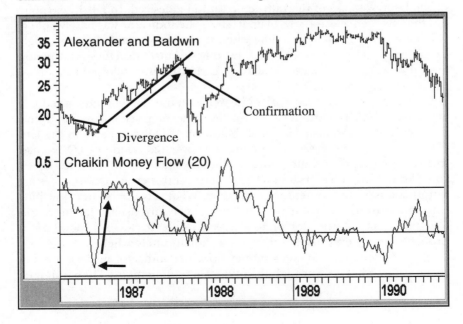

very sharply just prior to the point where the price took off on the upside. In fact, it was possible to construct a trendline marking the top of a small base for the price. The scene was then set for a worthwhile rally. Notice how the indicator gradually declined from early 1987 onward to the extent that by the time the final peak was seen, there was virtually no upside momentum. It was also possible to confirm this weak technical structure by observing a break below the 1986 to 1987 uptrend line prior to the market crash.

What I find incredible is that the 1987 low was slightly under that of 1986, yet the oscillator barely fell below zero (Chart 7-4). This indicated a very strong technical position. It was even possible to construct a downtrend line for the money flow indicator. The penetration of this line developed ahead of the decisive breakout in the price. The late 1988 to 1989 period was also associated with weak money flow (Chart 7-5). The price moved sideways while it traced out a head-and-shoulders top formation, but the oscillator spent a considerable amount of time below the zero line. When the actual breakdown in price took place, the money flow was well into negative territory. Sometimes the money flow indicator will give us an advanced warning that a pattern breakout may be imminent.

In Chart 7-6 of Merrill Lynch featuring a 20-period CMF, the spring 1992 lows experienced a small positive divergence with the price and this was confirmed by a trendline break. Later on, the price moved in a trading range.

Chart 7-4   Alexander and Baldwin and CMF divergences. (Source: *pring.com*)

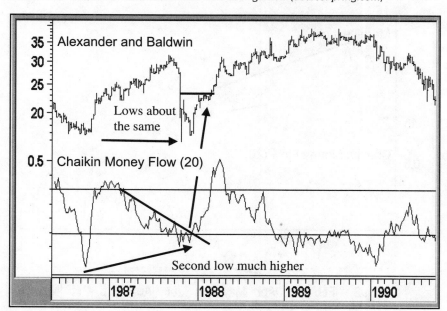

Chart 7-5   Alexander and Baldwin and CMF divergences. (Source: *pring.com*)

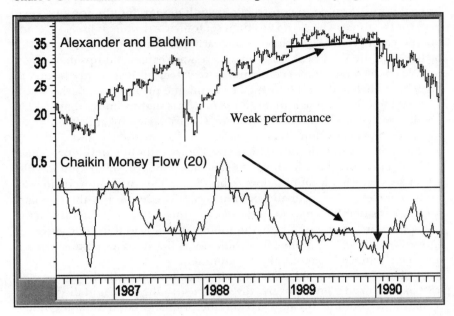

Chart 7-6   Merrill Lynch and CMF divergences. (Source: *pring.com*)

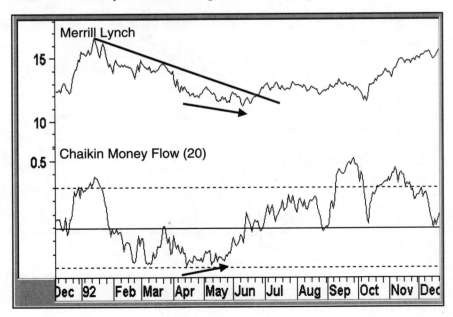

The top at point A in Chart 7-7 was associated with some positive money flow, but look at the next one (point B); the indicator is at a much higher level, indicating substantial accumulation, but the price had not yet decisively broken above the horizontal trendline. In actual fact, the oscillator was still rising as the price started to decline. It was surprising, though, to see the price then experience a sharp setback. However, while the price fell below its previous low, the money flow did not. This divergence has been flagged by the two *converging* lines. Later on, in Chart 7-8, the oscillator rallied into overbought territory once again (point C) as the price broke above the solid horizontal trendline. This is the type situation where the money flow can really be of help. On the surface, it looked as if the price weakness, once started, was likely to extend. However, the fact that the money flow indicator did not even cross below zero (at its October low) before it turned around indicated that selling pressure was really quite superficial. It is reasonable to have assumed that the neutral reading in the money flow in the ellipse would have indicated the potential for much further weakness. After all, the price could certainly have fallen quite a bit before the CMF would decline to an oversold level. The point is that the money flow is normally a *leading* indicator, so if it *was* going to register an oversold reading, it should have done this by now. Just remember that the earlier examples demon-

Chart 7-7 Merrill Lynch and CMF divergences. (Source: *pring.com*)

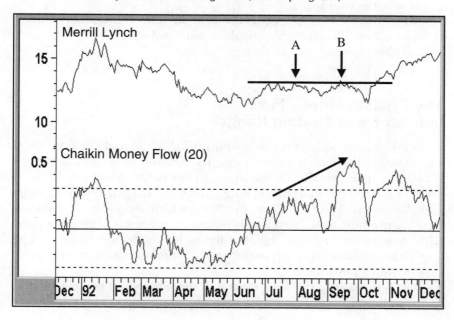

Chart 7-8　Merrill Lynch and CMF divergences. (Source: *pring.com*)

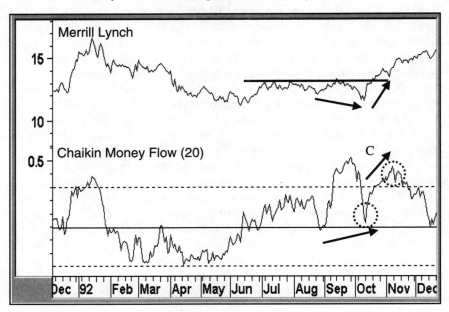

strated how the money flow was actually in negative territory when the price was at, or close to, a high.

This oscillator does not generally lend itself to trendline violations. However, Chart 7-9 offers an example in late 1993 wherein both the price and oscillator violate uptrend lines.

The Chaikin Money Flow Indicator and Trading Ranges

One of the ways in which I like to use the indicator is to study trading ranges and then compare the price action to the oscillator to see if it is giving a clue as to the direction of the eventual breakout. American Business Products was caught in a trading range in 1987 (Chart 7-10). Even though it held above the lower trendline, the 20-week CMF slipped quite decisively into negative territory. Then a rally followed at arrow A. The price came fairly close to the previous high, but the oscillator was well below it. This combination indicated vulnerability, so it was not surprising that the price experienced a nasty decline.

Chart 7-11 features the same stock, but the timespan is greater. In 1989 the price broke above a multiyear resistance trendline at point A. On the

Chart 7-9   Merrill Lynch and CMF divergences. (Source: *pring.com*)

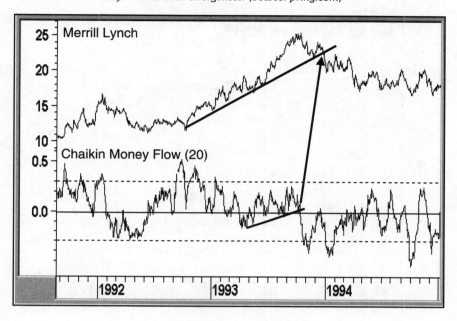

Chart 7-10   American Business Products and CMF divergences. (Source: *pring.com*)

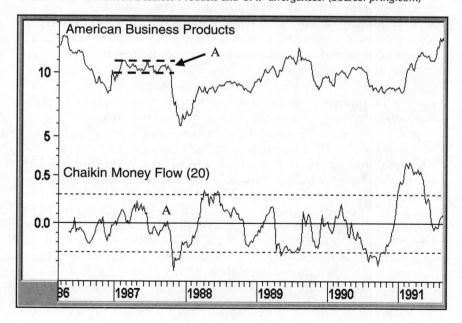

Chart 7-11   American Business Products and CMF divergences. (Source: *pring.com*)

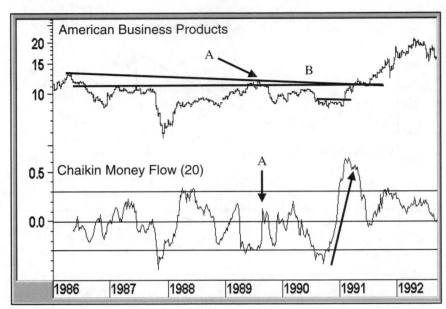

surface, this looked pretty good. However, the money flow indicator was barely able to rally above zero. This indicated that the breakout was not supported by positive volume characteristics and that a whipsaw was likely.

The price tried to rally back to the line once more in 1990 at point B, but the money flow again was headed south, thereby indicating that the attempt, as far as it was concerned, would not end in a successful way.

Now compare the difference in the technical situation in early 1991, when the price did manage to break to the upside. First, during the basing formation that preceded the rally, the money flow was in a sharp uptrend. See how prices were essentially flat, yet the oscillator moved quickly off its oversold bottom. By the time the price eventually broke above the lower horizontal trendline, the money flow indicator was at its highest level in 5 years. This indicated a tremendous amount of upside momentum and buying power. Holders of the stock were not disappointed.

In Chart 7-12 of Newmont Mining, a resistance trendline forms in the $45 to $50 area. There was no real reason why the 1993 and 1994 sharp price rallies accompanied by healthy readings in the money flow should not have resulted in a breakout. However, the mid-1995 attempt was doomed to failure, according to the money flow indicator, since this series barely made it to the halfway overbought zone. When the breakout did finally materialize, the oscillator was well above its previous high.

Chart 7-12   Newmont Mining and CMF divergences. (Source: *pring.com*)

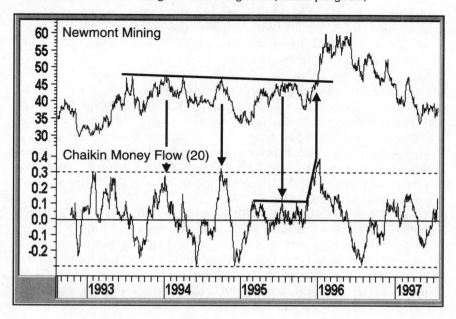

Chart 7-13   Newmont Mining and CMF divergences. (Source: *pring.com*)

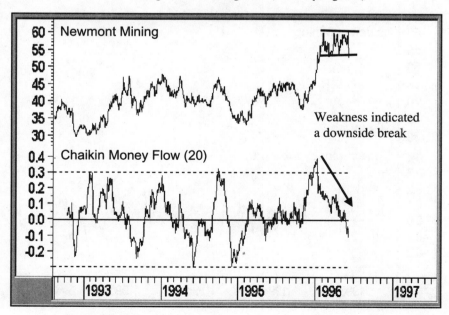

The top formation traced out in early 1996 was most instructive (Chart 7-13), since the price moved in a sideways trading range, which could have been resolved in either direction. However, the indicator started on a persistent declining trend that took it into negative territory just prior to the downside breakout, which is shown in Chart 7-14.

Chart 7-15 shows an unusual, but very powerful, combination of a double trendline break by the price and a 20-period CMF. This is a weekly chart, and the two lines extend back for several years. It was not surprising, therefore, that when the two breaks finally came, the price not only experienced a decline, but was unable to move to a new high for several years.

This same period also experienced a head-and-shoulders top in both series, as we can see in Chart 7-16. These two price pattern completions added greater weight to the two trendline violations, since they all developed around the same time.

Finally, Chart 7-17 shows the CMF in a less flattering light. In fall 1996, Western Deep, a South African gold mine, experienced a huge rally and a positive CMF. Then, in early November the price also advanced and broke above a small secondary trendline. Taken on face value, this looked to be a solid combination that would be followed by a very worthwhile rally. However, Chart 7-18 indicates that the breakout was a whipsaw. This example was included to warn you that the CMF is not an infallible indicator and

Chart 7-14 Newmont Mining and CMF divergences. (Source: *pring.com*)

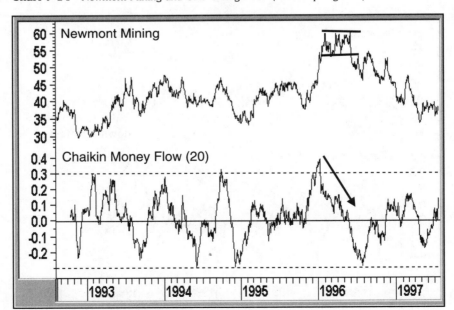

Chart 7-15 Alcoa and CMF divergences. (Source: *pring.com*)

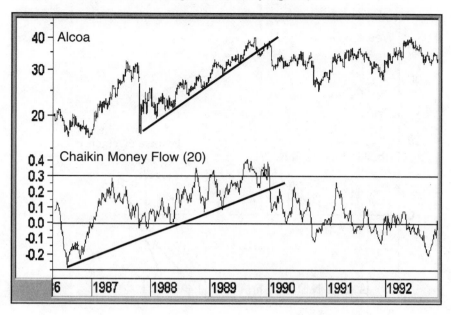

Chart 7-16 Alcoa and CMF trendline violations. (Source: *pring.com*)

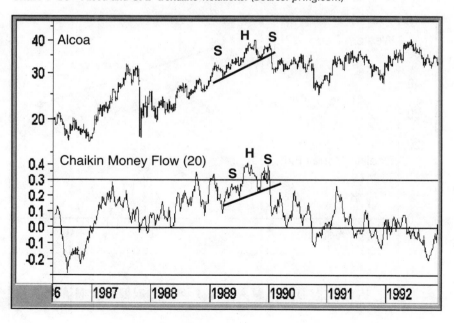

Chart 7-17   Western Deep and CMF price patterns. (Source: *pring.com*)

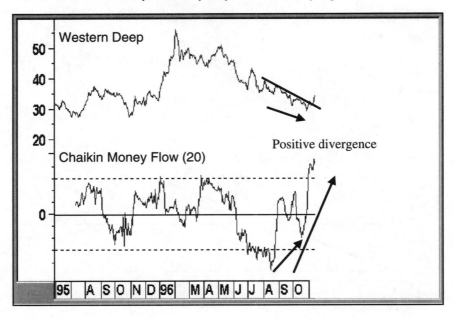

Chart 7-18   Western Deep and a false breakout. (Source: *pring.com*)

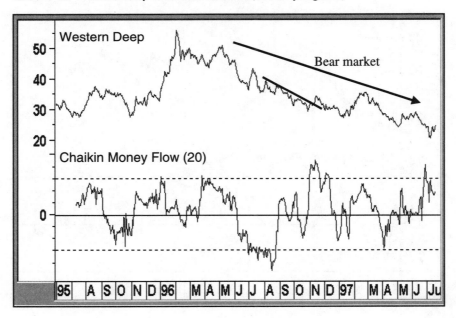

that even the best signals can sometimes fail to operate in the manner expected. All that can be said in the defense of this whipsaw is that the whole period covered by the chart was a bear market. Quite often, we find that if an otherwise very strong- and reliable-looking signal fails, it is typically a countercyclical one, and countercyclical signals have an unfortunate habit of being false. That is exactly what happened here.

Summary

1. The strength of the indicator is its ability to throw out blatant divergences, which have a reasonable degree of accuracy.

2. During sideways trading ranges, the indicator will often move decisively in one direction or another. This provides a valuable clue as to the direction of the price breakout when it ultimately takes place.

3. When prices reach resistance, look to the money flow for a clue as to whether it will hold or be violated.

4. When prices reach support, look to the money flow for a clue as to whether it will hold or be violated.

8
The Demand Index

The Indicator

Technicians have always been fascinated by the possibility of being able to separate volume-initiated-buy buyers from sellers. The former is known as *upside volume* and the latter as *downside activity*. Unless you are in possession of tick-by-tick data where it is possible to appropriate volume associated with up-ticks or down-ticks, it is not possible to accomplish this analysis. The Chaikin money flow indicator described in the previous chapter tries to achieve this objective statistically, as does the demand index. It was developed by Jim Sibbet, editor of the *Let's Talk Silver and Gold* market letter, and combines price and volume into one indicator. The demand index is based on the premise that volume leads price. Consequently, the objective is to end up with an indicator that leads market turning points. It is included in many charting packages and is interpreted in the following ways.

Six Methods of Interpretation

1. *Divergences between the indicator and the price indicate underlying strength or weakness, depending on whether it is a positive or negative one.*

2. *A long-term divergence between the index and the price indicates a major top or bottom.*

3. *Zero crossovers represent a change in trend.* Normally, this will occur after the fact, so it serves as a confirmatory indicator.

4. *Constant fluctuations around the zero indicates a weak price trend that will soon reverse.*

5. *Overbought-or-oversold crossovers generate good buy and sell signals in some markets.* Since the level of the demand index is affected by the volatility of the security being monitored, optimum overbought-or-oversold levels will vary and should be determined on a case-by-case approach. However, the ±25 levels appear to be a good compromise for most markets.

6. *The index sometimes forms price patterns and trendline violations.* They normally represent a reliable *advance* warning of an impending price trend reversal.

Let us consider each of these interpretive principles in turn.

Divergences

The interpretation of divergences between the price and the demand index is essentially the same as any other indicator. In Chart 8-1 you can see a positive and negative scenario. When the price makes its final peak in early March, the demand index has already started to decline fairly precipitously. This, of course, just warns that the underlying technical structure is not as

Chart 8-1 DuPont and demand index divergences. (Source: *pring.com*)

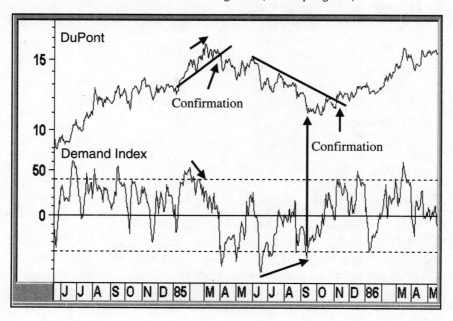

good as it looks on the surface. However, it is still necessary to observe some kind of trend-reversal signal in the price to confirm the probability that a new trend is underway. This signal comes when the uptrend line is violated.

The example on the right develops at the September 1985 bottom. See how the price makes its final low for the move there, but the demand index actually bottomed in June. The confirmation of this improving technical picture came later on, when the downtrend line was violated on the upside.

In Chart 8-2 the price makes a secondary peak at the end of 1992 (point A) that is ever so slightly below the first one. It's not, strictly speaking, a divergence, but in technical analysis, we are dealing as much in common sense as mechanical interpretation. The point being that the second peak was for all intents and purposes at the same level as the first one. However, momentum, in this case the demand index, was barely able to rally above zero. Consequently, the enthusiasm was just not there at the second peak. Ordinarily, when momentum is barely able to rally above zero at a time when the price makes a marginal new high or comes very close to it, this is usually followed by a sharp decline, once confirmed by a price trendbreak. That was certainly true in this particular case.

Chart 8-2   Rite Aid and demand index divergences. (Source: *pring.com*)

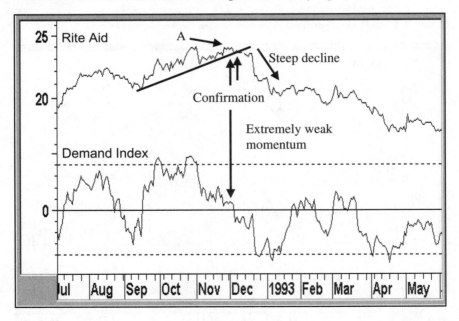

Long-Term Divergences

The divergences that we saw in the previous example were of relatively short-term duration. In Chart 8-3 we see that the demand index bottomed in April, 8 months prior to the December rally off the bottom formation. In the intervening period, it diverged several times in a positive manner with the price. Note that although the demand index did experience a series of higher bottoms between April and June, this occurred within the overall March-to-December downtrend. That is why we are able to count the April demand index low as part of the overall long-term divergence in this case.

A final point worthy of attention comes from the fact that the December low in the demand index was barely below the zero level (Chart 8-4), yet the price was within a whisker of the early October low. Hence, we have the exact opposite set of circumstances to that in Chart 8-2, where a demand index that was barely able to rally above zero was followed by a sharp decline. In this case, the inability of the demand index to fall much below zero was followed by a spectacular rally.

Chart 8-3   Rite Aid and demand index divergences. (Source: *pring.com*)

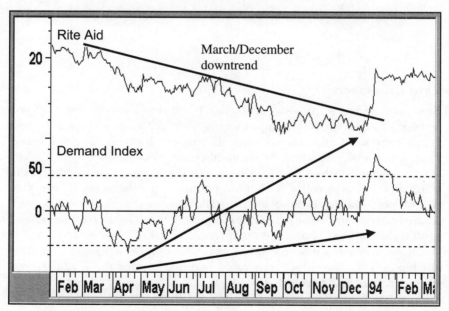

Chart 8-4   Rite Aid and demand index divergences. (Source: *pring.com*)

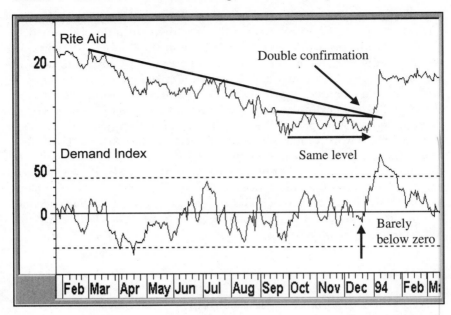

Zero Crossovers

Some people use zero crossovers by the demand index to generate buy-or-sell signals. Sometimes this can work quite well, as you can see from the position of the solid and dashed vertical lines in Chart 8-5. The solid lines represent buy signals when the demand crosses above zero and the dashed ones sell signals, when it crosses below. In these particular instances, this approach was very profitable. But what of the period between the two lines in April and May for Rohm and Haas? Here we see that the index whipped above zero on two occasions. Had we been following the zero crossover religiously, losses would have been incurred. Indeed, if you cast your eyes to the right, you will see several other examples of false signals contained in the boxes. This chart is not an isolated example because this is a fairly common occurrence. Therefore, my advice is to ignore zero crossovers unless you can spot instances when they turn out to be a good support or resistance point. Under such circumstances, the zero crossover will represent a form of support-or-resistance penetration and, therefore, has a tendency to be more reliable.

Chart 8-5   Rohm and Haas and demand index zero crossovers. (Source: *pring.com*)

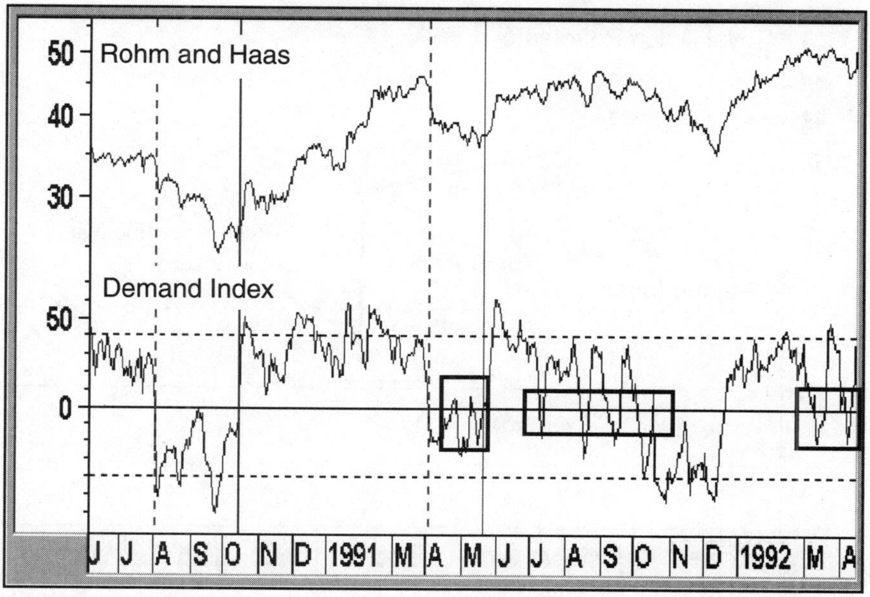

Constant Fluctuations around Zero

I had to search several charts and countless years of data to find the example in Chart 8-6 of what we might call a *zero-resistance crossover*. Even then,
the horizontal trendline is slightly above zero, so it does not really count. If
I have to do a lot of digging to find an example for an interpretive point
that I am trying to make, it really means that this interpretive characteristic is not particularly useful. Consequently, I am not really sold on Rule 4,
which states that if the index waffles closely around the zero level, it indicates a weak price trend that will soon reverse. In this case, I ask myself the
question, What constitutes "around" the zero level? After studying countless charts, I still cannot answer that question to my satisfaction, probably
because it is often very difficult to determine when the indicator has moved
sufficiently away from the zero level to constitute a change in trend. Most
of the time, when you can identify such situations, the horse has bolted from
the barn, anyway.

I have drawn two circles in Chart 8-7, featuring Royal Dutch Petroleum.
Both indicate what I would regard as indecisive price action around zero.
The first was followed by a break to the upside, and the one on the right, a
break to the downside. However, in both cases, the new price trend was
already well underway by the time it became obvious that the index had
moved away from its relatively narrow zero-based trading range.

Chart 8-6   Royal Dutch Petroleum and demand index zero crossovers. (Source: *pring.com*)

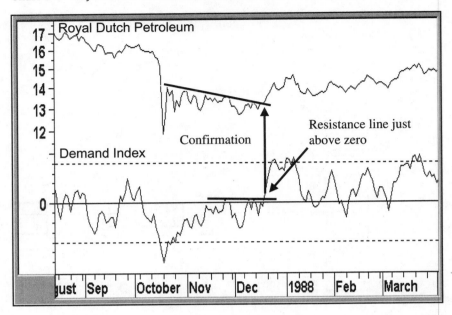

Chart 8-7   Royal Dutch Petroleum and demand index constant zero crossovers. (Source: *pring.com*)

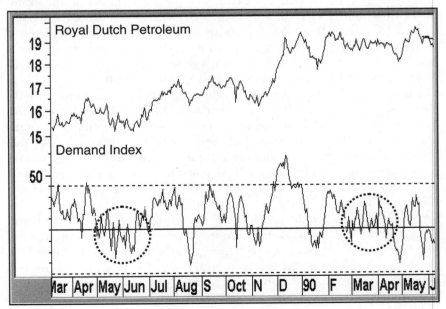

Overbought-or-Oversold Crossovers

I mentioned earlier that the construction of the demand index is such that overbought-or-oversold levels will differ with the volatility of the security being monitored. As you may have noticed, most of the examples used so far have placed the lines at ±40. That seems to work out quite well in a lot of situations. But it is very important to examine the security being analyzed on a case-by-case basis to make sure that the price history of that particular one is consistent with where the lines have been placed.

In Chart 8-8 the downward-pointing arrows indicate the price where the index crossed below its overbought level. Two types of market activity are covered. The first was between May 1981 and May 1982. This was a trading-range environment. During this phase, the overbought crossovers, with the exception of the first one contained within the ellipse, worked reasonably well. The period following this was an uptrend, or bull market. In this environment, the demand index gave a couple of reasonable signals. However, in other instances, the price only experienced a small decline prior to resuming the uptrend.

There were really two signals in the area of the ellipse. The first had absolutely no effect on the price because it still continued to run up. The second was followed by a pretty nasty decline. Had someone sold on the first

Chart 8-8 Royal Dutch Petroleum and demand index overbought/oversold crossovers. (Source: *pring.com*)

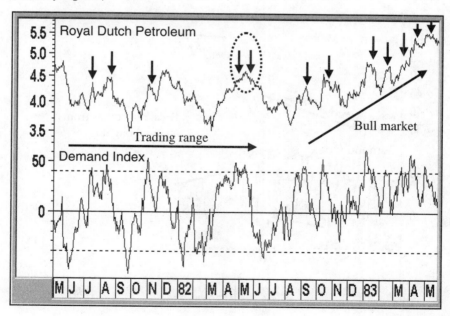

ellipse signal, the benefit of hindsight would have called this particular one a fairly good signal.

Obviously, it is not possible to know at the time whether the sell signal from an overbought crossover will be followed by a small or a large decline. We need to look at other indicators to obtain clues. Is the long-term KST in a bearish or bullish mode? Has the price recently completed a major head-and-shoulders top, indicating a bear market? And so on. However, I think that it is fair to say that when the demand index does cross below its overbought zone, the odds of at least a small decline are pretty high. This is the place where you might want to take at least partial profits, depending on your interpretation of the direction and maturity of the main trend.

The opposite is also true of oversold crossovers. In the vast majority of the charts that I have studied, these observations appear to hold true.

Price Patterns and Trendlines

My own feeling is that the demand index really comes into its own when it is possible to identify price patterns and trendline violations. In Chart 8-9 we see a head-and-shoulders violation in September 1995. The break develops a little bit below the zero line, so the downside potential was partially limited. However, the nice neckline break combined with the violation of

Chart 8-9 Newmont Mining and demand index price patterns. (Source: *pring.com*)

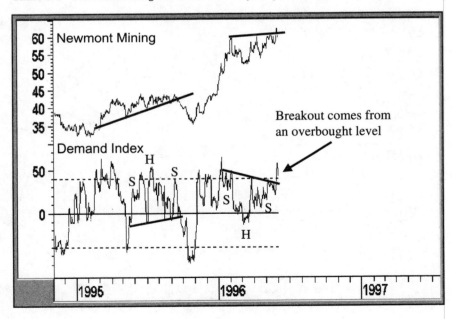

the uptrendline in the price offered a fairly timely signal. The next one that developed in May 1996 was not. See how the demand index breaks out from a reverse head-and-shoulders pattern. This was confirmed by a break in the price above its early-1996 trading range. The problem was that the head-and-shoulders momentum break came very close to the overbought level and was, therefore, suspect.

Chart 8-10 shows that it could have been better used as an opportunity to watch for additional weakness and a sell signal, not as a buy signal. Ironically, the day after the peak was an outside day, although that is not apparent from this line chart. The rule, then, is to look for a pattern completion from an overextended level, which is subsequently confirmed with a price break in the opposite direction to that of the breakout. This whipsaw activity can then be used as a basis from which a short position may be placed. This is because whipsaw signals are almost invariably followed by a very strong move in the opposite direction to that indicated by the original break.

Speaking of false breaks, look at the trendline on the extreme left-hand part of Chart 8-11. It marks the neckline of a head-and-shoulders pattern that did not "work." Once again, we have a form of whipsaw, but this time the indicated direction was downward, so when the pattern was not com-

Chart 8-10   Newmont Mining and demand index price patterns. (Source: *pring.com*)

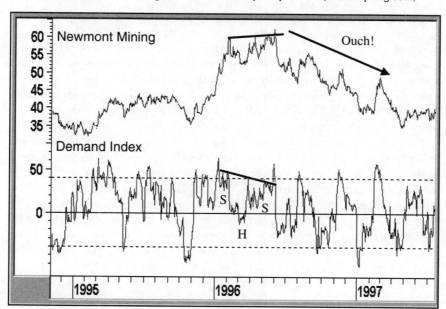

Chart 8-11 Newmont Mining and demand index price patterns. (Source: *pring.com*)

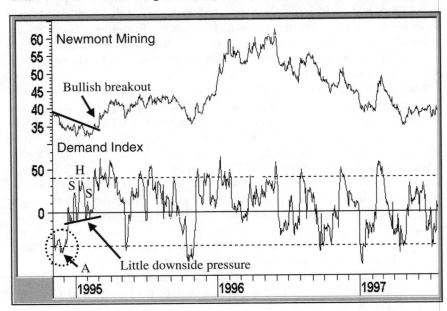

pleted *and* the price confirmed by rallying above the downtrendline, the price literally exploded on the upside.

Since this is a momentum indicator based partially on volume, we can interpret this situation in another way. See how the index was down at an oversold condition in November at arrow A. This indicated severe selling pressure. However, by the start of the new year, this downside pressure had abated until there was virtually none at the February bottom, as the right shoulder was being formed—this, despite the fact that the price was testing its December low. Little wonder that when the buyers began to come back, there was very little selling pressure and the price rose very sharply.

The patterns that seem to work best are the head-and-shoulders variety at both tops and bottoms. In Chart 8-12 a small top develops in the demand index. It was then confirmed by a break in the price in September. The decline does not amount to much, but that is not surprising, given the relatively small size of the two patterns. The next example on the right also coincided with a major uptrend line break in the demand index. The decline following this break was far more substantial. It represents a classic example of the neckline and trendline breaks in the demand index reinforcing each other in confirmation of a reversal in trend. One of the reasons trendline and pattern completions seem to work so well with the demand index, as opposed to a momentum indicator based solely on price, is that a trend break in the demand index reflects changes in the volume as well. So in a sense, there are two pieces of evidence pointing to a trend reversal. This same data (in Chart 8-13) also features several overbought/oversold crossovers that generate timely buy-or-sell signals. Indeed, the head of the head-and-shoulders top on the right is associated with an overbought crossover that develops right at the top of the rally.

Chart 8-14 offers some bullish examples. I would have thought that the rally following the breakout from the first set of downtrend lines would have been larger. After all these are quite long and well-tested lines. However, in retrospect it is evident that this was a bear market rally. The thrust off the February bottom was indicated by the demand index breaking out from a small triangle formation. This was then confirmed by a price break.

You may have noticed that I drew the first trendline in the demand index, so that it was violated by the late November rally (see Chart 8-15). Some may say that this is not a legitimate line because of the break. However, I believe that a good trendline reflects the underlying trend and should represent strong resistance in a downtrend and support in an uptrend. In this instance, the line is a very good reflection of the downtrend, for despite the false break, it is touched or approached on no less than nine occasions.

Chart 8-12 Schlumberger and demand index price patterns. (Source: *pring.com*)

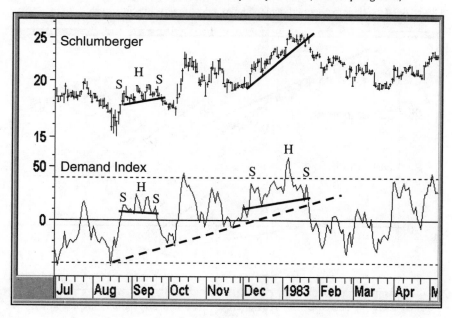

Chart 8-13 Schlumberger and demand index price patterns. (Source: *pring.com*)

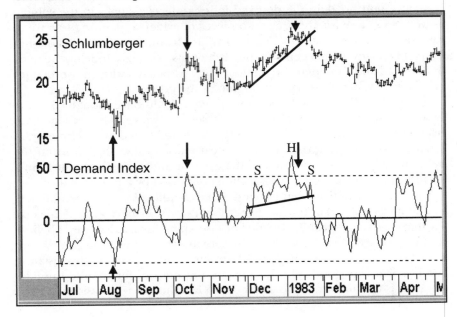

Chart 8-14 Schlumberger and demand index price patterns. (Source: *pring.com*)

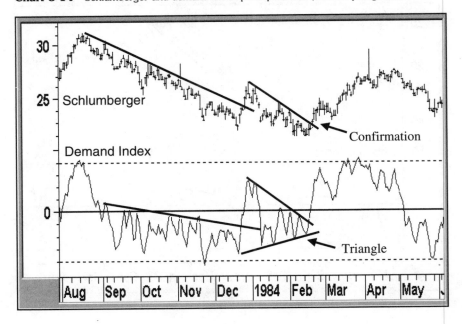

Chart 8-15   Schlumberger and demand index price patterns. (Source: *pring.com*)

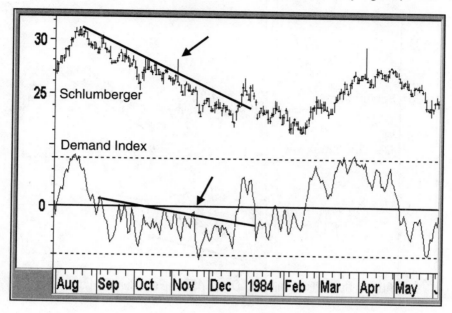

You can see a similar break earlier on in the trendline for the price. The same principle holds here, as well. Had I constructed the line to intersect with the intraday high, it would actually have been briefly whipped during the subsequent rally. In actual fact, the one-day break above this particular line that I drew was an exhaustion move, for once the price fell back below the line, it was unable to mount a rally for about 2 months. In retrospect, this exhaustion break shows that the line was indeed a better reflection of the underlying trend.

Before we leave Schlumberger, there are two other points to cover. First, in Chart 8-16 notice how the demand index reached its low in November, and by the time the price reached the end of its decline, the oscillator had diverged positively with it on several occasions.

Finally, note the head-and-shoulders top in the demand index that signaled the end of the rally and the trendline break in the price that confirmed it. In actual fact, this is the neckline of an upward-sloping head-and-shoulders formation.

Chart 8-17 shows Schlumberger in a different period. This time we see a giant reverse head-and-shoulders pattern in the index. There was also a positive divergence with the price (flagged by the converging arrows), and after the breakout, we see a normal retracement move back to the extended trendline. This is classic stuff, but where is the strong rally that should have

Chart 8-16 Schlumberger and demand index price patterns. (Source: *pring.com*)

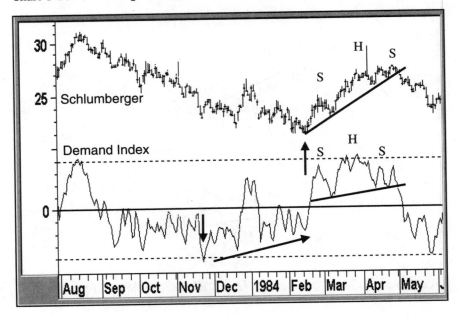

Chart 8-17 Schlumberger and demand index price patterns. (Source: *pring.com*)

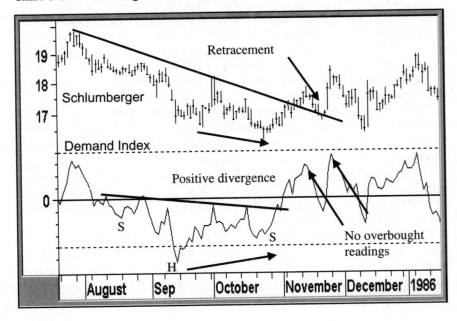

Chart 8-18   Schlumberger and demand index price patterns. (Source: *pring.com*)

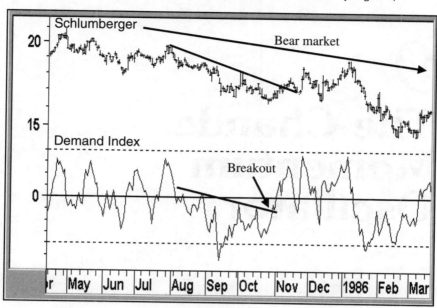

followed the retracement? It just was not there. Later on, we get a clue as to what may have happened because the demand index is unable to reach the overbought level on either the first or second rally following the breakout. This throws up a cautionary signal because momentum indicators that cannot reach an overbought reading are either indicating a trading range or more likely a bear market environment. This action is particularly suspect because of the two very nice trendline breaks in the price and demand index that took place in October.

Chart 8-18 shows that this period was part of an overall downtrend, so the action was typical of what we should expect in a bear market environment.

Summary

The demand index

1. Is constructed from both price and volume data
2. Experiences divergences with the price
3. Is better used with overbought-or-oversold crossovers
4. Is best used with trendline breaks and price pattern completions

9
The Chande Momentum Oscillator

Comparison with the Relative Strength Indicator

The Chande momentum oscillator (CMO), named after its inventor Dr. Tushar Chande, is a variation on the relative strength indicator (RSI), yet it is uniquely different. The CMO has three characteristics. First, the calculations are based on data that have not been smoothed. This means that extreme short-term movements are not hidden. Second, the scale is confined within the −100 to +100 range. This means that the zero level becomes the equilibrium point. With the RSI 50, l is the equilibrium point and is not always readily identifiable. With zero as the pivotal point, it is easier to see those periods when momentum is positive and those when it is negative. The zero equilibrium also makes comparisons between different securities that much easier. Finally, the calculation also uses both up and down days.

The CMO, as it is sometimes called, is interpreted in a similar way to other oscillators. Chart 9-1 compares the CMO with a 20-day RSI and a 20-day ROC. The 20-day period has been selected because it is the default for the CMO. What is striking is that the performance of all three (in terms of the swings) is very similar.

Chart 9-1 ASA comparing the CMO, RSI, and ROC. (Source: *pring.com*)

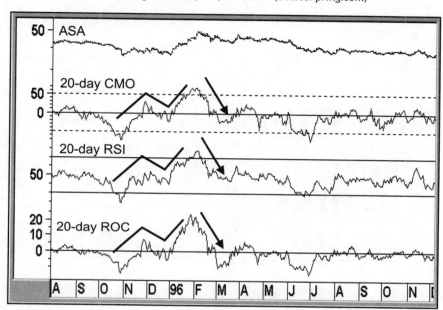

The three-wave advance between October and December 1995 is reflected in all three indicators. The January/February 1995 decline is also apparent.

Chart 9-2 limits the comparison to the RSI. The first thing that becomes apparent is that the RSI is much smoother. The November/December 1995 rally for the RSI is a zigzag ascending affair, but for the CMO, it is more of a spike. The April and June 1996 declines are also represented by spikes in the CMO, but not in the RSI. In fact, it is readily apparent that while the CMO does diverge from the price, the diverging characteristics of the RSI are much stronger in this instance.

Alternately, the CMO lends itself to trendline construction better than the RSI. Look at the rally between October and November 1995 in Chart 9-3. It was possible to construct a good uptrend line for the CMO, but not for the RSI. Similarly, in the March April 1996 period it was possible to draw a line only for the CMO. In this particular instance, it was not of much use, since the price had already peaked. However, the important point is the establishment of the principle that it is easier to construct trendlines for the CMO.

Chart 9-2   ASA comparing the CMO and the RSI. (Source: *pring.com*)

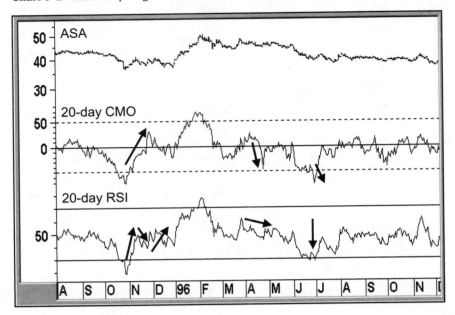

Chart 9-3   ASA comparing the CMO and the RSI. (Source: *pring.com*)

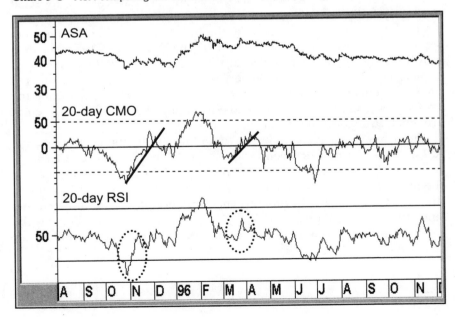

Comparison with the ROC

In Chart 9-4 the CMO is compared to the ROC. The individual swings are almost identical. Look at the fall 1995 rally and the February/March 1996 decline contained in the rectangles; the peaks are also very similar.

I have also drawn several trendlines for each indicator in Chart 9-5, and once again they are extremely close. It would be possible to say that the CMO is no better than the ROC. However, there is one very important point that should be taken into consideration and that is that the CMO is constrained by its calculation within the +50 or −50 zone. This means that it is possible to construct some standard overbought-or-oversold lines, that is, ones adaptable for all securities. This is not possible with the ROC because the volatility factor differs from security to security. With the CMO, it is possible to compare one security with another if the same timeframe is adopted. In other words, compare a 14-day CMO of security A with that of security B. What cannot be done is to compare a 14-day CMO for one security against a 30-day period for another.

For example, Chart 9-6 displays the 20-day ROC of two different securities on the left and the 20-day CMO of the same securities on the right. It is quite clear that while the swings in both oscillators differ from time to time, the scaling is much closer and the comparison much easier to make on the CMO side.

Chart 9-4 ASA comparing the CMO and the ROC. (Source: *pring.com*)

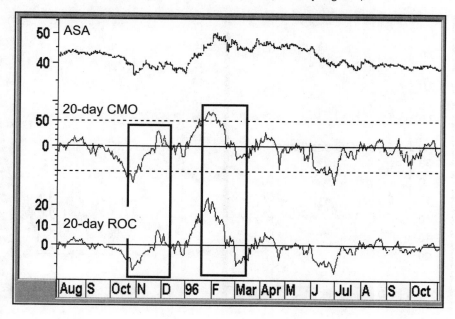

Chart 9-5　ASA comparing the CMO and the ROC. (Source: *pring.com*)

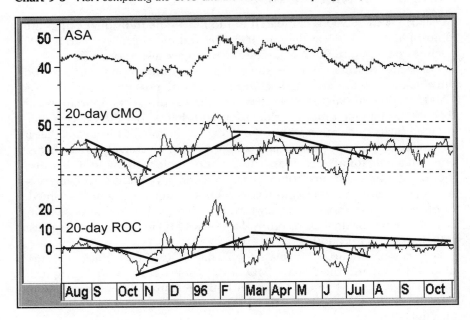

Chart 9-6　Comparing two securities—the CMO versus the ROC. (Source: *pring.com*)

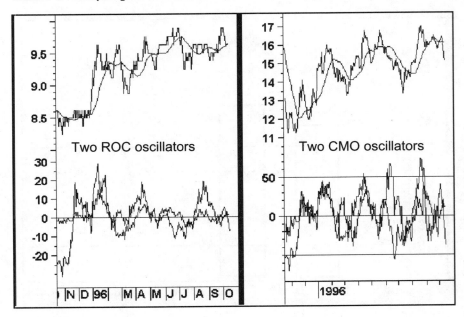

Interpreting the CMO
with Trendlines

One approach that I often use with the ROC indicator is to construct trendlines. When the trendline is violated, I then look around for a trend confirmation from the price itself. In Chart 9-7 several buy signals using this approach with the CMO have been highlighted. In late 1996, the CMO experiences a downtrend break, which is followed a little time later by one in the price. More than one vertical line marks the spot. The July 1996 trend break combination on the right also worked out well. It is also flagged by a vertical line.

I have displayed the February/May 1996 downtrend line as a dashed line because it was only half a signal, since the price of IBM was never able to rally above its downtrend line.

Chart 9-8 goes through the same exercise but from the point of view of sell signals. This time a 45-day CMO is being used. Note that the oversold line is barely visible. This is because swings in the CMO become less pronounced the longer the timespan is used in the calculation. The RSI has exactly the same characteristic. Therefore, it is appropriate to narrow the overbought-or-oversold lines with longer-term timespans. In this case, there

Chart 9-7 IBM showing CMO trendline breaks. (Source: *pring.com*)

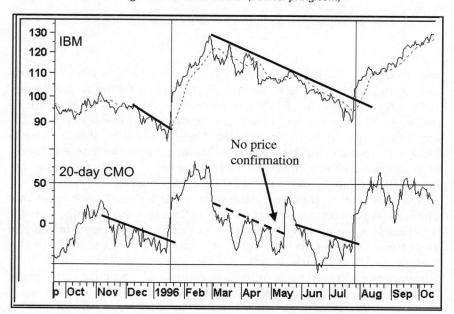

Chart 9-8   Philippine Fund and CMO trendline breaks. (Source: *pring.com*)

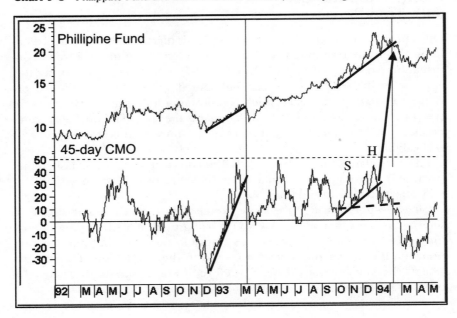

are two sell signals. The one on the left, in March 1993, is almost immediately confirmed by the price. Alternately, the one on the right, in February 1994, is not confirmed until just over a month later. At the time of the trendline break in the price, we actually get another trend break in the oscillator. If you look carefully, you will see that this was a breakdown from a head-and-shoulders top. At the time of the break there were several pieces of evidence suggesting that the trend had reversed, that is the two trendline breaks and the CMO head-and-shoulders completion.

It is important to note that these joint trend breaks do not occur that often. This chart, for instance, covers about 2 years. Consequently, patience is definitely a requirement in searching out this type of opportunity. Not every trend break results in a worthwhile move but most generally do. It is best to wait for a fairly lengthy trendline that has been touched or approached on at least three or four occasions, and if a similar setup in the price is observed, it is even better.

Smoothing the CMO

One approach that I have found helpful is to create a custom indicator of the CMO, smoothing, say, a 20-day CMO with a 10-day simple moving average. An example is shown in Chart 9-9. The dashed line plotted against the CMO is a 10-day exponential moving average. EMA crossovers are then used to generate buy or sell alerts. If these signals can be augmented with trend breaks in the price itself, then it makes sense to take some action. Since there are a lot of moving-average crossovers, it is important to filter out those that are not likely to work out. For example, a buy signal that is triggered when the indicator is overbought greatly reduces the odds of success, so do not use them. Generally speaking, though, even when you get broad swings in the oscillator, it is rare that you can rely solely on the EMA crossovers. A more accurate approach is to draw a trendline on the smoothed CMO, just as we did earlier with the CMO, using raw data. The upside breakout (Chart 9-9) in mid 1994 represented an excellent signal when it was finally confirmed by the price.

In March 1995 we have an EMA crossover from an oversold condition. Then the price breaks a trendline confirming the momentum trend reversal (Chart 9-10). But look at the smoothed CMO; it, too, is violating a downtrend line, thereby offering a third piece of evidence that the trend is

Chart 9-9 Echo Bay and a smoothed CMO. (Source: *pring.com*)

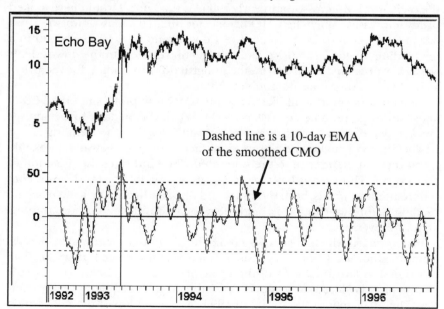

Chart 9-10   Echo Bay and a smoothed CMO. (Source: *pring.com*)

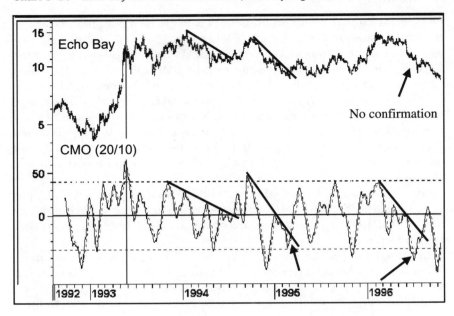

reversing. You can see the wisdom of waiting for a price trend reversal from the oscillator EMA crossover in early 1996. At the time, it would have looked pretty impressive, since the CMO has just terminated a long downswing and was extremely oversold. It also broke a downtrend line. However, within a few trading sessions, the price had once again reversed to the downside. It was never possible to construct a meaningful downtrend line for the price, so in this case there was no double signal.

One final way in which I like to use the CMO is to plot a smoothed CMO above an r-square indicator (Chart 9-11). When the 30-day r-square moves above 0.9 and then starts to reverse, this indicates that the trending factor has begun to dissipate and the random factor increase, causing a possible trend reversal. Reference to the smoothed CMO indicates the direction of the reversal. However, it has to come from an oversold-or-overbought condition. In other words, both the CMO and r-square have to be at an extreme reading before we can have a high degree of confidence that the trend is about to reverse.

In this chart, which covers $4^{1}/_{2}$ years, we do not get many such signals. But when they do appear, they result in some very interesting situations. The buy signal in late 1992 met all the principles I have outlined. However, it cannot be considered successful because the price subsequently made a new low. The sell signal in the spring of 1993 caught the top of the rally, which

Chart 9-11 Echo Bay, a smoothed CMO, and an r-square. (Source: *pring.com*)

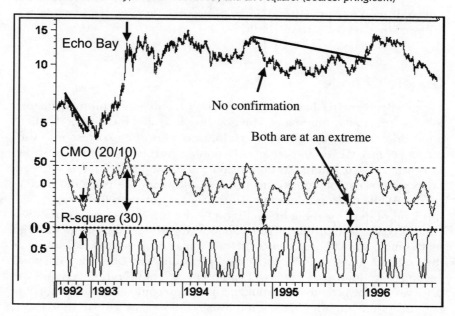

Chart 9-12 ASA comparing two CMOs. (Source: *pring.com*)

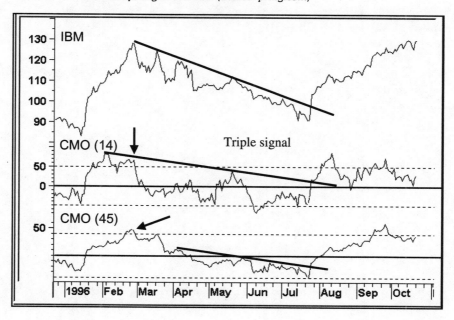

was pretty close to the final top. The next buy signal in December 1994 was not confirmed by a price trend break. However, that in November 1995 was followed by a very worthwhile rally.

Double Chande

The arrangement in Chart 9-12 features two Chande momentum oscillators, with 14- and 45-day timespans. The objective is to spot those periods where both series are overbought or oversold, since this often corresponds with turning points. We see an example of a double overbought by the two arrows in February 1996. There was no possibility to draw a trendline or witness a price pattern completion in this instance, although the price did decline sharply. While the conditions for a short sale did not, therefore, materialize, this kind of joint overbought condition by the two oscillators is certainly a great place to take profits or write options, for while the price may not go down much, it usually experiences at least a small drop or consolidation. This then offers enough time for the option premium burn-off. There is a good example of a joint trend break in July 1996. See how both CMOs and the price violate downtrend lines simultaneously. This combination does not happen that often, but when it does, it is usually followed by a worthwhile move.

10

The Relative Momentum Index

Basic Concepts

The *relative momentum index,* or *RMI* as it is known, is a variation on the RSI. In the calculation of the RMI the standard formula for the RSI is modified to allow for a momentum factor. This modification has two effects. First, it smoothes the indicator, and second, it accentuates the degree of the fluctuation. The result is a less jagged oscillator that experiences more rhythmic fluctuations. The effect is that more overbought-or-oversold crossovers are generated. The RMI requires two parameters. The first, as with the RSI, is the timeframe. The second is the momentum factor.

Chart 10-1 shows a 20-day RMI and a 20-day RSI. The two are identical, since the RMI contains a momentum factor of 1, which makes it identical to the RSI.

In Chart 10-2 the RMI momentum factor has been changed to 5, which results in a substantial difference. The RMI is far smoother. Note also that the overbought-or-oversold lines have been drawn at 25 and 75 for both series, but you can see that the RSI reaches the overbought zone on far fewer occasions than the RMI.

Chart 10-3 substitutes a 30-period RMI with a momentum factor of 10 for the RSI. As you can see, this series is even smoother than the 20/5 combination.

Chart 10-4 shows the 30/10 combination on its own. The downward-pointing arrows indicate those points where the RMI crosses below the overbought line on its way toward the neutral 50 level. The upward-pointing ones

Chart 10-1   Heinz comparing an RMI with an RSI. (Source: *pring.com*)

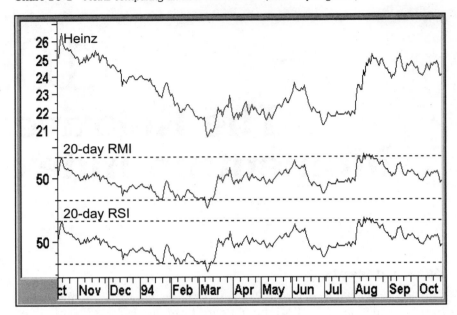

Chart 10-2   Heinz comparing an RMI with an RSI. (Source: *pring.com*)

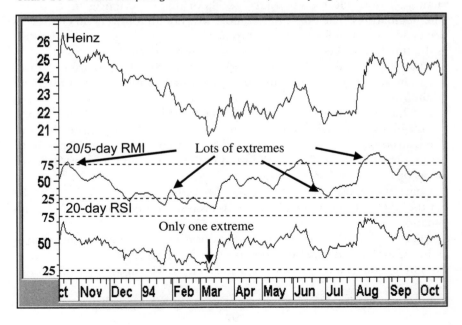

Chart 10-3 Italian Government Bonds two RMI's. (Source: *pring.com*)

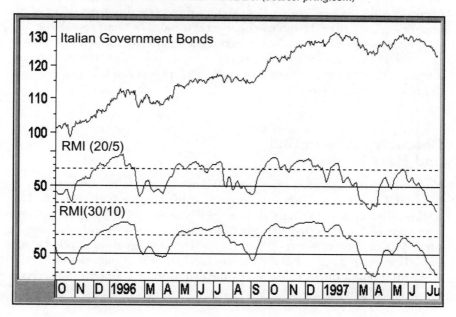

Chart 10-4 Italian Government Bonds with a 30/10 RMI. (Source: *pring.com*)

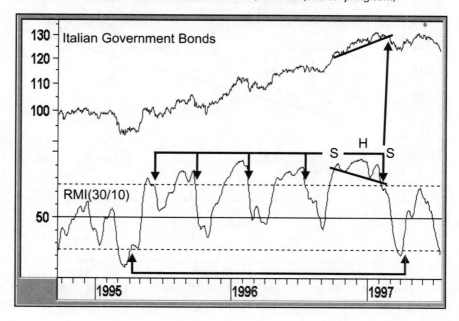

indicate the opposite set of conditions, where the RMI is crossing above its oversold zone. By and large, these signals provide a timely warning of an impending change in the intermediate-term trend. The chart reveals the fact that this versatile indicator also traces out price patterns, though this is quite rare when the momentum factor is as large as it is in this instance. A head-and-shoulders top is completed in early 1997, just as the bond price starts to break in a major way.

Characteristics in Bull and Bear Markets

No momentum indicator, however well-devised, is able to generate timely buy-or-sell alerts in a market undergoing a linear up- or downtrend. The RMI is no exception. In Chart 10-5 we see it with the S & P Composite. Some negative overbought crossovers are followed by a sideways trend, or even a small decline. But for the most part, they offer false signals of implied weakness. This again goes to emphasize the fact that it is of paramount importance for momentum signals to be confirmed by some kind of trend-reversal signal in the price.

Chart 10-5   S & P Composite with a 30/10 RMI. (Source: *pring.com*)

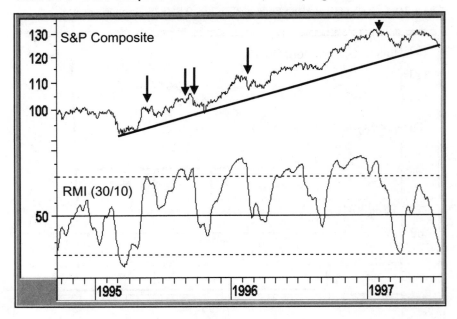

Chart 10-6 of the Japanese Topix Index can be roughly divided into two bear and one bull periods. The first bearish environment developed between 1994 and 1995: the bullish one between mid 1995 and early 1996, and the second bear in early 1997.

Now look at the performance of this 30/10 RMI. During the bear phase, it is rarely able to rise above zero but spends a lot of time in the oversold area. This is indicative of the kind of characteristic we should expect from a momentum indicator in a bear market. Note that none of the oversold conditions are able to trigger very much in the way of a rally. Then, in mid 1995, the situation changes dramatically, as the indicator moves to an overbought condition. But during the whole rise it is unable to slip back into oversold territory. This is the way we would normally expect a momentum indicator to act during a bull market. In effect its action is providing us with a vital clue as to whether the Topix is in a primary bull or bear market.

Then, in early August of 1996 the RMI falls back into the oversold zone for the first time in over a year. Not every oversold condition following a long uptrend in the price signals a bear market, but quite often when a

Chart 10-6 Topix Index with a 30/10 RMI. (Source: *pring.com*)

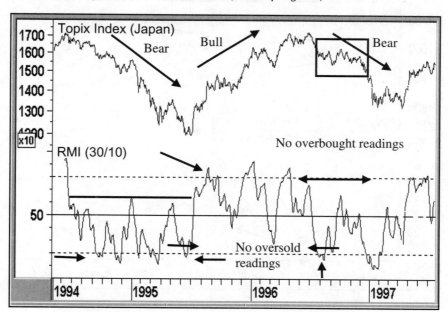

short-term momentum indicator reaches an oversold reading that surpasses anything seen in the previous 12 months or so, this increases the odds that a bear trend is underway. In this case, a new primary trend was in force and the RMI entered a period when it did not experience an overbought reading yet fell into oversold territory three times. Look also at how the price rallies after this second attempt to fall into oversold territory fails. The character of the rally gives us two clues that the bear market is still alive at this point. I am now going to focus on the bear market consolidation contained in the rectangle.

First, the momentum indicator peaks from a fairly low level (Chart 10-7). This failure to reach an overbought condition, especially following the small positive momentum divergence in September 1996, is indicative once again of tired bear market activity. The second clue came from the fact that the price rallied above this trading range and then fell back below it again. False breakouts are unusual and are, again, a characteristic of a negative primary trend.

Chart 10-7   Topix Index with a 30/10 RMI. (Source: *pring.com*)

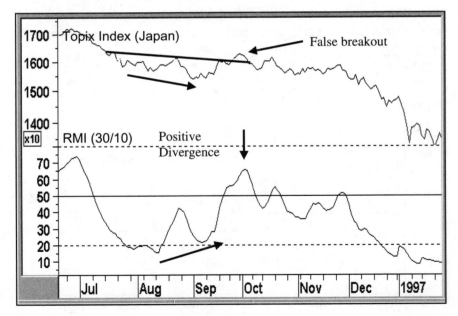

RMI and Trendline Construction

Chart 10-8 shows us how the RMI occasionally lends itself to trendline construction and analysis. See how it was possible to construct a good downtrend line for the RMI. Just shortly after its penetration, the price experiences a double trendline violation. Not surprisingly, a very nice rally followed.

The RMI versus The RSI

Chart 10-9 compares the performance of a simple 30-day RSI with that of an RMI with a 10-day momentum factor. First of all, the overbought-or-oversold zones are set at different parameters. The RSI is at a fairly narrow 65/35, whereas the RMI is at 75/25. The action of the RMI is much smoother and gives clearer signals. For instance, the arrows point out those periods in 1996 when the RMI falls to its oversold zone and then crosses the dashed horizontal line on its way back to the equilibrium point. Given the neutral/bearish environment, these are reasonably good signals. However, the RSI, despite the narrower bands, does not reach the oversold zone on

Chart 10-8   Topix Index with a 30/10 RMI. (Source: *pring.com*)

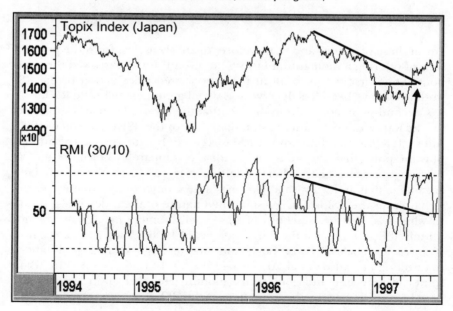

Chart 10-9   TVX Gold with an RMI and an RSI. (Source: *pring.com*)

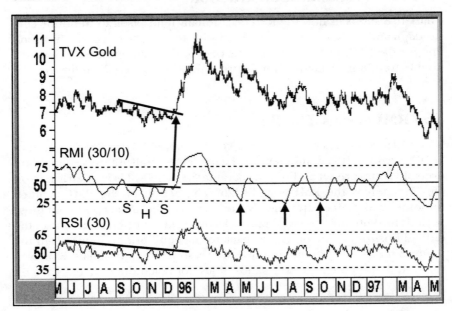

any of these occasions and is, therefore, relatively useless from the point of
view of offering a momentum buy signal. Even if I had narrowed the overbought-or-oversold zones still further, the jagged price action of the RSI
would still have been less decisive as a signal generator than the RMI.

A second point comes from the fact that the reverse head and shoulders
for the RMI was much easier to spot than that for the RSI at the end of 1995.
Alternately, the trendline for the RSI was certainly a lot longer. This under-
pins the point that it is often a good idea to compare two or more indicators on the same chart, thereby letting one reinforce the other. One
advantage that an RMI with a relatively large momentum quotient appears
to have over the RSI is that the smoothed nature of the index is less prone
to whipsaws. Yet the timelines of buy-or-sell momentum signals are not
unduly affected. Look at the RSI in January of 1996 (Chart 10-10). See how
it moves down below its overbought zone and then quickly rallies back above
it, resulting in a false signal. Alternately, the 30/10 RMI gives no hint what-
soever of a decline and goes on to smoothly roll over and cross its overbought zone at roughly the same time as the RSI.

Chart 10-10   TVX Gold with an RMI and an RSI. (Source: *pring.com*)

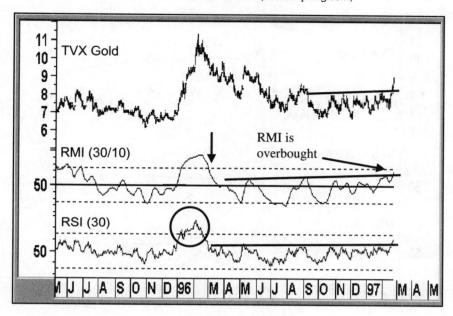

On the right-hand part of the chart, we see a good example of a momentum breakout from an overextended level. Normally, this kind of thing does not work, since a momentum breakout that develops close to an overbought zone indicates that the price is already overextended by the time the breakout takes place. This example was no exception, as Chart 10-11 shows the price experienced a false breakout.

RMI Variations and Arrangements

The RMI lends itself nicely to short-term trends when used with a smaller timespan. Chart 10-12 features an RMI with a 10-period timespan and a 5-period momentum factor. As the timespan is shifted to a smaller number of periods, so the indicator becomes increasingly volatile. As a result, it is less suitable for the construction of trendlines or the formation of price patterns. However, this disadvantage is partly offset by the fact that the movements between overbought-or-oversold zones become far more pronounced. The upward- and downward-pointing arrows indicate those periods when the RMI reaches an extreme and then turns back toward the equilibrium

Chart 10-11   TVX Gold with an RMI and an RSI. (Source: *pring.com*)

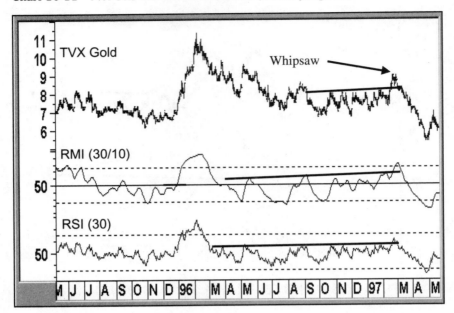

Chart 10-12   Homestake and two RMIs. (Source: *pring.com*)

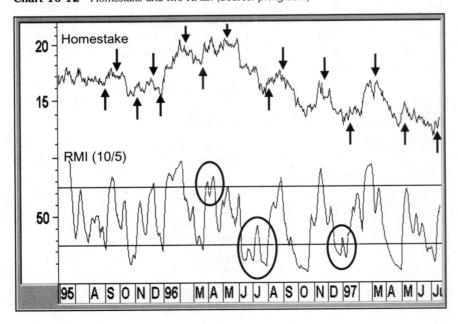

level. By and large, these signals are fairly good. However, the arrows were placed with the benefit of hindsight. In the three cases flagged by the ellipses, the RMI would have left us in doubt on a real-time basis, since it whipped above and below the overbought-or-oversold line on several occasions.

One solution for this problem is to also plot an RMI with a longer timespan and momentum factor on the same chart. In this way, it's possible to get a better perspective of what is really going on (Chart 10-13). The longer-term RMI is much smoother in nature. As a result, it is possible to use a more conservative interpretation by waiting for the smoothed RMI to reverse direction before taking any action. In most cases, this will delay the signal by a few sessions but will not substantially affect the result adversely.

You can also see that the short-term RMI in the center area is not very helpful from the point of view of interpreting whether the current primary trend is bullish or bearish (Chart 10-14). Note how the lower series fails to reach an overbought reading in the March/December period in 1996, yet

Chart 10-13   Homestake and two RMIs. (Source: *pring.com*)

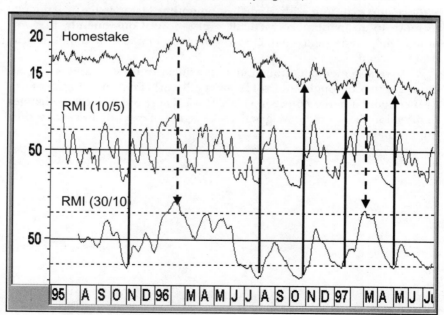

Chart 10-14   Homestake and two RMIs. (Source: *pring.com*)

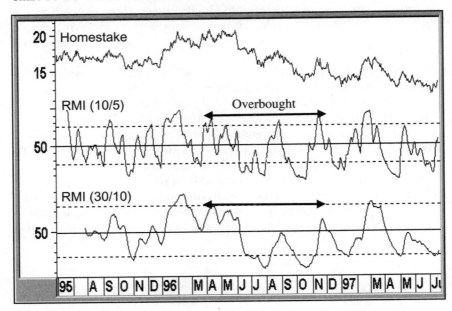

its short-term counterpart did. This is because the RMI is calculated from a short timespan and with a small momentum factor it has a tendency to move to an extreme on virtually every move. Consequently, they are of little help in trying to characterize whether a market is in a bull or bear primary trend.

We have to remember, though, that in a linear trend such as this one, no momentum overbought/oversold system will work. Look at the longer-term RMI contained in the ellipse in Chart 10-15. There are numerous changes in direction that would have given a false signal of extended weakness during this period.

Chart 10-15 Merrill Lynch and two RMIs. (Source: *pring.com*)

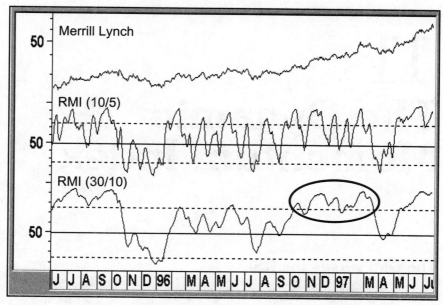

Summary

The RMI

1. Is a modification of the RSI indicator
2. Has a tendency to exaggerate oscillations and generate overbought-or-oversold signals more often than other indicators
3. Becomes smoother when the momentum and time factors are increased. In this format, it lends itself to trendline construction.

11
The Dynamic Momentum Index

The DMI versus the RSI

The *dynamic momentum index*, or *DMI*, is a variation on the RSI index. The principle difference is that the period of calculation is fixed with the RSI, but in the case of the DMI, it is not. This is because the DMI controls the periods in the calculation based on the volatility of recent price changes. Consequently, during quiet trading periods, the DMI will use a smaller time-span in the calculation than when things are more volatile. The index can use as many as 30, and as little as 3, periods.

For those who are mathematically inclined, the DMI is based on a calculation that uses a 5-period standard deviation and a 10-period average standard deviation.

The index is justified on the grounds that the variable time lengths enhance short-term movements that are often obscured by the regular RSI calculation. This enables it to turn faster than the regular RSI. Both indicators have been plotted in Chart 11-1. There is no question that the DMI is more volatile and turns ahead of the RSI. However, if you look very carefully, you will find that there is very little difference between the two, as each little rally and reaction in the RSI is reflected in the DMI.

The big difference is in the volatility. In Chart 11-2 the DMI has been overlaid on the RSI. The DMI is the dashed line. There is no doubt that the DMI reaches an overbought-or-oversold reading ahead of the RSI. It also touches extreme levels when the RSI does not, as in December 1983 and again in May 1984. Indeed, the DMI warns us of a possible trend reversal when the

Chart 11-1   Dow Jones Bond Index comparing an RSI with a DMI. (Source: *pring.com*)

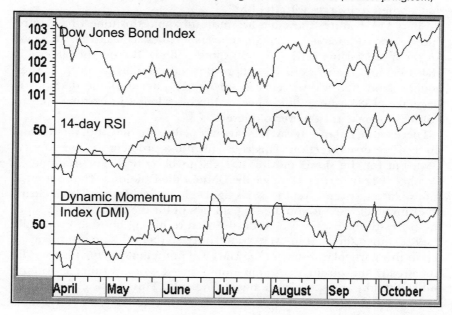

Chart 11-2   Dow Jones Transports comparing an RSI with a DMI. (Source: *pring.com*)

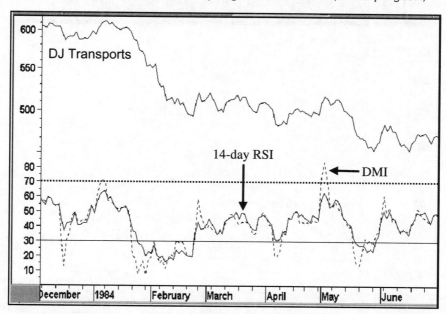

RSI does not. This leads us to arguably the best occasion for this index, and that is when it diverges with the RSI.

Chart 11-3 features the same two indicators, but this time I have introduced some additional overbought-or-oversold lines at 80 and 20. These are for the more volatile DMI. Now you can see the DMI cross the 80 level in May 1984 and then reverse direction. But the RSI fails to reach its overbought zone, and a divergence is set up. Another example develops in December 1983, where the dashed DMI crosses below its extreme, yet the RSI fails to make the 30 oversold level.

There is one important caveat: you must make sure that both the RSI and the DMI reverse direction. This is usually not a problem for the sensitive DMI, but for the slower-moving RSI, it can be critical. For example, in October 1987 (Chart 11-4) we see the DMI for the Dow Jones Transportation Index is at an extreme, yet the RSI is right at its oversold zone. This is clearly an example of when it would have paid to wait for the RSI to reverse, since the price still had some way to decline before hitting bottom. Eventually, the RSI joined the DMI in oversold territory, so there was no divergence at all. In this particular instance, the DMI was not telling us anything we did not already know from an examination of the RSI or any other short-term index: that the transports were deeply oversold. This approach works well most of the time. But as with all signals, it is important to check out the situation with other indicators to make sure that they agree.

Chart 11-3   Dow Jones Transports RSI/DMI divergences. (Source: *pring.com*)

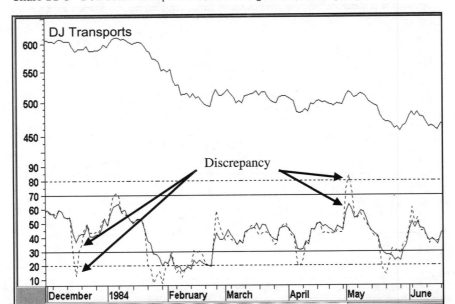

Chart 11-4 Dow Jones Transports RSI/DMI divergences. (Source: *pring.com*)

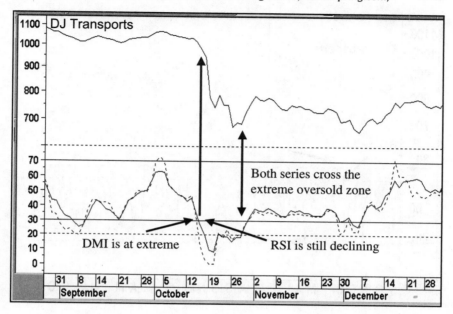

The Cluster Rule

There is another way in which I like to use the DMI, and that is with the cluster rule. The cluster rule states that if, after an advance or decline, the DMI makes three peaks or troughs above the extreme overbought level or below the oversold zone within a period of roughly 90 days, then expect a reversal of the prevailing trend. A peak is defined as a rally that takes the index above 80, where this is followed by a reaction below the extreme level, as shown in Chart 11-5. Then, when the index rises above the 80 zone again, a new peak is formed. However, one or more of the two reactions must push the indicator below the normal overbought parameter at 70. In effect, the second and third peaks will be separated by two valleys, at least one of which will find its bottom somewhere below the regular overbought zone. The condition for a bottom will be exactly the reverse.

Chart 11-6 shows a far longer period, and you can see several instances that have been highlighted with the boxes. Each was followed by an important advance, decline, or consolidation. Now let us take a closer look at one such situation.

Chart 11-7 focuses on the period contained in the large box in the 1992 to 1993 period. The three peaks in January, February, and April 1993 are

Chart 11-5   Dow Jones Transports and a DMI. (Source: *pring.com*)

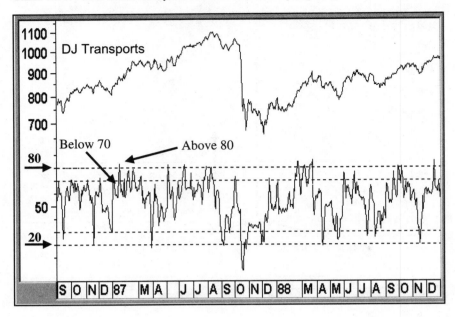

Chart 11-6   Dow Jones Transports and the three-cluster rule. (Source: *pring.com*)

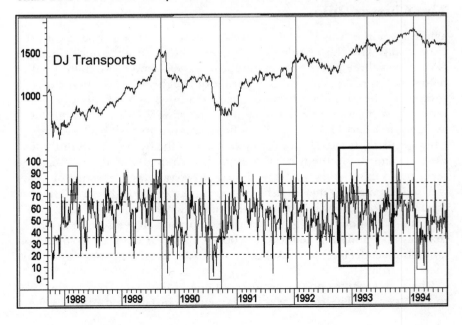

Chart 11-7 Dow Jones Transports and the three-cluster rule. (Source: *pring.com*)

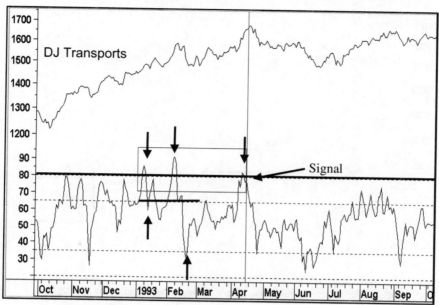

flagged by the downward-pointing arrows. Each one is separated by a reaction, where the DMI registers a low below the regular overbought condition. These are flagged by the upward-pointing arrows. Then, when the third peak crosses below the extreme zone, the indicator triggers a three-cluster sell signal. You can see that the first and third peaks are separated by just a little over 3 months. I do not like to see a separation greater than 3½ months as a general rule. The idea behind the 3-months-or-less rule is that after a rally, three overbought extremes within a 90-day period indicate exhaustion. If the peaks are separated by 5 or 6 months, this means that the price trend has had time to take a rest and recuperate. Consequently, there will be less chance of a reaction. The opposite set of principles apply to a reversal from a downtrend to an uptrend.

If you look at the July to August period in Chart 11-8, you may come to the conclusion that this is another cluster sell signal. However, while the DMI does move into overbought territory, it never reaches an extreme position. Therefore, it is not a valid signal.

Chart 11-9 shows buy and sell signals that are very close to each other. In this case, the sell signal in February 1994 is followed by relatively short-lived decline. The three bottoms in early 1994 are separated by less than 3 months. Both rallies separating the bottoms are halted well above the oversold zone. In this instance, the cluster buy signal was not followed by a rally, but by a 3-month consolidation.

Chart 11-8   Dow Jones Transports and the three-cluster rule. (Source: *pring.com*)

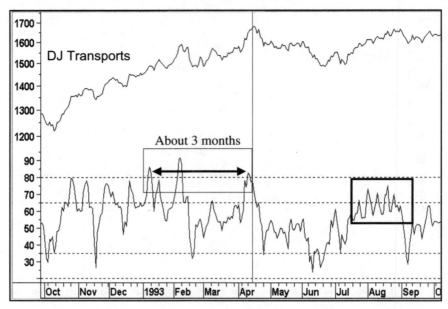

Chart 11-9   Dow Jones Transports and the three-cluster rule. (Source: *pring.com*)

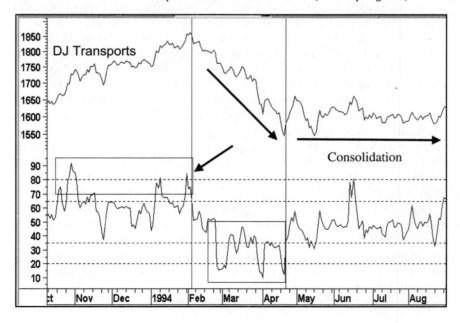

Smoothing the DMI

Another idea is to plot two exponential moving averages and use over-bought-or-oversold crossovers as buy-or-sell points. In Chart 11-10 I have plotted an 8-day EMA and a 25-day EMA of the DMI. When the 8-day series moves into the extreme overbought-or-oversold zone, this puts me on the alert that the trend in the price may be about to reverse. As you can see, there are not many instances, but when these momentum buy-or-sell signals are triggered, the price itself usually undergoes an important trend reversal. Narrowing the zones a little will increase the number of signals, but some of them are likely to be less reliable. It is really a matter of trial and error with each security to see which might fit the best. Remember to plot as much data as possible in your experimentation, so that your chart encompasses different market situations. The fall 1994 sell signal is a bit of a stretch because the indicator never quite made the overbought level.

In Chart 11-11 the overbought-or-oversold zones are not quite so extreme as the previous ones. They have been narrowed from an 80/20 zone to a 75/25 zone. The reason for this is that we are now dealing with a smoothing of the data rather than the raw series itself. The technique is to wait for the 8-day EMA to move to the extreme zone above 75 or below 25 and cross the 25-day series. It is the crossing that generates the signal. Examples are flagged with the vertical lines. They are not triggered very often, but when they are, there is a good chance that the prevailing trend is about to

Chart 11-10   ASE Biotech Index and two smoothed DMIs. (Source: *pring.com*)

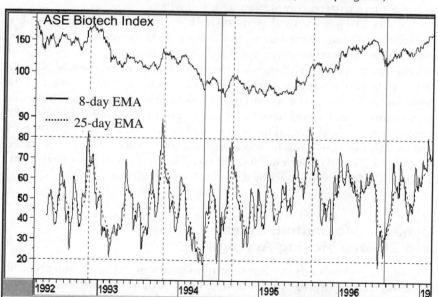

Chart 11-11   ASE Biotech Index and two smoothed DMIs. (Source: *pring.com*)

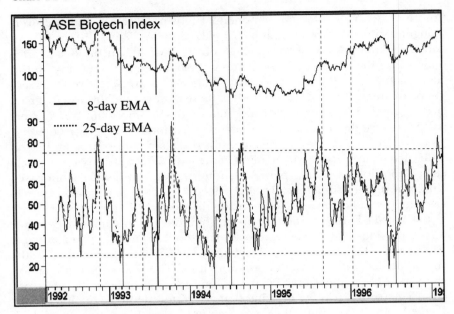

reverse. Of course, this is only a momentum sell signal, so then it is necessary to look around to see what price trend-reversal signals may be in the offing. This could be a crossover of a reliable moving average, a trendline break, a price pattern completion, and so forth.

Chart 11-11 shows several years of trading for the ASE Biotech index. There are not many occasions when the 8-day EMA moves into the extreme overbought-or-oversold zone. But nearly all of them trigger some kind of trend change. Chart 11-12 offers a closer look at some of these signals. In January 1994, the 8-day series did not make it to the extreme zone, but the crossover did confirm the second top in a double top formation. The actual momentum signal would have been given at point A, where the solid DMI crossed the dashed one. The signal in August 1994 was followed by a decline. Though there was no way in which a trendline could be constructed for the price, it did experience a small top. The final sell signal on the chart in August 1995 was followed by a 3-month consolidation.

Dynamic Momentum Index and 10-Day Moving Average

Chart 11-13 features a dynamic momentum indicator in the bottom area and its 10-day moving average in the center. The DMI itself is useful for flagging overbought-or-oversold conditions. However, the 10-day moving average

Chart 11-12 ASE Biotech Index and two smoothed DMIs. (Source: *pring.com*)

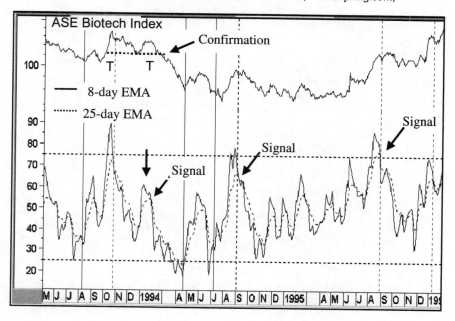

Chart 11-13 Nolose and two DMIs. (Source: *pring.com*)

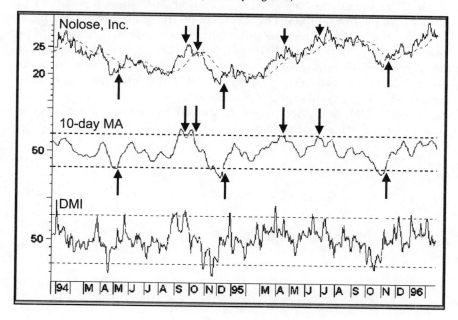

Chart 11-14   Nolose and two DMIs. (Source: *pring.com*)

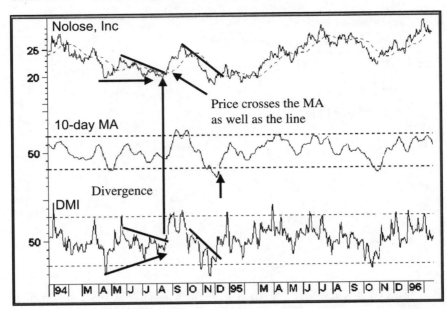

offers a more stable indication of these extreme reversals, which are indicated in the chart with the upward- and downward-pointing arrows.

The DMI sometimes lends itself to trendline construction. Chart 11-14 shows a couple of examples. The trendline on the left experiences a trend break for both the DMI and the price. Note that it was not confirmed by an oversold reading in the smoothed DMI, but that does not really matter, since this indicator is diverging for a second time in a positive way with the price. Note also that this action was also confirmed by the price crossing its moving average. The second example, in early 1995, was confirmed with a trend break in the DMI and price, as well as a positive crossover of the oversold line by the smoothed DMI.

12
The Klinger Oscillator

Basic Concepts

The *Klinger oscillator* was developed by Stephen J. Klinger with two objectives. The first is to have an indicator that is sensitive enough to signal short-term price reversals and the second is to reflect the long-term flow of money in and out of a specific security. This oscillator uses both price and volume. The price range is the measure of movement and the volume reflects the force behind the movement. Price is defined as the high minus the low for a specific period. If this number is larger than the previous period, then the formula treats it as accumulation. And if it is lower, the formula treats it as distribution.

Volume is then introduced into the calculation as a positive or negative force, depending on whether the price is classified as being in an accumulation or distribution phase. It is a general technical principle that volume leads price. This means that the Klinger oscillator should peak ahead of price in uptrends and bottom out ahead of prices during downtrends.

The indicator is represented in the chart as the difference between a 39- and 55-period exponential moving average of the resulting volume-price calculation. A trigger line, somewhat along the lines of the MACD trigger line, is also part of the approach.

This indicator seems to have its definite strong and weak points. First of all, the signal line is not of much help. Crossovers by the oscillator are so frequent that many whipsaw signals are generated (Chart 12-1). Zero crossovers by the signal line are also of little help in identifying trend reversals, as can be seen from Chart 12-2 of Coca-Cola around the year's end, 1992.

Chart 12-1   Coca-Cola and a 13-day Klinger. (Source: *pring.com*)

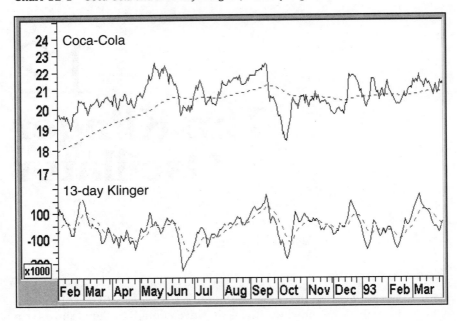

Chart 12-2   Coca-Cola and 13-day Klinger zero crossovers. (Source: *pring.com*)

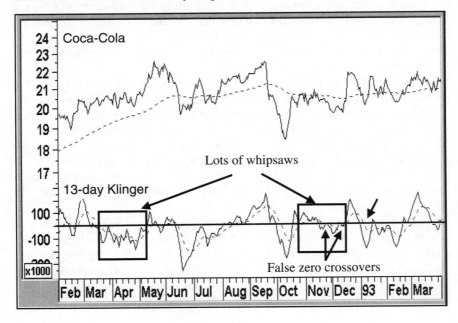

Relating Klinger Signals to an 89-Period EMA

It is recommended that the oscillator be compared to the price in relationship to its 89-period EMA. The idea is that when the price is above its 89-period EMA, it is in a bull trend, and when it is below, this indicates that the trend is down. One interpretive rule states that when the price is above its EMA and the Klinger oscillator falls to an unusually low level, this is a buying opportunity. Chart 12-3 contains an oversold line for the oscillator. The vertical lines indicate where the price is above its EMA *and* the oscillator falls decisively below the oversold line. They all seem to work quite well, but remember this was a strongly trending market, so they should do so. In effect, what we are saying is buy on a short-term oversold in a bull market, and vice versa. The best situations seem to occur when the price experiences a decline that takes it close to the EMA, but not through it. Of course, you do not know at the time that the decline will halt at the average, but that is where the extreme reading in the Klinger oscillator comes in.

Chart 12-4 focuses on the two signals contained in the rectangle in Chart 12-3. The first one in late May turns out to be okay, but only after a little decline takes place. Then in September, the price declines close to the EMA and the oscillator moves well into extreme oversold territory and actually

Chart 12-3   Coca-Cola relating Klinger signals to an 89-day EMA. (Source: *pring.com*)

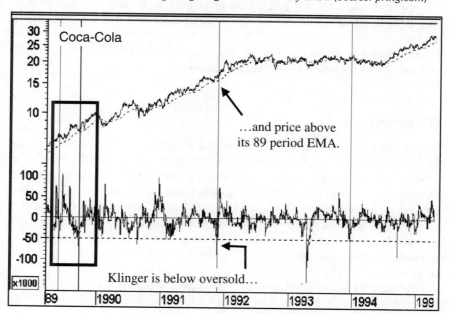

Chart 12-4   Coca-Cola relating Klinger signals to an 89-day EMA. (Source: *pring.com*)

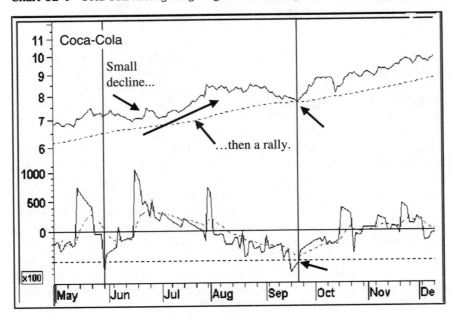

rises, as the price touches its EMA. A good rally follows. This is an interesting approach, but by and large, I do not find it to be any better than a lot of other indicators. The choice of 89 periods for the EMA is interesting, though I have never found the period to test particularly well. Innovative readers might wish to experiment with other timeframes, such as a 200-day MA for the purposes of defining the long-term trend.

Divergences

The strongest point I can find in favor of the oscillator is its ability to diverge from the price during both uptrends and downtrends. Chart 12-5 shows an example using Heinz, where a double top formation develops between December 1992 and March 1993. It is fairly evident that the second is accompanied by a very weak reading in the oscillator. This warned of potential underlying technical weakness, and sure enough, the price did decline quite sharply. Note that up to the time of the first top, the indicator was in gear, because it makes a series of ascending peaks. Only later did it diverge in a serious way.

One final idea is to construct a 10-day EMA of the Klinger oscillator and observe at what point it becomes overbought. In Chart 12-6 you can see that

Chart 12-5 Coca-Cola relating and a 10-day Klinger. (Source: *pring.com*)

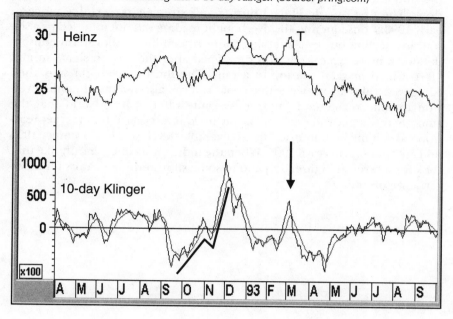

Chart 12-6 Coca-Cola and a 10-day EMA Klinger. (Source: *pring.com*)

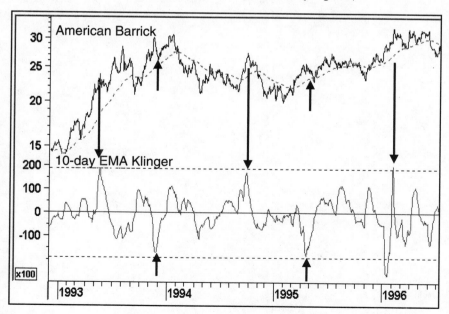

the smoothed oscillator rallies up to the overbought zone on three occasions. The first one developed during an extremely powerful advance in early 1993. Consequently, the overbought reading was not followed by a significant decline but by something more resembling a short-term consolidation. A more typical reaction developed after the second signal in mid 1994, which marked the top of a rally. The third overbought smoothed Klinger was also associated with a peak. You can also use this smoothed version to time reactions in uptrends. Quite often you will find that the smoothed Klinger will decline sharply in countercyclical bull market reactions, as volume literally dries up. An example developed in November 1993 and another one in April 1995. When the indictor declines sharply like this, look for a reversal in direction and to some short-term indicators for a better sense of timing.

13

The Herrick
Payoff Index

The Concept

The *Herrick payoff index* tries to measure money flowing into, and out of, a security. It does this by incorporating open interest into the formula by calculating the difference between the current period (usually a day) to the previous period's open interest. The formula is as follows.

$$HPI = (Ky + (K1 - Ky)S/100,000$$

Ky is yesterday's HPI, S is the user-entered smoothing factor (0.1 is the default), y is yesterday's value, and K1 (wait for it) is $CV(M - My)[1 \pm 2I/g]$.

In this case, M represents the mean and is calculated as half the value of the high plus the low. C is the value of a 1c move, V is the volume, and I is the absolute value of today's open interest.

The plus sign in the right-hand part of the formula occurs if M is greater than My (yesterday's mean). It would be a minus sign if yesterday's mean was below today's mean, that is, My < M.

Since the formula incorporates open interest, *this indicator can only be applied to the futures markets where open interest data are available.*

There are two variables that can be set by the user. The first is an exponential smoothing factor. As you might expect, the greater the smoothing factor, the smoother the oscillator. Chart 13-1 features a payoff index with a 2-day smoothing in the middle area and a 75-day smoothing in the lower one. As you can see, there is a tremendous difference in the volatility of the two series. The second user-determined variable is the value of a 1c move for the futures contract being monitored (for example, $400 for cattle, $50 for soybeans, and so on). This does not affect the shape of the index and has no bearing on the signals and interpretation.

One problem in the calculation of the index results from the fact that most data services only provide data for the total volume and open interest on *all* contracts. This causes a predicament for many agricultural commodities, where for seasonal reasons, price movements in the nearby contracts can differ considerably from more distant ones. This dilemma is not so acute for financial futures, because their price movements are more interrelated between the various contract months, generally fluctuating due to changes in interest rate differentials. Where commodities are subject to such seasonal differences, a single contract system is recommended. In other words, use the volume and open interest pertaining to that specific contract.

This can be quite an onerous task unless the data can be conveniently downloaded electronically from a data vendor. If that is not possible, it is probably better to limit payoff analysis to financial futures and other markets not seriously affected by seasonal variations. Except when it comes close to expiration, the nearby contract typically attracts the majority of the trading volume. For most futures contracts where there is little or no seasonal variation, a 3-month perpetual contact will provide a satisfactory compromise.

Chart 13-1   London Copper and two payoff indexes. (Source: *pring.com*)

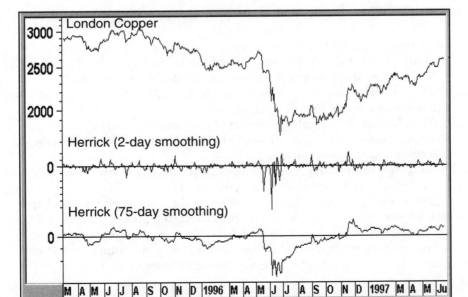

The perpetual contract is a continuous contract with a theoretical life for a specific period, say, 3, 6, or 9 months, with a theoretical life of 3 months. Carrying costs and other differentials are calculated with reference to more distant contract months. It offers the best compromise of obtaining a continuous series for contracts that would otherwise expire every 3 months. Data for these contracts are provided by CSI Data of Boca Raton, Florida (csidata.com).

Finally, one should always be on the lookout for contracts that often undergo a sharp reduction in open interest purely because of quarterly contract expiration. An example is shown in Chart 13-2, featuring the Euroyen contract. See how the open interest takes a sharp drop every quarter.

Interpretation

Zero Crossovers

The first step is to determine whether the payoff indicator is above or below zero, as this gives a good indication of whether money is flowing into, or out of, the market. Readings above zero indicate that interest is growing,

Chart 13-2 3-month Euroyen and open interest. (Source: *pring.com*)

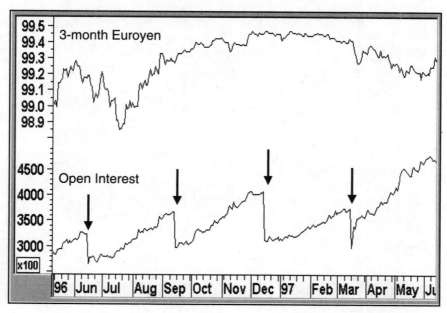

and they are regarded as a positive sign. Readings below zero indicate a contraction of activity, and they are bearish. The choice of timespan for the smoothing factor is obviously quite critical; the shorter the span, the greater the number of zero crossovers. In Chart 13-3, featuring Comex Silver, the payoff index is calculated with a 30-day span. The idea is that when the indicator experiences a decisive zero crossover, this often signals that a new sustainable short or intermediate trend is under way. There are several good buy signals labeled 1 to 5. When I say "decisive," I am just considering those signals that come from below zero and cross it in an almost vertical fashion. In a fast-moving market, it is possible, when the rally turns out to be sub par, for a substantial part of the move to have already been seen by the time it is realized that a sharp zero crossover has been achieved. For this reason, it seems that the best signals come from a situation where the index has been below zero for a while, say, 2 or 3 months.

You may have noticed that the August 1996 crossover has been flagged with an ellipse. This is because it was a failure. See how the signal was given right at the top of a whipsaw downtrend line break.

Generally speaking, decisive zero crossovers tend to give long-term signals *relative* to the timeframe under consideration. For example, if the average short-term rally lasts for 3 weeks and gains 5 percent, a good Herrick zero crossover might be expected to signal, say, a 5-week rally with a gain of 10

Chart 13-3   Comex Silver and a Herrick payoff index. (Source: *pring.com*)

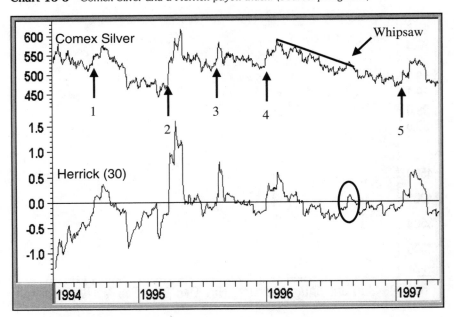

percent. Having said that, it is important that each security is analyzed on its own merit from the point of view of the reliability and timeliness of zero crossovers. If a particular timespan or market proves undependable, then disregard or significantly downplay the zero crossover concept. While I regard zero crossovers in many securities to be a useful concept, it should be noted that the innovator of the payoff system, John Herrick, has discounted their importance.

Overbought/Oversold Crossovers

An alternative approach is to construct overbought-or-oversold lines for the payoff index, using those periods when it crosses these extreme levels on its way back to zero as buy-or-sell alerts. Chart 13-4 features Live Hogs. I have drawn overbought-or-oversold lines at +3 or −3, respectively. This is by no means a perfect approach, but it is amazing how often it warns of probable trend-reversal points. I have labeled all the sell signals, using this method. You can see that most of them came early. The second signal, for instance, was triggered about three-quarters of the way up. After the signal, the price lost a lot of upside momentum, but eventually went on to reach a new high. The third was far too early; the fourth came too far off the top. The fifth and sixth were spot on, and the seventh was early again.

Chart 13-4 Live Hogs and a Herrick payoff index. (Source: *pring.com*)

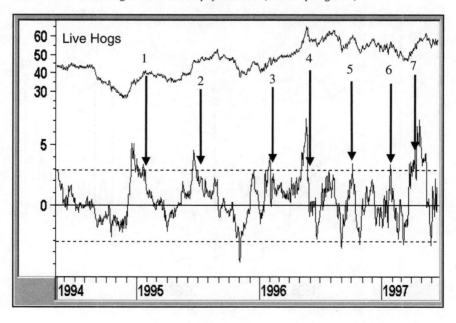

The buy signals in Chart 13-5 (numbered 8–12) were far more timely as a group. All of them were triggered fairly close to the lows. Why is this? Well, the answer probably lies in two areas. First, there is a general tendency in markets for prices to appreciate at a slower pace than they retreat. Remember, it takes a lot longer to construct a building than to tear it down. The same is true of markets. This means that momentum indicators have a greater tendency to lead during uptrends. Second and perhaps more to the point, this chart covers what we might term a *bullish* period, since the price moves from a November/December 1994 low of about 27c to a 1997 high more than double that amount. As explained previously, short-term indicators in a bull market have a tendency to move to higher levels and stay there longer than in a bear market. Oversold conditions are rarer in a bull market, as prices are much more sensitive to them.

Recognizing this fact, one way to improve the results is to use the Herrick payoff extreme signals as an alert and then use some kind of moving-average crossover as an actual sell signal. This is not going to improve every signal, but it will definitely help. Also, you may find that some signals are less profitable because they are delayed too long. What I have done in Chart 13-6 is to display dashed vertical lines where the payoff index crosses its overbought line and solid ones where this is later confirmed by an MA crossover in the price. You can see that there is a substantial difference. While the MA

Chart 13-5 Live Hogs and a Herrick payoff index. (Source: *pring.com*)

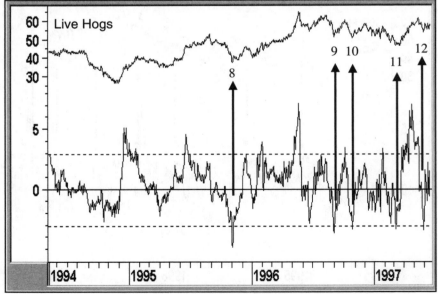

Chart 13-6   Live Hogs and a Herrick payoff index. (Source: *pring.com*)

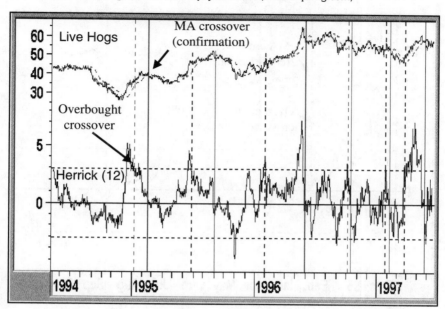

crossovers all come after the peaks, they are still sufficiently timely to enable participation in the majority of the up-move that follows the Herrick extreme signal. Where the arrows are close together, the MA filtering approach would not have worked so well. However, in most instances, they are quite far apart, indicating that the filtering approach was more profitable.

Chart 13-7 shows the December 1994 to October 1995 period in greater detail. See how the 12-period payoff index breaks below its overbought zone in January 1995, thereby triggering a premature sell signal. Only in February, a little time after the peak, does the hog price cross below its moving average. We see a similar set of circumstances later on in the June to August 1995 period.

Trendlines and Divergences

Supplementary analysis should look for positive and negative divergences, as well as trendline violations and price configurations. It is also possible to look for moving-average crossovers. In this respect, a lot will depend on the smoothing factor used in the formula.

Chart 13-7   Live Hogs and a Herrick payoff index. (Source: *pring.com*)

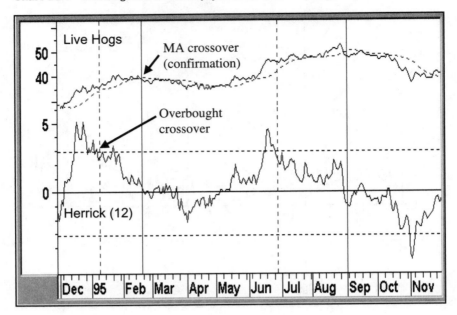

As discussed previously, payoff indexes calculated over a longer timespan are much smoother and more deliberate than those based on a shorter one. You can see this by comparing the difference in characteristics between the two lower areas in Chart 13-8, where payoff indexes have been plotted using 2- and 10-week smoothings, respectively. See how it was possible to construct a trendline for both the price and the 2-period smoothing in March 1995. It was not possible to do this for the 10-period smoothing at the bottom.

There are a couple of examples of divergences. See how the final March low in the silver price was not confirmed by either of the indexes. Later on, we see a negative divergence, as the February 1996 high was not confirmed by the August 1995 high in either of the indexes. Note also how this rally was signaled by a price and payoff trendline break. The natures of the two payoff trend breaks were different, but the results were still valid.

Extreme Swings

One other important characteristic of the payoff index that appears to be very useful from a short-term trading aspect is the fact that from time to time, the index moves to an extreme, often reversing quite sharply. An example

Chart 13-8 Comex Silver and two Herrick payoffs indexes. (Source: *pring.com*)

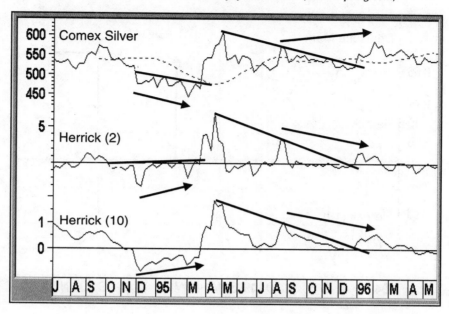

is shown in Chart 13-9, which features two payoff indexes. See how the 2-day series reaches extreme readings on the upside on three different occasions. The first two reverse simultaneously with the price and the third one is followed by some sideways trading action before the price continues on the last leg of its rally. These are also confirmed by an extreme reading in the 10-day series. The only buy signal on the chart using this approach is triggered in May 1995, but this is not confirmed by the 10-day series.

Chart 13-10 features Euro deutsche marks. The vertical lines indicate when the index reverses from an extreme reading. Solid ones indicate good signals and dashed ones indicate poor or questionable signals. In this case, the reliable ones beat the poor signals on a two-to-one basis. However, it is important to note that this is basically a bull market and that all the bad signals develop on the sell side. This only goes to underscore the importance of making an attempt not only to understand the direction of the main trend, but also whether it possesses a lot of momentum. Typically, short-term signals that go against the main or primary trend run a far greater risk of being false.

When a market does not respond to an extreme reading in the way that it should, a strong warning is given that a powerful trend is under way. The false signal in early 1995 is a classic example. The price should have moved

Chart 13-9   German mark and two Herrick payoffs indexes. (Source: *pring.com*)

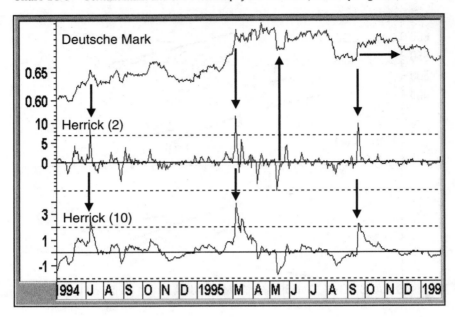

Chart 13-10   Euro deutsche mark and a payoff index. (Source: *pring.com*)

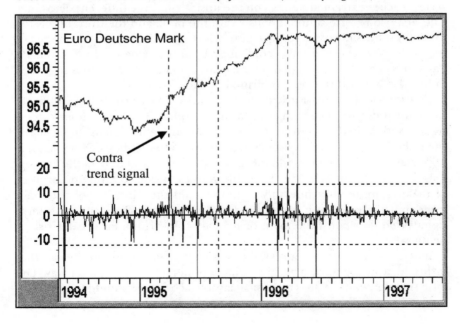

down or at least sideways, following this extreme reading. Instead, it just kept on barreling upward, thereby indicating that this was a very strong trend, indeed. Problems with this false signal could have been avoided, had we waited for some kind of confirmation of a trend reversal by the price itself. In this particular case, it was not possible to identify a price pattern, construct a trendline, or even witness a moving-average crossover, so no such confirmation was given.

Chart 13-11 shows an example of an extreme oversold reading in January 1996, following a strong advance. The first thing to note is that this is by far the most extreme oversold in the previous year. In fact, my data go back to 1994, and nothing surpasses this reading on the downside. This clearly indicates a major reversal in sentiment. And under the rules set out in Volume I of our momentum series, this characteristic is indicative of a bear market. Consequently, it would be reasonable to expect that any rally developing from this extreme reading would be countercyclical. The odds of a worthwhile move on the upside would, therefore, be relatively low. That certainly turned out to be the case even at the next signal, indicated by the second vertical line. The extreme reading at the third line was also followed by weak action in the form of a trading range. Note how the final low in June was associated with a relatively mild reading in the index, as it diverged posi-

Chart 13-11 German Bunds and a payoff index. (Source: *pring.com*)

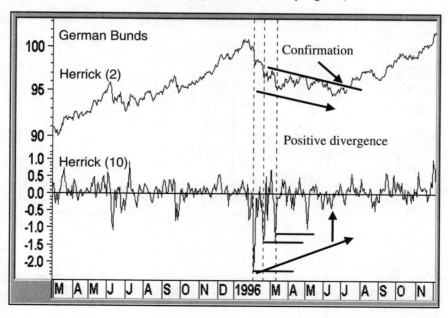

tively with the price for the sixth time. Then, when the price violated a nice downtrend line, a buy signal was given.

Moving Averages

The payoff index can also be used with moving averages. Chart 13-12 features a 30-day simple moving average (the solid line) and an 8-day EMA (the dashed line). This combination has not been selected on an optimized basis, so I am sure you could come up with a better combination. However, I am showing it here to indicate that it is possible to use moving-average crossovers as a basis for interpreting the payoff index. The idea is that when the shorter-term average is above the longer one, this represents a bullish environment, and vice versa. This approach certainly worked well for the Topix in the second half of 1995 and the first half of 1996. However, this was a good trending environment, so in the latter half of 1996, this technique was very disappointing. It really does not matter what combination of averages you use. I am sure that a trading-range whipsaw-inspired period such as this will defeat even the most intelligently designed systems. That is why I prefer to study the averages themselves and then use trendline breaks in combination with those of the price to filter out good buy-or-sell signals.

Chart 13-12   Topix Index and two smoothed payoff indexes. (Source: *pring.com*)

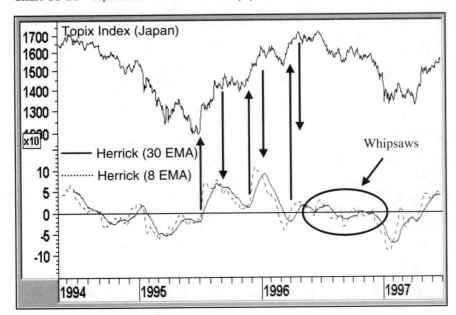

Chart 13-13   Topix Index and two smoothed payoff indexes. (Source: *pring.com*)

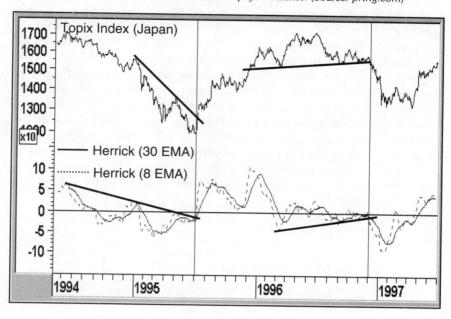

Chart 13-14   Topix Index and two smoothed payoff indexes. (Source: *pring.com*)

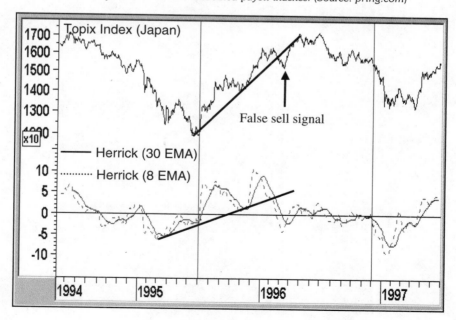

Chart 13-13 also shows some more signals using trendlines as confirmation. This time we are rewarded with a good buy in 1995 and a good sell in late 1996.

Chart 13-14 shows the same period, but this time a false sell signal has been indicated. The two trendlines are perfectly legitimate using the technique that I have described. Why, then, do we get a false signal? First of all, it is important to understand that technical analysis is concerned with probabilities. While the probabilities favor a combination, such as this being followed by a worthwhile trend reversal, they by no means guarantee it. In this particular case, though, you can see that the solid 30-day moving average of the payoff index did not diverge negatively with the price. Since a divergence is the norm, a small clue that the subsequent joint break might fail was given—not a strong discrepancy, but one that definitely lowered the odds of a reliable signal.

14

The TRIX Index

The Calculation

The TRIX index is a rate of change of a closing price smoothed by a triple exponentially smoothed moving average. That sounds like a big mouthful, but it is really quite simple. The process merely requires calculating an EMA of a 1-period rate of change, then smoothing the result with another EMA, then a second, and finally smoothing it again with a third EMA. The result is an EMA of an EMA of an EMA.

Chart 14-1 features the price in the top area, along with a 1-day rate of change in the lower one. This thicker line is a 12-day EMA of the ROC. Now, when I extend this a little further, Chart 14-2 includes an additional panel. The smoother dashed line in the lower panel (A) is a 12-day exponential smoothing of the first EMA (B). The dashed line in the lower panel is a 12-day EMA of the thick line in the middle and lower panels.

Finally, in Chart 14-3 we see B again. It is smoothed again by another 12-day EMA, which is the thick line in the bottom panel. This is the TRIX indicator.

The result is a very smooth curve. Indicators always represent a trade-off between sensitivity (reliability) and timeliness. One would think that the triple EMA smoothing would give the indicator good characteristics so far as reliability is concerned but would leave it lacking in the timeliness department. Obviously, the longer the timespan, the less timely an indicator will be. Nevertheless, it is surprising how well the TRIX, though far from perfect, can balance these two different characteristics.

Chart 14-4 shows three timespans for a 2-, 12-, and 45-day TRIX. You can see that the shorter 2-day span is almost as volatile as a short-spanned RSI or ROC indicator. The 12-day series is certainly a lot smoother but still suffers a significant amount of whipsaw directional changes, as highlighted in

Chart 14-1   DuPont and two indicators. (Source: *pring.com*)

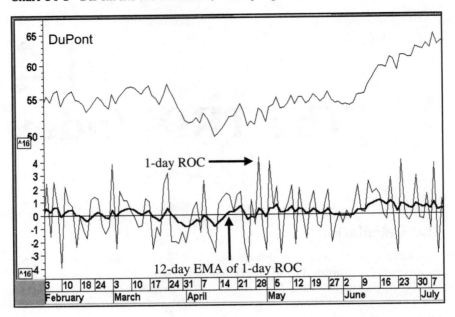

Chart 14-2   DuPont: Some exponential smoothings. (Source: *pring.com*)

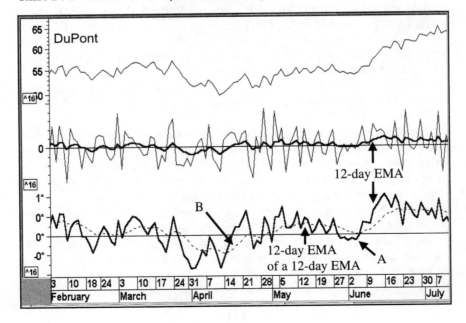

Chart 14-3 DuPont and a TRIX Indicator. (Source: *pring.com*)

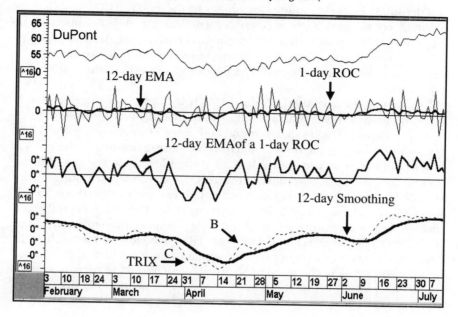

Chart 14-4 National Semiconductor and three TRIX Indicators. (Source: *pring.com*)

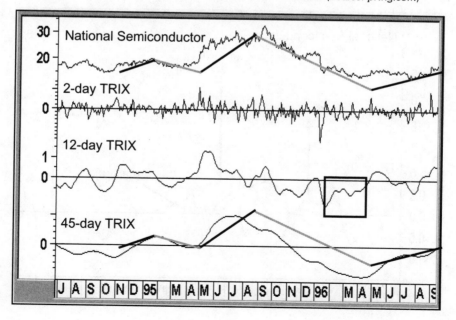

this box. The 45-day series captures the flavor of the intermediate moves but definitely lacks the timing capabilities of the 12-day TRIX.

When considering what is often regarded as the default timespan of 12-periods, it is apparent that changes in direction are not particularly helpful for triggering consistently accurate buy-or-sell signals. An alternative approach is to run a moving average for the TRIX and use these as buy-or-sell alerts.

In Chart 14-5 I have used a 9-day EMA. It is still far from perfect, but it does eliminate a substantial amount of whipsaws. If you look closely at this spring 1995 period, you will see several false signals of weakness as the TRIX reverses direction to the downside. However, during this phase, the EMA is never penetrated on the downside. Use of the EMA crossover as a filtering system does not appear to adversely affect the sensitivity or timing of the signals. However, there are some notable failures, such as the three bullish signals that took place just before a nasty decline. They have been flagged with the upward-pointing arrows. Even so, it is important to note, first, that two of these signals developed when the TRIX was close to an overbought reading and, second, that none of these signals were confirmed by a meaningful trend break in the price of National Semiconductor, such as a trendline break, pattern completion, or MA crossover. The moral of the story, as

Chart 14-5   National Semiconductor and a 9-day TRIX. (Source: *pring.com*)

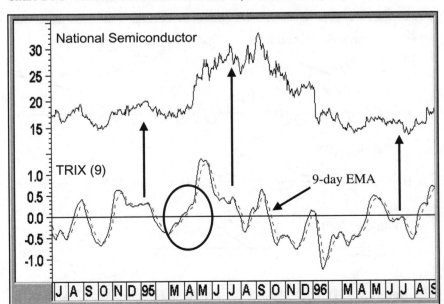

with all momentum interpretation, is to use the analysis first as a filtering approach, which is later confirmed by actual trend analysis in the price, before any serious action is taken.

Divergence and Overbought/Oversold Analysis

The TRIX indicator also lends itself to divergence and overbought/oversold analysis. Chart 14-6, for instance, contains some overbought-or-oversold lines. Movements that recross the lines on their way back to equilibrium are indicated by the arrows. The buy signal in October 1994 and the sell signal almost a year later catch the bottom and top on a very timely basis. In Chart 14-7 the sells in November 1994 (point A) and summer 1995 (point B) were also associated with a change in trend, but this time it was a sideways movement. However, the buy signals later in October and November 1995 were far too premature to be of much help, since they developed in a pervasive downtrend. Let us take a closer look at them, since the overall technical position of the TRIX in this period is quite instructive.

First, notice that the period between 1994 and fall 1995 was a bull market environment (Chart 14-8). You can see that the TRIX spent quite a bit

Chart 14-6 National Semiconductor and a 12-day TRIX. (Source: *pring.com*)

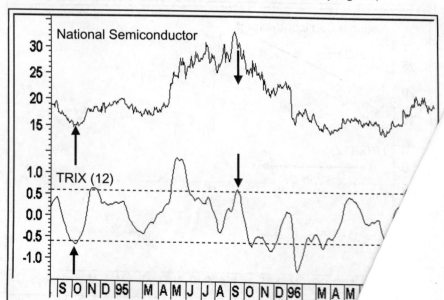

Chart 14-7   National Semiconductor and a 12-day TRIX. (Source: *pring.com*)

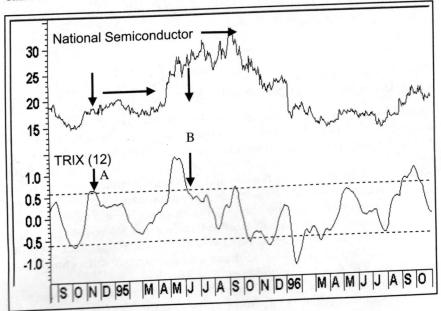

Chart 14-8   National Semiconductor and a 12-day TRIX. (Source: *pring.com*)

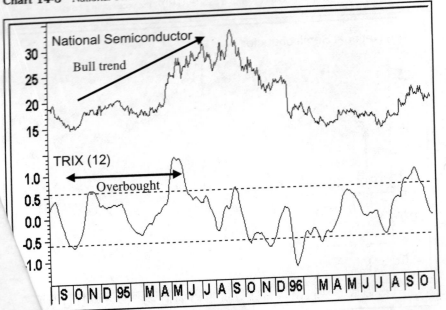

of time in an overbought condition and not that much time in oversold territory, again a characteristic of a bull market environment. The fact that it was able to reach an extreme overbought reading in May 1995 offers additional evidence. Note what happens in September 1995: the TRIX experiences a negative divergence as the price reaches a new high (Chart 14-9). This is a bearish sign, but not in-and-of-itself a signal that a bear market had begun. Later on, the price completes a 6-month top, which does suggest that something more serious is in the air. Now look at the TRIX: it falls to an oversold reading (point A) for the first time in well over a year. The failure of the price to bounce and the previous top completion both indicate that the odds of a bear market have increased substantially. Any doubt in this regard would be erased when the TRIX rally reversed, quickly sending it back to an oversold condition once again (point B). Remembering the principle that oversold conditions often fail to trigger rallies in a bear market, the action of the TRIX would have warned a trader that he would need much stronger evidence than an oversold TRIX crossover to take a position from the long side.

I do not wish to leave you with the idea that this type of interpretation will work perfectly well at all times because it certainly does not. In Chart 14-10 National Semiconductor experiences an almost identical replay in the

Chart 14-9 National Semiconductor and a 12-day TRIX. (Source: *pring.com*)

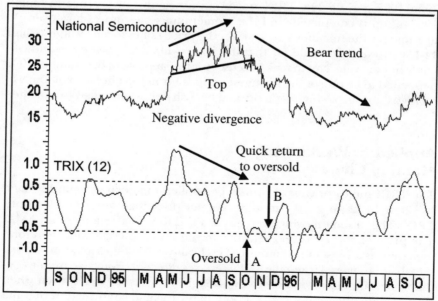

Chart 14-10 National Semiconductor and a 12-day TRIX. (Source: *pring.com*)

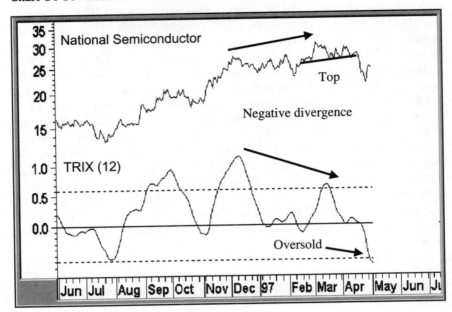

1996–1997 period. The TRIX traces out a negative divergence in March 1997, a top is completed, and the momentum series moves into oversold territory for the first time in a year. Yet the price rallies to a new high (Chart 14-11). However, I would say that this is very much the exception and certainly not the rule. Not to make excuses for this approach, but summer 1997 happened to be one of the strongest periods for market breadth on record. So it was not surprising that a normal bearish condition failed to operate.

Applied to Weekly and Monthly Charts

The TRIX indicator can, of course, be applied to weekly or monthly data. In Chart 14-12 we see the monthly copper price together with a 9-month TRIX. The dashed moving average for the TRIX itself is a 9-month EMA. The price of copper is very sensitive to the business cycle and, therefore, experiences a substantial amount of cyclicality. Sometimes great buy-or-sell signals are triggered when the TRIX reverses direction from an extreme condition beyond either of the two overbought or oversold zones. Even when they are late, they still serve as a reasonably reliable confirmation that the

Chart 14-11   National Semiconductor and a 12-day TRIX. (Source: *pring.com*)

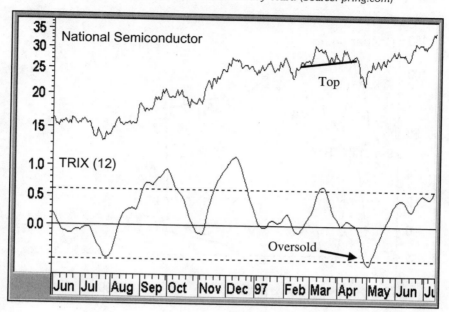

Chart 14-12   Copper and a 9-month TRIX. (Source: *pring.com*)

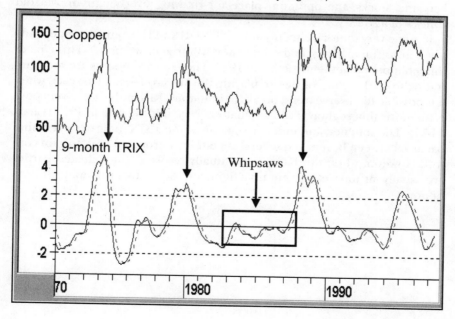

Chart 14-13   Copper and a 9-month TRIX. (Source: *pring.com*)

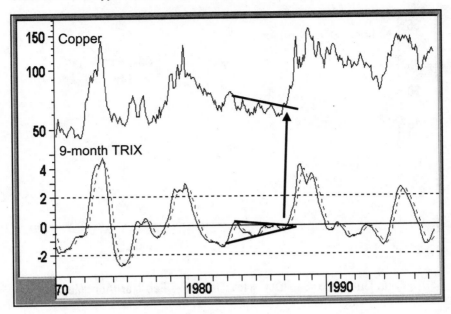

primary trend has reversed. Incidentally, since volatility differs between markets and stocks, the optimum place for drawing overbought-or-oversold zones will also vary.

In some very unusual circumstances, the TRIX will become extremely subdued in its fluctuations, and such action will trigger whipsaws. This type of thing happened between 1982 and 1987. These environments are very frustrating from the point of view of playing the MA crossovers. However, when it is possible to observe trend breaks in both the TRIX and price, a very powerful move almost always follows. That was certainly the case in 1987 (Chart 14-13). The subdued and indecisive action of the TRIX indicates a very fine balance between buyers and sellers, as neither is strong enough to gain control. However, when this battle is eventually resolved, the defeated parties are usually far too weak to put up a fight, and the victors run away with the honors.

15
Aroon

The Indicator

The *Aroon indicator* has a very different appearance than the other items covered in this book. It was developed by Tushar Chande and the indicator's name is a Sanskrit word meaning *dawn's early light,* or the change from night to day. The objective of Aroon is to warn the trader when market action is going to change from a trading range to a trending condition.

The Aroon measures two conditions. The first is the number of days that have passed since the last high. The period in question is determined by the user. Thus a 10-period Aroon will measure the number of days that have elapsed when the price did not make a 10-day high. That is displayed by the solid line in Chart 15-1. The dashed line measures the number of days that have passed since the price made a 10-day low. The solid line is known as the *Aroon up* and the dashed line as the *Aroon down.* The range for this indicator is 0 to 100. A reading of 100 in the Aroon up means that the security has just made a new high over the timespan specified in the calculation. Thus a reading of 100 in this 10-day Aroon means that the price has registered a 10-day high. A reading of 0 in the Aroon up means that the price has not recorded a high for 10 days, and vice versa, for the Aroon down.

Interpretation

There are three principal methods of interpretation. First, look for extremes when the indicators are at 100 or 0. In theory, when the Aroon up is at 100, strength is indicated. A persistent reading between 70 and 100 means that a new uptrend has been signaled. And a strong uptrend is indicted when

Chart 15-1   IBM and a 10-day Aroon. (Source: *pring.com*)

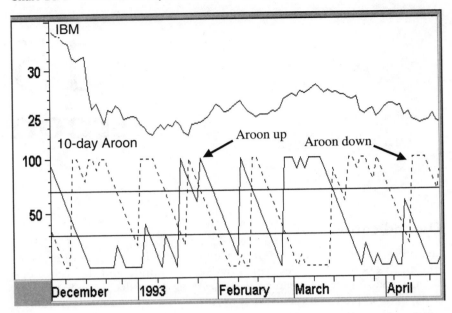

the Aroon up remains above the 70 level and the Aroon down stays below the 30 level.

The problem I have with this approach is that the trend is usually well under way by the time you realize that the up and down indicators are persistently at an extreme, that is, above 70 for the up and below 30 for the down. Look at Chart 15-2 of IBM in early 1993. See how the Aroon is trading up in the 100 zone in ellipse A. However, once it appears that it is persistently hovering in the 100 zone, at about this point, the trend is more or less over. The same could be said of the rally here in 1993 at ellipse B. When it is obvious that the indicator has been persistently above 70, the rally falters once again.

The second rule of interpretation is that when the up and down lines move in a parallel manner with each other, expect a consolidation. In Chart 15-3 we see the two lines in a parallel formation in the ellipse, and this is followed by a small trading range. Unfortunately, in my experience with the indicator (and I have to say that it is a fairly limited experience), this does not always occur. Chart 15-4 shows another situation in September 1989. The two lines in the ellipse are parallel, so we should expect to see a trading range. You can see that the price fell dramatically later on.

Chart 15-2   IBM and a 14-day Aroon. (Source: *pring.com*)

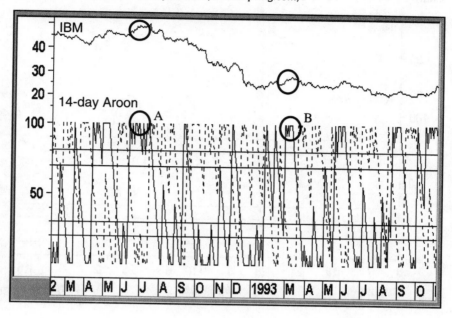

Chart 15-3   Biomet and a 12-day Aroon. (Source: *pring.com*)

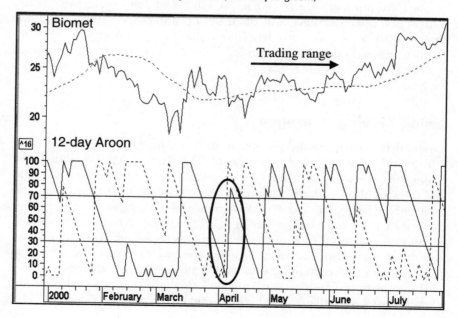

Chart 15-4 IBM and a 10-day Aroon. (Source: *pring.com*)

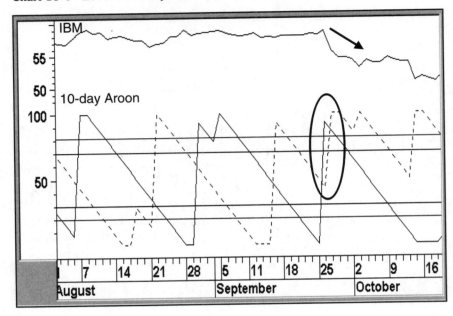

The third interpretive rule is that when the down line crosses the up line, expect potential weakness, and when the up line crosses above the down line, look for a rally. The problem here is that this system generates far too many whipsaws. Look at Chart 15-5. The indicators are far too volatile to generate any consistent results.

Using Moving Averages

One way that I have found the Aroon to be of practical help is to smooth the up and down series with a 30-day EMA. In Chart 15-6 the smoothed version of the Aroon up is displayed as a dashed line and the Aroon down as the thick solid one. I have also put in an overbought reading at 80 and an oversold one at 20. The idea is that when the dashed (up) series moves below 20 and then rises above it, a buy signal is triggered. When it rallies above 80 and then reverses direction, a sell signal is triggered. You can also use the Aroon down for confirmation. When the two are juxtaposed, the situation becomes clearer than if just one indicator is positioned at an extreme. Unfortunately, this approach will not work in a persistent up- or downtrend and, as with any oscillator, it will give premature buy-or-sell signals.

Chart 15-5 IBM and a 10-day Aroon. (Source: *pring.com*)

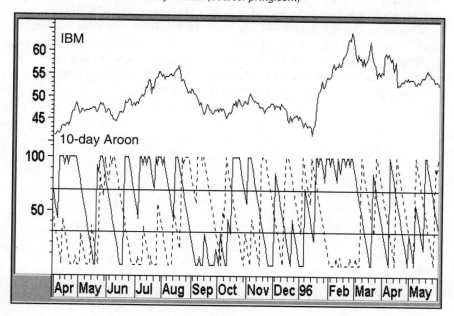

Chart 15-6 IBM and a smoothed 10-day Aroon. (Source: *pring.com*)

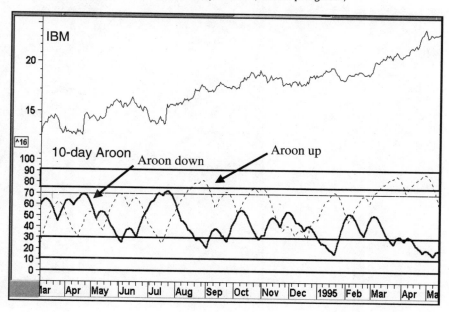

As you may gather, I do not find the established interpretive rules to be very helpful. However, when used with this MA approach, its seems to work reasonably well—which is good because I believe that the basic concept is sound and builds on a form of peak-and-trough analysis, a basic building block of technical analysis. Incidentally, I am suggesting a 30-day EMA, but this was established on a quick trial-and-error basis. If you like this approach, I encourage you to experiment with other possibilities.

16
Qstick

The Concept

The *Qstick indicator* is a momentum series that uses a basic concept incorporated in candlestick charting: that the open and close are the two pivotal points in any trading period. The important point concerning these data points is whether the closing price is higher or lower than the opening. If it is lower, then this is generally regarded as a bullish factor. If the opening is higher than the close, then in a general sense, a bearish interpretation is given. The Qstick indicator essentially calculates a simple MA of the difference between the open and closing prices. The result is displayed as an oscillator. In Chart 16-1 I have shown the price in candlestick format. Qstick is often used with divergence analysis. We see here, for instance, that the indicator makes a peak in late April, and by the time the price itself reaches its high, the Qstick diverges from it in a negative way. Then, when the price violates the trendline in mid May, a sell signal is triggered.

Chart 16-2 shows the same indicator, only this time I have constructed an overbought-or-oversold line. In this case, the lines are at ±0.6. Positioning of these lines is done on a trial-and-error basis, so the levels chosen will depend a great deal on the volatility of the security being monitored. The idea is that when the Qstick touches, or goes through, the overbought-or-oversold zones and then reverses direction, a buy-or-sell alert is triggered. I have highlighted these points with arrows. I deliberately use the word *alert* because it is usually a good idea to make sure that these types of momentum signal are confirmed by some kind of price reversal. That is not much of a problem if you were already long, because you could have taken profits in early December 1995. However, if you were considering entering a short position at the first peak in December 1995, you would have had to undergo

Chart 16-1   JP Morgan and an 8-day Qstick. (Source: *pring.com*)

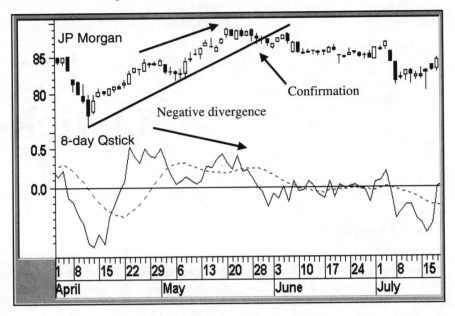

Chart 16-2   JP Morgan and an 8-day Qstick. (Source: *pring.com*)

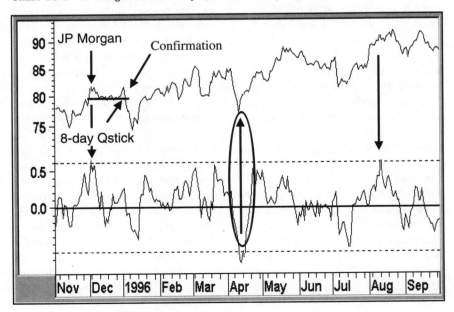

a scary-looking rally. Better to have gone short when the Qstick was being confirmed by a price trend break, which in this case would have been a penetration of the horizontal trendline in late December.

A buy alert developed in April, but there was no meaningful trend-reversal signal by the price. However, had a trader been lucky enough to be short at this point, then it would have represented a great covering point (reasonably close to the day of the low).

Price Patterns and Moving Averages

The two examples of Qstick shown so far have been plotted with an 8-day timespan. However, the indicator lends itself better to trendline and other types of analysis when longer timeframes are calculated.

For instance, Chart 16-3 uses a 25-day span. Now it is easier to construct a trendline and, when the line is violated, to wait for a confirmation by the price. A buy signal is then triggered.

The Qstick often forms price patterns when the timespan is extended. In Chart 16-4, using a 25-period series, I have been able to mark quite a few tops. There is a broadening formation with a flat bottom in the

Chart 16-3 General Motors and a 25-day Qstick. (Source: *pring.com*)

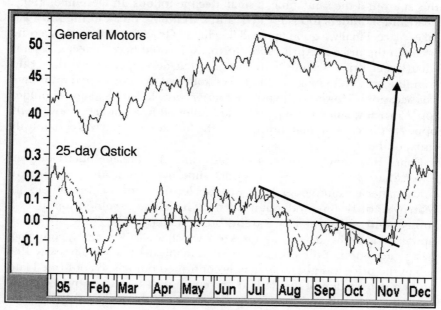

Chart 16-4   JP Morgan and a 25-day Qstick. (Source: *pring.com*)

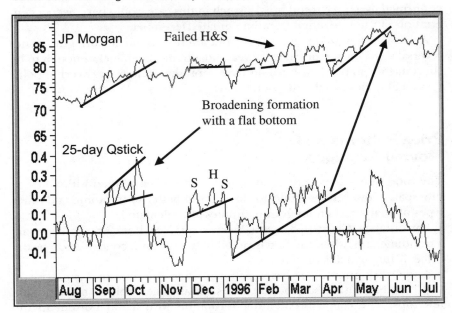

September/October 1995 period. The trendline break in the price confirms this at around the same time; a small decline follows. In December 1995 a head-and-shoulders top is formed, and a trendline break in the price also takes place. Finally, a good uptrend line in the Qstick is confirmed by a trend break in the price in April 1996. Normally, I would have expected a somewhat larger price decline than the one that developed, since the Qstick trendline was quite long and had been touched or approached on numerous occasions. However, the price experienced a failed head-and-shoulders top. Normally, failed price patterns are followed by a powerful move in the opposite direction to that indicated by the formation. That was certainly the situation here.

Chart 16-5 shows another example using the Philadelphia Gold and Silver Share Index. The 30-day Qstick timespan again offers some useful price pattern examples. I have not labeled the one on the left in the March/April 1995 period, but it is a small head-and-shoulders top that was subsequently confirmed by a trend break. Later in May/June, we see an upward-sloping head-and-shoulders top, which was subsequently confirmed by a penetration of the neckline in July. Finally, the late 1995 to early 1996 top in the price was not immediately confirmed but was so confirmed later on by a penetration of the dashed uptrend line. The price moved sideways for about a month and then broke below the solid line. Note also how the

Chart 16-5 Philadelphia Gold and Silver Share Index and a 30-day Qstick. (Source: *pring.com*)

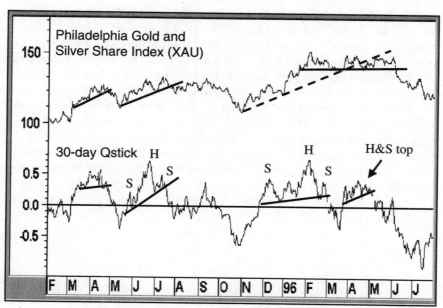

Chart 16-6 General Motors and a 25-day MA of a 25-day Qstick. (Source: *pring.com*)

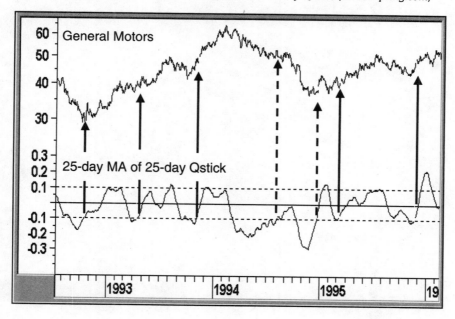

Qstick also traced out a small head-and-shoulders top and its completion occurred just about 4 weeks before the final price breakdown.

One final way in which I find the Qstick to be of help is to calculate an MA and to use the average to trigger buy-or-sell alerts as it crosses an over-bought-or-oversold zone on its way toward equilibrium. The vertical arrows in Chart 16-6 flag such instances. The solid ones are relatively timely signals and the dashed ones are less timely. In all these instances, the signals flagged by the solid lines were followed by a rising trend of some kind. The only exception was that triggered in August 1994, which was followed by a con-solidation and then a sharp decline. This, however, is one of the faults of all momentum indicators, for in a persistent up- or downtrend, nothing works. That is why it makes sense to wait for some kind of trend reversal in the price itself. Even this does not always work out, but it certainly improves your odds of success.

17

The Relative Volatility Indicator

The Concept

The *Relative Volatility Index* (or *RVI* for short) was introduced by Donald Dorsey. It is used to measure the direction of volatility. The calculation is very similar to the RSI, except that the RVI incorporates the standard deviation of price changes instead of absolute price changes. The indicator is used to enhance the results from MA crossover systems. The following are the rules devised by Dorsey.

The first rule is: only act on positive MA crossovers when the RVI is above 50. Chart 17-1 features a 25-day simple MA, which has been advanced by 5 days. The upward-pointing arrows indicate when these two conditions have been met. The dashed arrow indicates a poor signal. The two dotted arrows indicate when the MA crossover occurred, but the RVI was still below 50. The one on the left (point A) in November 1989 was very successful. The one in February (point B) was a more or less breakeven situation. The April signal (point C) was a definite disaster. The signal in July 1990 (point D) experienced a small rally, but by the time the price recrossed below the average, the trade would have barely broken even. Unfortunately, the November 1990 buy signal was followed by a worthwhile rally but did not qualify, because the RVI was below 50. The signal in late 1991 (point E), was followed by a small rally but then whipsawed. Finally, the last signal developed when the indicator was below 50 and was not, therefore, a valid one.

Chart 17-2 shows the sell signals, where the rules are reversed. The October 1990 sell was followed by a small decline. The next couple of signals

Chart 17-1   DuPont and a 14-day RVI. (Source: *pring.com*)

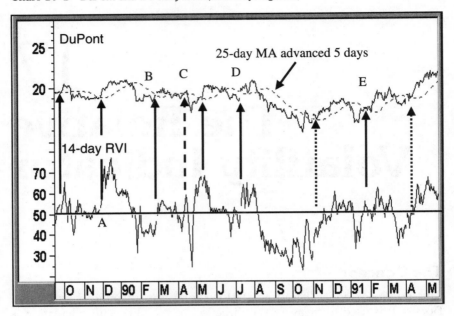

Chart 17-2   DuPont and a 14-day RVI. (Source: *pring.com*)

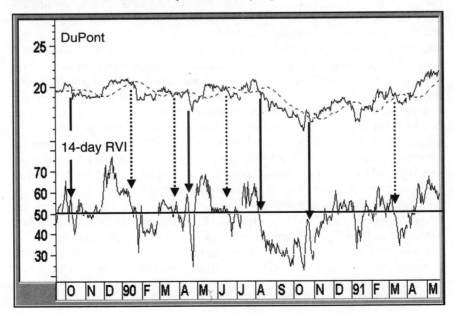

Chart 17-3   Heinz and a 14-day RVI. (Source: *pring.com*)

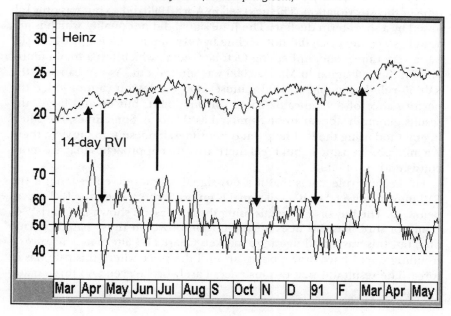

Chart 17-4   Heinz and a 14-day RVI. (Source: *pring.com*)

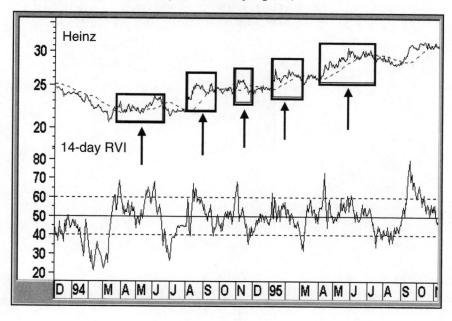

in 1990 did not qualify because the RVI was just above, or at, 50 during the time of the MA violation. The next sell in April 1990 did so but was only followed by a short-term decline. The June signal did not qualify, which is just as well, since the price did not decline by very much. The August 1990 sell was a very timely one, unlike the October signal, which was a total failure. Finally, the sell signal in March 2000 was filtered out. As you can see, the RVI 50 rule has its plusses and minuses. Obviously, you cannot judge the performance of an indicator based on one chart, but by and large, the results generally appear to be as mixed as this one. Sometimes, the filtering method using the RVI helps; at other times, it doesn't. In my view, there is a mild plus in using it, but I feel there are other approaches that are more consistently profitable.

The second rule states that if a buy signal is ignored, enter long; if the RVI moves above 60 or if a sell signal is ignored, short when the RVI moves below 40. The buy-or-sell signals using these rules are shown in Chart 17-3. I am not sure that this does anything to improve on those based on rule one, but this was a trading-range market. Chart 17-4 alternately features a trending one. I have drawn boxes around the price where this rule was in force. The result was that two instances barely broke even and three made a profit.

18

The Inertia
Indicator

The Concept

The *inertia indicator* was developed by Donald Dorsey and is an outgrowth of Dorsey's relative volatility index (see Chapter 17). The name *inertia* was chosen because of his definition of a trend. He states that a trend is simply the "outward result of inertia." It takes significantly more energy for a market to reverse direction than to continue along the same path. Therefore, a trend is a measurement of market inertia. Dorsey asserts that volatility may be the simplest and most accurate measurement of inertia. The inertia indicator is simply a smoothed RVI. The smoothing mechanism is a linear-regression indicator.

Chart 18-1 features a 14-day RVI setting for the inertia. At the bottom is a 21-day inertia overlaid on a 21-period linear-regression indicator of the RVI. As you can see, both indicators are identical.

The trend is indicated as bullish when this indicator is over 50 and bearish when below 50. In Chart 18-2 the bullish periods have been highlighted with the thin line and bearish ones with the thick line. Most of the time, this approach appears to work quite well. However, it is as well to bear in mind that this is a trending market.

Chart 18-3, alternately, shows a trading-range market, and you can see that the approach was far from satisfactory, since there were several periods, such as September/October 1992 and April/May 1993, when the price declined sharply and persistently in a bullish period. Conversely, in the bearish October/November period, the price rallied. This is not typical, though. In

Chart 18-1 Heinz comparing the inertia to a linear regression of the RVI. (Source: *pring.com*)

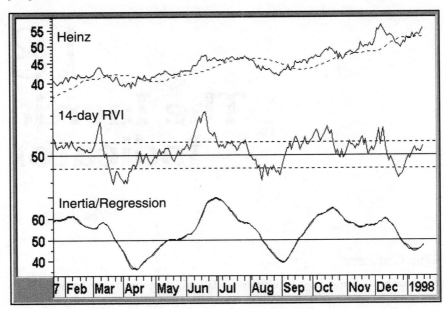

Chart 18-2 Newmont Mining and a 45/21 inertia. (Source: *pring.com*)

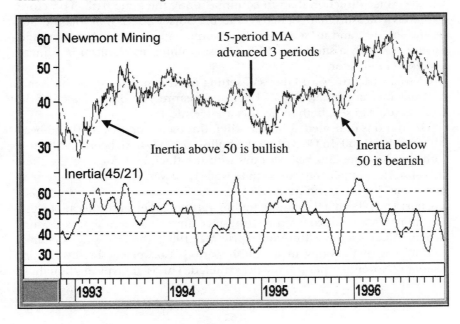

Chart 18-3   Coca-Cola and a 21/14 inertia. (Source: *pring.com*)

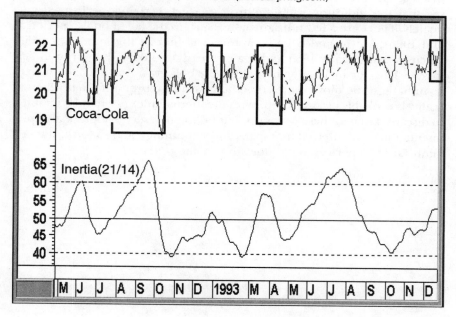

Chart 18-4   Newmont Mining and a 45/21 inertia. (Source: *pring.com*)

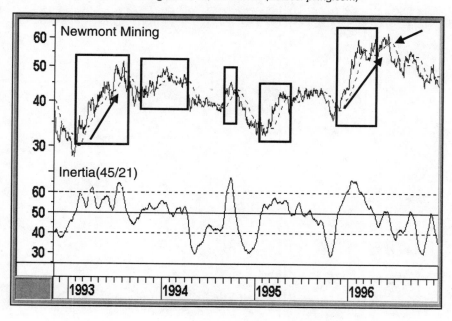

this regard, Chart 18-4 shows the trading range for Newmont Gold. You can see that the indicator, while far from perfect, certainly performed adequately. There are a few transgressions (such as the failed bullish period in mid 1996), but by and large it captures the bulk of the important rallies (such as that in early 1993 and again in early 1996). With a lot of indicators, we have the inclination to look for the holy grail. And if a new one fails its initial test, we move on to something far more promising but which in reality is probably just as flawed. With the inertia index, we may be tempted to discard it due to these whipsaws, but I think it deserves additional experimentation with different timespans and smoothings, and so forth. It is certainly far from perfect, but it does show some promise.

19

The Directional Movement System

The Objective

One of the key problems faced by all traders is to determine whether the future characteristics of the market in which they are involved is going to be of the trending or trading-range variety. This is very important, since a trading-range market should be attacked by selling into an overbought reading and buying into an oversold one. Short positions would be initiated with an overbought condition and covered with an oversold one. Alternately, if it is known ahead of time that a market is likely to trend, greater emphasis would be placed on trend-following devices such as moving averages, trendlines, and so on, and less on oscillators.

After all, if you believe that a market will continue to rally, why take decisions based on a momentum indicator that is likely to undergo several negative divergences with the price before the final peak?

There is, of course, no precise way in which this task can consistently be achieved. However, in *New Concepts in Technical Trading*, Wells Wilder outlines an approach that tries to identify when a market is likely to break out of a trading range. He called it the *directional movement system*.

Most of the techniques described here deal with a description of technical systems, but the directional movement approach tries to fit a system relative to the likely market action. In other words, if we apply a particular system to a market, it's rather like trying to ski regardless of whether it is summer or winter, which is really like putting the cart before the horse. The directional movement system, alternately, tells us what the prevailing season is likely to be, so we can decide whether to use momentum indicators

171

that are suitable to trading-range environments or MAs, which work more profitably in trending markets. In my experience, the approach does not do a very good job in discriminating between these two key trading environments. However, there are some useful and practical twists to its application, as we shall learn later.

What Is the Directional Movement?

In order to measure directional movement, two periods are required, so a comparison can be made. In short-term trading, these would be represented by days, but there is no reason why weekly, or even monthly, data could not be used. Taken to the other extreme, the comparison could be made between hourly bars in an intraday chart, and so forth.

In this explanation I will use days, but please remember that these principles can be applied to any period. In essence, the directional movement is defined as the difference between the extreme part of the current period (today) that falls outside the previous period's (yesterday) range. Let us consider some examples.

In Fig. 19-1 the range of day 1 is AB and day 2 is ED. Part of the price range in day 2, namely, the distance between C and D, retraces some of the ground covered in day 1. It is the distance between C and E in day 2 that

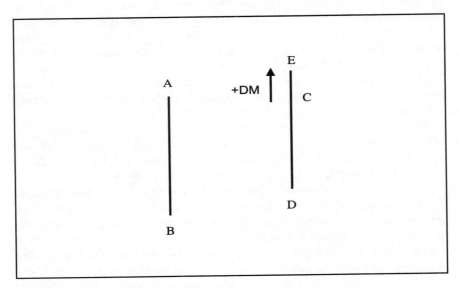

Figure 19-1   Plus directional movement.

really earmarks the directional movement. The difference between point E in day 2 (that is, the high and point A in day 1, meaning the high) is called *plus DM* (*+DM*) because the movement is an upward one.

Minus DM (*−DM*) would occur when the price declined between the two periods, as in Fig. 19-2. In effect, the distance between the low today and the low yesterday would represent the −DM.

There are some other possibilities to consider. The first is shown in Fig. 19-3, where the trading range in day 2 is so great that it encompasses all of day 1 and then some. How should this example be treated? In effect, this situation offers both a +DM and a −DM, but for the purposes of calculation, we take the *greater* of the two. In this example, this would be recorded as a +DM, because the distance between A and E is greater than that between B and D. Figure 19-4 shows the same idea, but this time day 1 encompasses day 2, so there is no directional movement.

Alternately, we might get an example where the two trading ranges are identical, as in Fig. 19-5. Again the directional movement would be nonexistent.

In futures trading, many contracts are subject to limit moves, which must also be addressed. Figure 19-6 shows a limit up day. Please note that the +DM is *not* the extent of the limit, that is, the distance between day 1's close

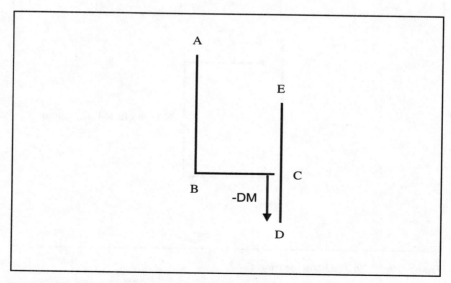

Figure 19-2 Minus directional movement.

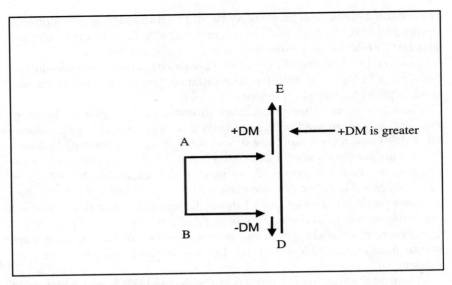

Figure 19-3   Plus directional movement variation.

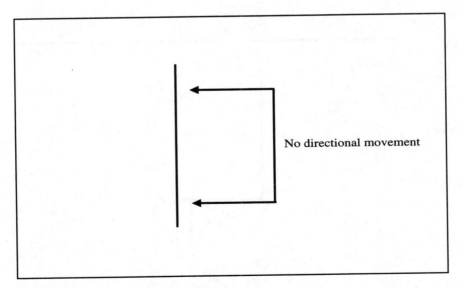

Figure 19-4   No directional movement.

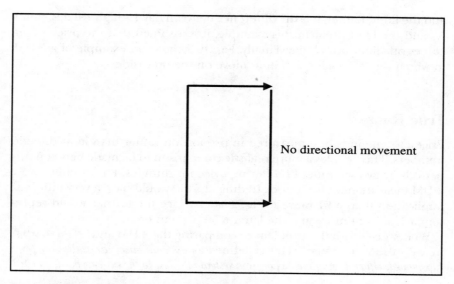

Figure 19-5   No directional movement variation.

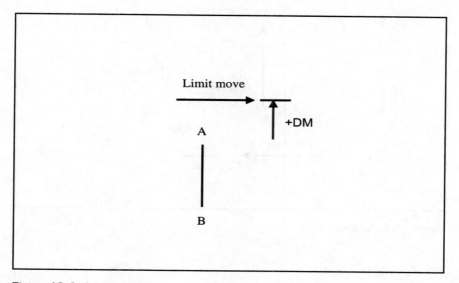

Figure 19-6   Limit up move.

and the limit. Rather, it is the difference between day 1's high (that is, point A) and the limit itself. In this example, it is assumed that the price never comes off "limit up" all day. Finally, Fig. 19-7 shows an example of a −DM in which we are looking at a limit move on the downside.

True Range*

Price movement is best measured in proportion rather than in arithmetic numbers. This enables a more realistic comparison to be made between two periods or two securities of differing price magnitudes. For example, a $1 +DM measurement for a stock trading at $100 would have a very different implication than a $1 move for a $2 stock, since the former would represent a 1 percent move and the latter a 50 percent one.

Wilder deals with this problem by comparing the +DM and −DM to what he calls the "true range." This is defined as *the maximum range that the price has moved, either during the day or from yesterday's close to the extreme point reached*

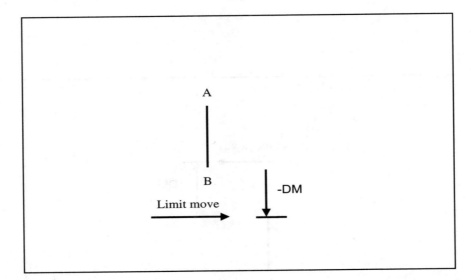

Figure 19-7 Limit down move.

*For a full discussion on this concept, please refer to *New Concepts in Technical Trading* by Wells Wilder (Trend Research).

during the day. This means, in effect, that the true range is the greatest of the following:

1. The distance between today's high and today's low
2. The distance between yesterday's close to today's high
3. The distance between yesterday's close to today's low

Introducing the Directional Indicators (DIs)

When the directional movement is related to the true range, two indicators, the plus and minus DIs, are born. Since the resultant series is unduly volatile, they are each calculated as an average over a specific time period, and the result is plotted on a chart. Normally, they are overlaid in the same panel, so that it is possible to observe when they cross each other. The standard, or default, timespan for the DIs is 14 periods. Chart 19-1 shows the two DIs using a 14-day span. Crossovers of the DIs are then used as buy-or-sell signals, but we will discuss that later.

Chart 19-1   Singapore Fund and two DIs. (Source: *pring.com*)

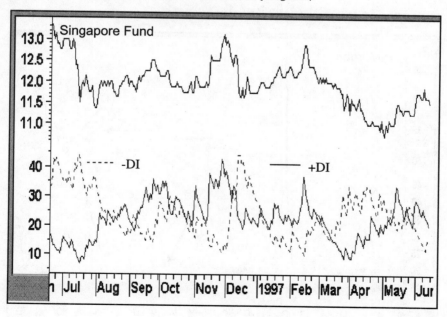

Introducing the ADX

There is one other important indicator incorporated in this system, and that is the *ADX*. The ADX is simply an average of the +DI and −DI over a specific period. In effect, it subtracts the days of negative directional movement from the positive ones. However, when the −DI is greater than the +DI, the negative sign is ignored. This means that ADX only tells us whether the security in question is experiencing directional movement or not. Again, the normal default timespan is 14 days.

The ADX is calculated in such a way that the plot is always contained within the scale of 0 to 100. High readings indicate that the security is in a trending mode (that is, has a lot of directional movement), and low readings indicate a lack of directional movement and are more indicative of trading-range markets. Unlike other oscillators, the ADX tells us nothing about the direction in which a price is moving, only its trending or non-trending characteristics. We need to use other oscillators for this task.

In this respect, note that the two highs in the index at points A and B in Chart 19-2 are each associated with a top and bottom, respectively. For example, if the price moves down sharply and then stabilizes, the ADX will move from a high number, as it did between points B and C. Then as the price

Chart 19-2 JP Morgan and a 14-period ADX. (Source: *pring.com*)

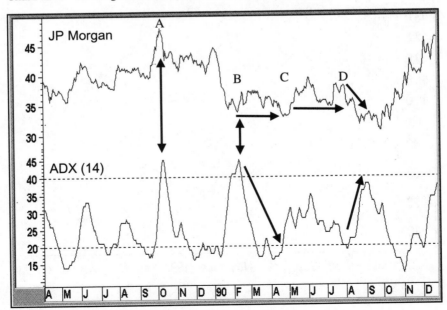

continues to rally or starts to decline again, as it did in this example, the ADX rallies once again. The low ADX numbers between points C and D indicate low directional movement. Only after prices resume their decline does the ADX rally again. This low reading between C and D arises because the difference between +DI14 and −DI14 is decreasing, occasionally touching zero.

A high ADX reading does not tell us then that the market is overbought and about to go down. What it does do is inform us that when the indicator is at a high reading and starts to reverse, the prevailing trend has probably run its course. From here on in, we should expect a *change* in trend. This is different from a reversal in trend, since a change in trend can either be from up to down or up to sideways. Similarly, a downtrend could change to a trading range or to an uptrend.

I mentioned earlier that the ADX is normally calculated with a 14-day span. However, it is possible to vary this number in the same way you might for an MA or other oscillator. Chart 19-3 features a 32-day ADX in the lower area. You can see that this is a more smoothed version, compared to the 14-period variety featured in the middle area. Because of the smoothing effect, longer-term timespans or averaging also experience lower levels of volatility. The overbought level for the 14-day series has been drawn at 40,

Chart 19-3 JP Morgan and two ADX indicators. (Source: *pring.com*)

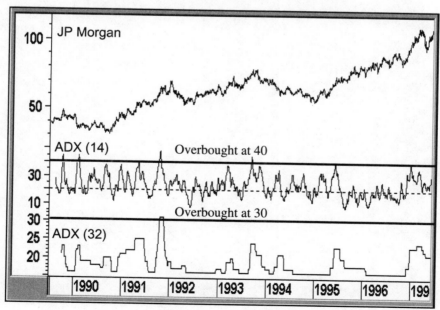

for example, yet the 32-day series in the lower area never reaches 40. In fact, it is only able to register a 30 reading once in 8 years! You can also appreciate from this chart that an ADX calculated from a longer timespan is also much more step-like in nature, compared to the 14-day series, which is more jagged.

The other principal point to grasp is that reversals in the ADX that develop from an extremely high reading indicate an exhausted price trend. The actual reversal point in this indicator tells us when the security in question has become tired of moving in an up or down direction and is ready for a *change* in trend. Since the reversals, when they come, are usually pretty deliberate, a peaking-out action usually indicates that the ADX has begun a move to a far lower reading. This compares to many oscillators, whereby a reversal from a high level can often result in a double or even triple top formation. Since the ADX is far less prone to such misleading signals, a reversal in its direction is usually a reliable signal that the ADX has peaked. As a general rule, I would say that the higher the level at which the reversal takes place, the more reliable the signal is likely to be.

20

Interpreting the ADX and the Directional Indicators

High and Low ADX Readings

Since the ADX only tells us about the trending qualities of the price and not its direction, we need some system to warn us of which way a price is likely to trend once a directional signal has been given. One possibility would be to compare the ADX with a regular oscillator, as in Chart 20-1, where I have compared an ADX with a smoothed 9-day RSI. See how the 14-day ADX for JP Morgan reverses from a peak trend reading in October 1989 at roughly the same time that the smoothed RSI crosses below its overbought zone. Then a little later on, the reverse set of circumstances develop as the ADX once again peaks out, but this time when the RSI is crossing above its oversold zone. In this instance, the trend reversal was from down to sideways. This, then, is a sharp reminder that a trend change does not have to be a 180-degree turn from up to down, or from down to up, but can also be a 90-degree one from up to sideways, or from down to sideways.

Low readings in the ADX indicate a trendless market. This can also be used to some advantage. For example, if the ADX slips to an unusually low reading, as in Chart 20-2, and it is then possible to construct a trendline for the ADX. The subsequent break above the line indicates that the market is likely to trend again. This type of signal needs to be confirmed by some kind

Chart 20-1   JP Morgan, an ADX, and an RSI. (Source: *pring.com*)

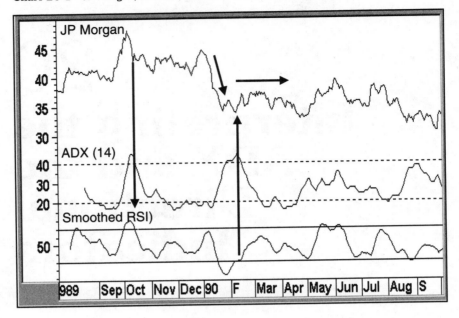

Chart 20-2   JP Morgan and a 14-period ADX. (Source: *pring.com*)

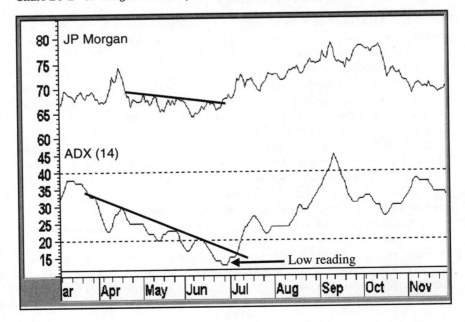

of breakout in the price itself. In Chart 20-2 the oversold reading for the ADX has been set at 20. You can also see that it was possible to draw a trend-line for both the ADX and the price. The signal to buy would have developed after both lines had been violated.

It is not always possible to draw lines for the ADX. In Chart 20-3, for instance, the ADX reaches a low reading, but there is no convenient series of peaks against which a line could be plotted. In this instance, the trend break in the price would be used to confirm that the period of relatively trendless price activity is over. A quick glance at the chart may give the impression that the price was not trendless, but declining. This is true, but at the point where the ADX makes its low, you can look back and see that the previous period was essentially flat. This has been flagged on the chart with the two horizontal arrows.

The other point to bear in mind is that these signals are relatively short-term in nature. The first one (on the left) was followed by a one-month rally after the breakout. The second was followed by a more sustainable 3-month advance. The reason the first was so anemic was because this whole period was one within the confines of a bear market. This once again underscores the idea that it is very important to make an attempt at discovering the direction of the primary trend, whether you are a trader or an investor. A rising tide lifts all boats, but a falling one takes them all down again.

Chart 20-3 JP Morgan and a 14-period ADX. (Source: *pring.com*)

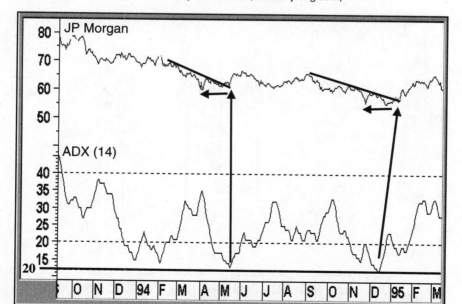

On balance, I find that the reversals from a high reading in the ADX are far stronger and more reliable than reversals from low, nontrending readings.

DI Crossovers

Another way in which the directional movement concept can be used is to compare the progress of the plus and minus directional indexes, or DIs. Remember the 14-day +DI measures the average of the directional movement when the price is rallying and the −DI the average directional movement when the price is declining. The average in this case will depend on the time period over which the calculation is made, the default or norm being 14 days. When the two are overlaid, as we see in Chart 20-4, the crossovers act as buy-or-sell signals.

In Fig. 20-1, points A, B, and C represent the equilibrium points, that is, the places where the DIs cross. This example shows that there is a fair degree of volatility, but unfortunately, the profit potential from buying at A, and selling at B, is not very great (Fig. 20-2). According to Wilder, this type of market would have a *low* ADX rating. Figure 20-3 shows a small profit from a short sale between B and C.

Chart 20-4   Singapore Fund and two 14-day DIs. (Source: *pring.com*)

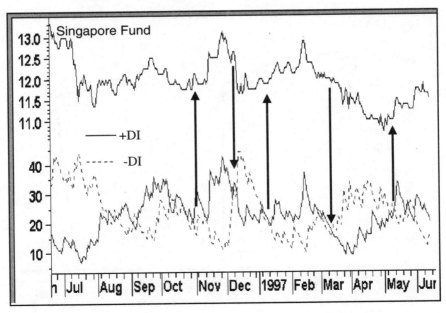

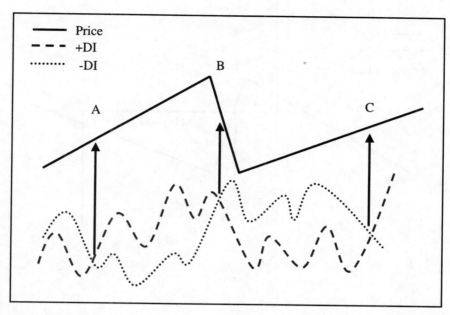

Figure 20-1   DI crossover.

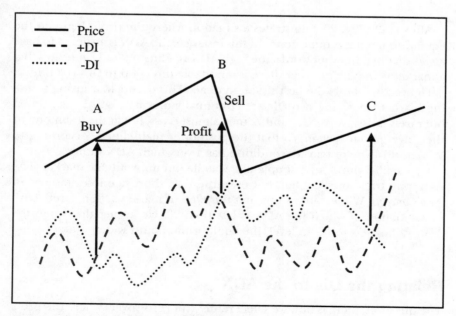

Figure 20-2   DI crossover and small long profits.

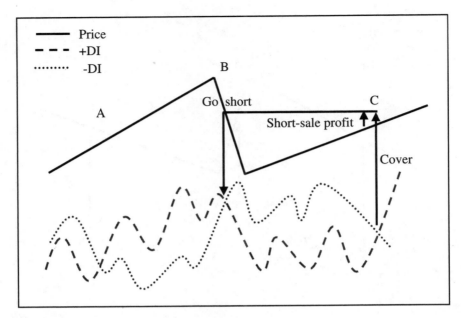

Figure 20-3 DI crossover and small short sale profits.

Alternately, Fig. 20-4 illustrates a situation where the profit between the equilibrium point is quite good. In this instance, the ADX is assumed to have a *high* reading. In other words, the high ADX reading not only indicates that a market is volatile but that there is a tradable direction to this volatility.

Figure 20-5 shows the best situation of all. This occurs in a strong trending market where the two DIs are continually moving toward each other, but rarely cross. At W, X, Y, and Z, they almost cross, but at the last moment they diverge once again, so that the position is maintained. According to Wilder, this type of market condition has a very high ADX rating.

Figure 20-6 shows an example of a volatile but unprofitable market. The A–B long trade breaks even, but even the B–C short sale loses money. In *New Concepts,* Wilder points out that this type of market action is reflective of a situation in which the ADX is less than 20. He argues that when the ADX rallies above the 25 level, the equilibrium points widen out.

Relating the DIs to the ADX

The question, then, is how we select trades from crossovers where the probability of making a good profit is high. According to Wilder, the first step is

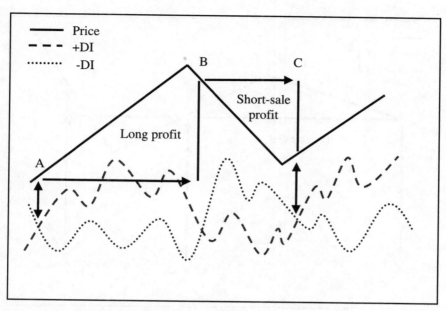

Figure 20-4 DI crossover and large profits.

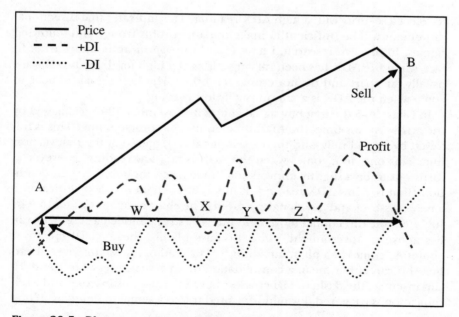

Figure 20-5 DI crossovers in a very bullish market.

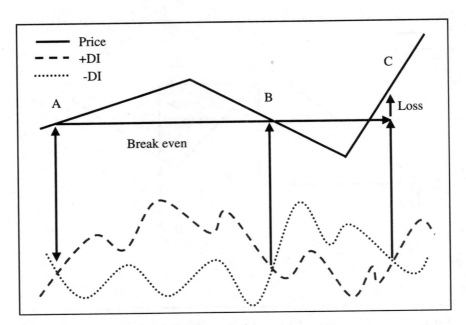

Figure 20-6 DI crossovers and breakeven trades.

to select a security with a high ADX reading. This indicates that directional movement will be sufficient to make tradable profits from trend-following signals. In my own research, I have found the *opposite* to be more true. In fact, when the ADX has been rallying and is at a high level, the two DIs are usually far apart and do not cross each other. The best signals appear to come when the ADX is at an unusually low reading.

In Chart 20-5 the first buy signal comes in November 1992, as flagged by the arrow. At this time, the ADX is below its solid oversold line. This is followed by a good rally, and then a sell signal is triggered at the first vertical line. This one, too, comes when the ADX is at a low reading. However, it turns out to be a slightly unprofitable trade, even though the right condition (that is, a low ADX reading) is in force. Then, at the next vertical line a new crossover and buy signal are given. The chart clearly indicates that by July 1993 the directional movement was very strong indeed as the ADX rallies above its "overbought" zone. Because of this, the next DI crossover (point A) comes at a high, but falling, ADX reading. As we discovered earlier, this can either mean a consolidation or an actual reversal in trend. In this instance, the dashed −DI crosses above the solid positive one and a sell indication is triggered. I would have used this as a signal to liquidate a long

Chart 20-5 General Motors, an ADX, and two 14-day DIs. (Source: *pring.com*)

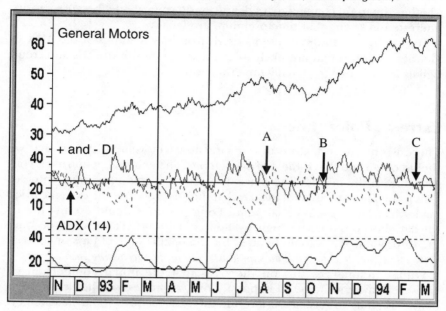

position, but not necessarily to put on a short. As it happened, the price declined, so a profit would have been made. However, there was no guarantee at that point that the price was not about to enter an unprofitable trading range. Indeed, if you look at the two DIs between August and September, you can see that they came very close to a crossover on two occasions.

The next buy crossover developed in mid October. However, it was not triggered at a time when the ADX was at a particularly low reading. This was then followed by a quick whipsaw crossover, which can hardly be detected on this chart. What is interesting is that the ADX subsequently fell back to its oversold reading, and when the DIs crossed again, a powerful rally ensued (point B). The last sell signal in February 1994 (point C) developed at a fairly high ADX reading. This, too, proved to be unprofitable as a buy signal was given right at the end of the chart.

This example featured both good and bad signals, but by and large, the best ones came when the ADX was at an unusually low reading. I will not deny that some good signals are triggered just as, or just after, the ADX has peaked at a high ADX reading. However, this system does not tell us whether a trading range or trend reversal is going to take place, so it is a bit like rolling the dice unless we can get some pointers from other indicators. Of course, if you are writing or selling options, you do not care whether the trend changes to a sideways or downward one, because you are interested in seeing that time premium erode away.

To sum up our findings, use reversals from low readings in the ADX to identify securities that are likely to trend and then use the DIs and trend signals in the price to actually time the move.

Extreme Point Rule

There is one more feature of the directional movement system that we should cover, and that is the *extreme point rule.* The extreme point rule is concerned with the best level to place a stop once a trade has been entered. This principle states that on the day that the DIs cross, use the extreme price made that day as the reversal point. Long positions would use the low of the day, short positions the high, as shown in Fig. 20-7. These, then, become the stop points that should be used for the next couple of days or so, *even if the DIs signal that the position should be liquidated by recrossing each other.*

Wilder rationalizes this on the basis that the initial equilibrium or crossover day tends to be an important one, regardless of whether or not a market is going to reverse. As a result, the extreme price point reached on

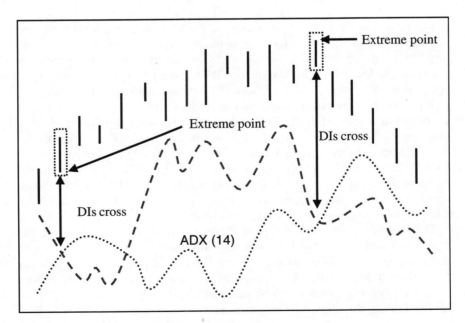

Figure 20-7 Extreme point rules.

that day is psychologically important to market participants. For this reason it is not normally breached, but if it is, then this typically indicates that the DI crossover was a whipsaw.

Overlaying the ADX on the DIs

One approach that is sometimes used for enhancing the interpretation of the directional movement system is to overlay the ADX on the two DIs. Important turns are indicated when the ADX reverses direction *after it has moved above both DIs.* In Fig. 20-8 the ADX reverses direction at point A, and after one more rally, the price also peaks. The actual signal would have occurred when the +DI14 crossed below the −DI14 but it would not have been a bad idea to take some profits at A, since the timing was better. In a really strong market, similar to that indicated in this example, the ADX will reverse direction from a high level, decline, and then move back up. Yet the DIs don't cross until much later, as at point B in this instance.

Conversely, when the ADX line moves below both DIs Wilder recommends staying away from trend-following systems.

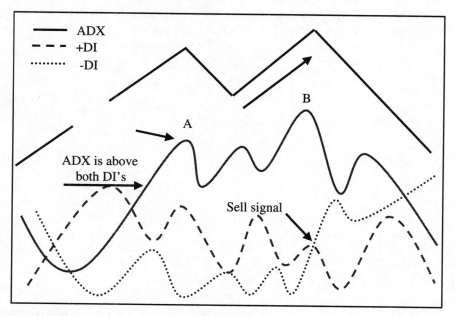

Figure 20-8 Relating the ADX to DI crossovers.

Summary

It is possible to set out a series of rules as explicitly proposed by Wilder. 1. *Only trade trend-following systems with securities that have a high ADX rating.* The ADX level reflects the degree of directional movement, not the direction itself. 2. *Use crossovers of the +DI14 and −DI14 as timing points for entering and exiting the markets.* 3. *The principal exception to rule 2 occurs when the extreme point trading rule takes effect.* It states that on the day of the DI crossover, use the extreme price point in the opposite direction to your position as a stop point. Long positions should use the low of the day, and short ones the high. This becomes the stop point regardless of whether the DIs subsequently and temporarily recross again. 4. *When the ADX moves above both DIs and reverses direction this represents an early indication that a trend reversal is about to take place.* Some profit-taking is in order. Final liquidation would occur with a DI crossover or an extreme point violation. If the +DI14 is above the −DI14 at the time of the ADX reversal, this would mean a change in trend from up to down, and vice versa. 5. *If the ADX is above both DIs and it is at an extreme reading, this means that the trend has been in force for some time and it is not a good point for entering new trades in the event that the DIs recross in the direction of the prevailing trend.* In other words, the high reading in the ADX is a form of overbought-or-oversold reading where new trades in the direction of the prevailing trend are not usually profitable. 6. *When the ADX is below both DIs avoid trend-following systems as little directional movement is indicated.* 7. *When the ADX is below the 20–25 area regardless of its position to the DIs, avoid trend-following systems, since little or no directional movement is indicated.*

21
Extremes in the ADX

Pring Alternative Interpretation

Technical analysis is an art rather than a science, so it would not be surprising if other methods of interpretation of the directional movement system were to evolve. In my own research, I have found different ways in which the directional movement system can be used. These comments are in no way intended to denigrate Mr. Wilder's contribution; rather, they are more to elaborate and expand on his ideas. You are free, of course, to choose whatever principles you find most useful.

In Chart 21-1 we move back to the DI arrangement. The idea is that buy signals are generated when the solid +DI crosses above the dashed −DI, and vice versa. In some market environments, this works very well. However, in others, a substantial number of whipsaws can be generated. In this example of the Singapore Fund, you can see that numerous whipsaws were, in fact, triggered.

One way around this is to smooth the DIs. In this respect Chart 21-2 is presented as an example. You can see that most of the whipsaws have been filtered out. In this instance, the trading action is so volatile that these smoothed crossovers would (in most instances) have occurred well after the turning points. So what was gained from fewer whipsaws was lost in tardy signals. However, since we know that these signals were more reliable, it is possible to pick and choose entry points. In other words, if a signal is given well after a turning point, ignore it and either wait for another one or look for another security.

Chart 21-1   Singapore Fund and two 14-day DIs. (Source: *pring.com*)

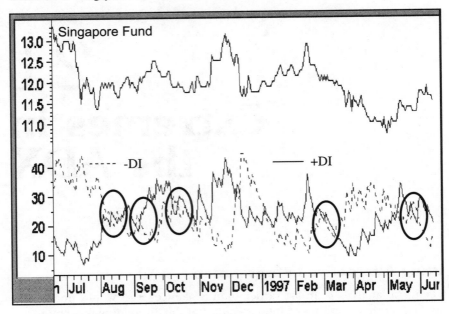

Chart 21-2   Singapore Fund and two smoothed 14-day DIs. (Source: *pring.com*)

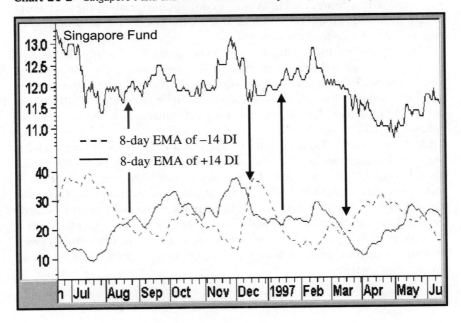

This approach works better in a trending market, where the price stalls sufficiently to trigger a quick whipsaw with the simple DI crossover approach but does not with the smoothed variety. Chart 21-3 of IBM displays two whipsaws with the DI crossover approach.

In Chart 21-4, though, the DIs have been smoothed. Consequently, a great deal of this whipsaw activity has been filtered out. Now it is true that the sell signal for IBM in January 1997 comes right at the bottom of the first down leg. However, the overall performance, allowing for slippage, commissions, and so forth, still beats the two whipsaws that developed in the ellipse using the raw DIs. Also, the actual DI crossover sell signal developed about halfway down the decline. So not much was lost overall with the smoothing approach, but a great deal was gained.

More on the ADX

These simple crossovers form only part of the system, of course, and should be related to the ADX. From my own observations, I have not found the concept of a high ADX rating as a selection tool for securities with a strong directional movement to be particularly helpful. Any momentum indicator in an overbought-or-oversold extreme can tell you that a market has been trend-

Chart 21-3 IBM and two 14-day DIs. (Source: *pring.com*)

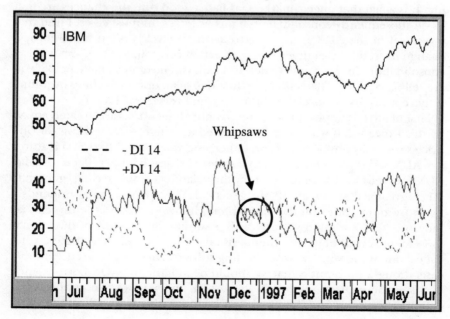

Chart 21-4   IBM and two smoothed 14-day DIs. (Source: *pring.com*)

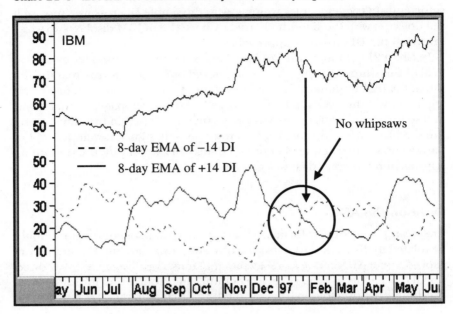

ing. It is a fact that once a market has had a good run, the chances are that it will subsequently consolidate its gains or losses. In most cases, I find that a reversal in the ADX from an extreme high level is often followed by a change in trend. Sometimes this is an actual reversal; at other times it is a consolidation. In this respect, such reversals can be of invaluable help if you are selling options. This is because the price of an option declines over time if there is no price movement or if the trend reverses direction.

First of all, it is important to note that not all securities are created equal. By this I mean that what may be regarded as a high ADX reading for one price series may not be high for another, and vice versa. Chart 21-5 features two ADX series plotted on the same scale. The dashed line reflects a 14-day ADX for Newmont Mining. See how the volatility for this series is generally much greater than for the JP Morgan solid ADX. JP Morgan also spends a lot more time under the horizontal line, indicating very little directional movement. If finding a security with a substantial amount of directional movement is your objective, then a visual comparison such as this, or a statistical one using your favorite charting software, makes good sense. In this case, though, my point is that we should be judging the ADX performance of a specific security relative to its past. In this way we can establish the extreme points or overbought levels in the ADX. Then when the ADX

Chart 21-5 JP Morgan and Newmont Mining ADX indicators. (Source: *pring.com*)

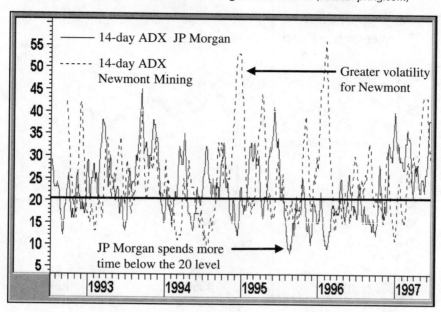

reverses direction, that is the time to anticipate a reversal in trend or the start of some trading-range action.

Chart 21-6 shows International Paper at the end of the 1980s and the start of the 1990s. The dashed line is an 8-day MA of the 14-day ADX. I have placed the extended zone for the ADX at 40. The vertical lines show those periods when the ADX, having crossed above the overbought zone, then crosses below the 8-day MA. On each occasion, the price reverses trend. The first signal in 1989 is followed by a small decline, but the ensuing price action is really an extended trading range. The next signal develops just before the August 1989 peak. Note how the end of the decline is signaled by another instance in which the ADX moves above its overbought zone and then crosses below its average. Finally, the whole of 1990, despite some volatile action, is totally devoid of any extreme directional movement. We have to wait until 1991 for the ADX to give us another signal. This time it is followed by a relatively short 3-month consolidation.

Chart 21-7 features DuPont. The detail is not so good because I wanted to show you the perspective over a long period. The vertical lines again signal the 8-day MA crossovers after the ADX reached an extreme. The solid horizontal lines indicate that almost all of the signals were followed by a consolidation. The two dashed vertical arrows in 1995 point up to those periods when nothing much happened. In fact, after a small decline, both

Chart 21-6   International Paper and an 8-day MA of a 14-day ADX. (Source: *pring.com*)

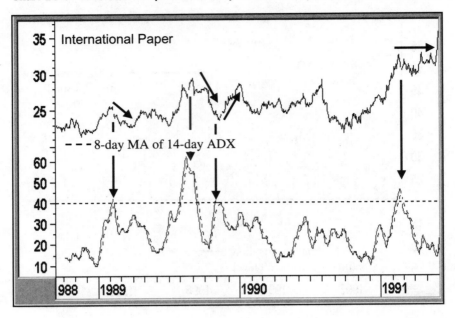

Chart 21-7   DuPont and an ADX. (Source: *pring.com*)

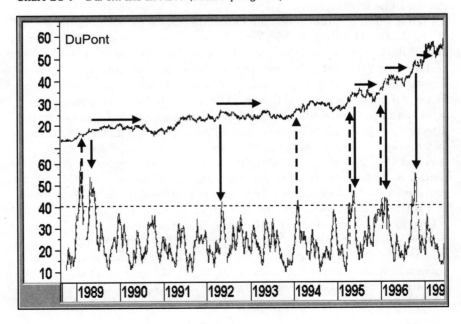

signals were followed by an extension of the previous advance. What is interesting is the fact that the next signals were not long in coming, and once they occurred, they were followed by an extensive consolidation. The other two dashed arrows in 1989 and 1994 also point up to failures. These examples all used a 14-day timespan. There is, of course, no reason why a different span cannot be used. However, in my experience, 14 days seems to work as well as any.

Low ADX Readings

I have found that some of the best trend-following moves begin when the ADX is at a low number and *starts to reverse* to the upside. In Chart 21-8 we can see that several major trending moves are all signaled by a DI crossover that occurs *when the ADX is at a low 20 reading.*

Low readings are very useful, since they tell us in a fairly graphic way those times when a market has *not* been trending. For other oscillators, such as an RSI, directionless markets are reflected in dull activity around the 50 level, which is relatively difficult to spot. In the case of the ADX, it is easier to detect, since the indicator falls to a low reading of 20 or less. Again, the

Chart 21-8   The XAU, two DIs, and an ADX. (Source: *pring.com*)

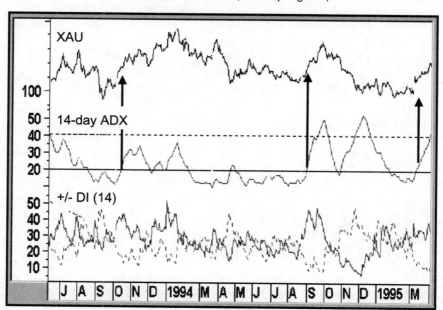

actual level for a specific security can best be obtained by a quick historical review to discover what is the norm for a trendless market. When the ADX starts to rally, it warns us that a directional move is on the way. The nature of the direction can be obtained from a review of other momentum series. The problem that I have found is that by the time the ADX starts to rally, the move is often well underway.

One way around this is to look for an abnormally low ADX reading and then wait to see if it is possible to construct a trendline for the price itself. Then, when the price violates the line (provided the ADX is still at a subdued reading), use the trendline break as a buy signal. It is even better if you can see a strong DI crossover or even a DI trend break. In Chart 21-9 of the Philadelphia Gold and Silver Share Index (XAU) I have plotted the lower ADX extreme at 20. The bottom area features a 14-period +/−DI. In any situation it is always best to have as many indicators offering signals as possible. This, then, increases the odds that they will work. In the example on the left-hand part of the chart in October 1993, we see that the ADX moves below the 20 level in August. However, we do not see a trendline violation in the price until October. At that time, the ADX and +DI also violate trendlines for a very strong buy signal. Later on (January 1994), the ADX once again slips below the 20 zone. In March the price breaks above

Chart 21-9   The XAU, two DIs, and an ADX. (Source: *pring.com*)

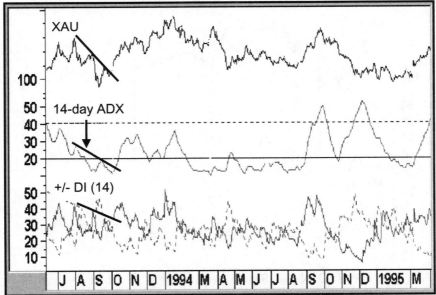

a nice downtrend line. It actually takes place when the ADX makes its low for the move. The price then rallies sharply. However, the advance is very short-lived and the signal is a bit of a failure. Based on our rules, it was quite legitimate, but we need to realize that not every situation is going to work out in a profitable way. In this particular instance, we could point to the fact that neither the ADX nor either of the two DIs violated a trendline. But even so, the result was a disappointment.

The next signal (in August 1994) was followed by a pretty good rally, but note how the ADX and +DI both broke above downtrend lines.

Chart 21-10 shows the same arrangement, but for a later time period. See how the ADX was below 20 in May and June 1995. Then we see a trend break in the price. This time it was followed by a small rally and consolidation—not a disaster, but certainly disappointing. Note also that neither the ADX nor the DIs violated trendlines in this instance, as in the previous weak signal.

Finally, look at the situation in October. The ADX had been in a non-trending mode below 20 for over $2^1/_2$ months. Then the price completed a top and the ADX violated a trendline. Following this, the price fell quite sharply. Note how the bottom was signaled by the ADX crossing below the 40 extreme.

Chart 21-10 The XAU, two DIs, and an ADX. (Source: *pring.com*)

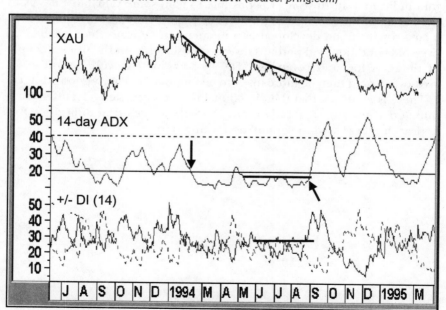

Chart 21-11   The XAU, two DIs, and an ADX. (Source: *pring.com*)

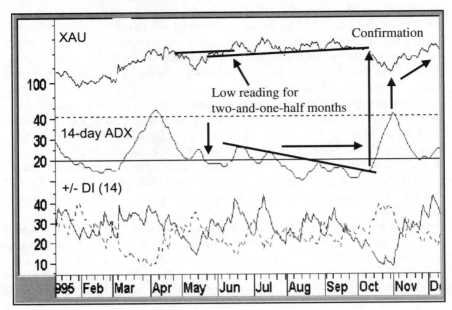

The DMI system should always be used in conjunction with other momentum indicators. In this way it is possible to gain some valuable clues as to the nature of the forthcoming trend. For example, we would expect to see a far stronger trend develop after a momentum indicator had reached an oversold condition and perhaps diverged positively with the price a couple of times. A low and reversing ADX in combination with a positive DI crossover would then be more likely to be followed by a fairly good advance.

There is no doubt that the directional movement system can offer some quite good trading signals. However, as with all technical indicators, this approach is best used in conjunction with others.

22

The Commodity Selection Index

The *commodity selection index* (CSI) is another Wells Wilder innovation. It was originally named the commodity selection index, but this oscillator can really be applied to any security for any timeframe.

The objective is to identify which securities are likely to give the trader the greatest bang for the buck. The characteristics measured by this oscillator are directional in nature. It also takes into consideration volatility, margin requirements, and commission costs. The result in theory is an indicator that allows for comparison and selection, the idea being to select the security with the greatest directional movement.

The CSI is not designed as a timing device in its own right but more as a method for finding out where the most leverage can be obtained relative to the implied volatility and trending characteristics of various contracts.

My own view is that this is a poor method for selecting potential trades, since it places emphasis on the greed factor, that is, how quickly and easily someone can make money. Anyone who has studied the psychology of trading or who has learned from his or her own errors in the markets knows without a shadow of doubt that one of most important psychological attributes is objectivity. Any hint of the greed factor substantially increases the odds of failure. Patience and discipline, not greed and speed, are the order of the day. Having said that, I have noticed that in some cases, when the selection index reaches an extreme and reverses, it can often warn of an important change in trend. In this sense, I am assuming that there are three trends: up, down, and sideways. A change in trend does not, therefore, mean the same thing as a reversal in trend. The CSI is not interpreted in the usual way in that a high reading indicates an overbought condition, and a low one an oversold. This is because it indicates the degree of direction. Thus a high

203

reading indicates lots of directional movement, and vice versa. When the CSI reaches an extreme and reverses, as it does in early 1996 (Chart 22-1), it indicates that the prevailing trend is likely to change. In this instance, it is from up to down. However, it might easily have been from up to sideways. Two other extremes (in September and December 1994) indicate reversals, one from an up to a down and one from a downtrend to a sideways congestion.

The question naturally arises as to what is an extreme. The answer is that it can really only be determined on a trial-and-error basis for a particular security. For this you will need a lot of historical data. I would suggest more than 5 years' worth. In Chart 22-2 featuring the U.S. dollar index I have placed the overextended extreme line at 200, since this appears to catch most of the sharp rallies in the CSI. The chart covers a 12-year period in which there were roughly nine extreme CSI movements: of the nine, six were followed by a change of trend lasting about 3 months or more, and three were failures (flagged by the dashed arrows). In some instances, especially when a price is in a linear up- or downtrend, the CSI does not work as well.

Chart 22-1   ASA and a 14-day CSI (Source: *pring.com*)

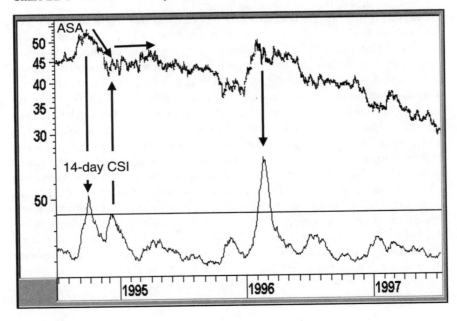

Chart 22-2   U.S. dollar index and a 14-day CSI (Source: *pring.com*)

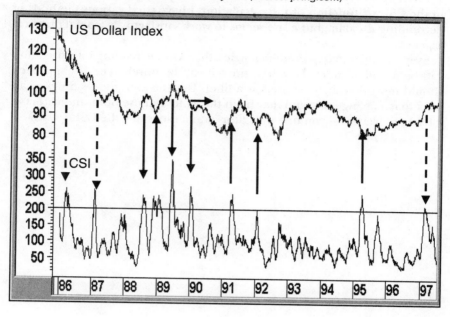

Chart 22-3   Abbott Labs and a 14-day CSI. (Source: *pring.com*)

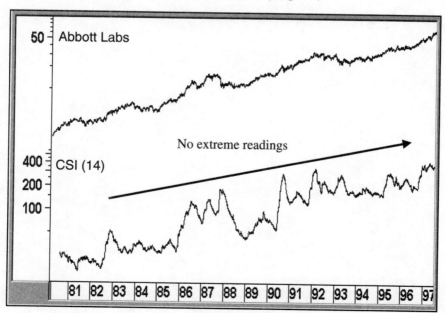

Chart 22-3 of Abbott Labs illustrates an example. This long-term uptrend in the CSI is a function of the calculation. I have tried various methods of detrending the data, but none seems to work satisfactorily from a practical aspect.

Even though it has many deficiencies, the extreme reading interpretation can be useful at times. However, since it can be unreliable, this approach should most definitely be used as a filter. Use the extreme readings as an alert that a change of trend may be in the wind, but use other indicators as a backup. Never rely on one indicator alone, especially the CSI.

23

The Parabolic
Indicator

Introduction

The *parabolic indicator*, devised by Wells Wilder, is not a momentum indicator and so, strictly speaking, does not fall within the scope of this book. However, it is being mentioned briefly, since it has become a very popular trading mechanism and can be used with momentum indicators to generate timely stop-loss signals.

One of the most valid criticisms of trend-following systems is that the implied lags between the turning points and the trend-reversal signals obliterate a significant amount of the potential profitability of a trade. The parabolic system is designed to address this problem by increasing the speed of the trend, so far as stops are concerned, whenever prices reach new profitable levels. The concept draws on the idea that time is an enemy, and unless a trade or investment can continue to generate more profits over time, it should be liquidated. Since it is a stop-loss system, it can be used with any momentum series, once that indicator has been used to filter out a good entry point for a trade. It is also a trailing stop-loss system, which means that the stop is continually being moved in the direction of the position, that is, up for a long position and down for a short.

The parabolic stop reversal system is a trailing stop technique. The formula is designed so that the stop is constantly being tightened as the market moves in your favor. The disadvantage is that when the position is first initiated, it is given a relatively long leash, so to speak. Then as time passes and the price increases, the stop is gradually tightened. The expression *par-*

abolic derives from the shape of the curve of the stops as it appears on the chart. In a rising market, the stop is continually being raised, never lowered. In a declining market, the opposite will hold true.

How Does It Work?

The parabolic shows up on the chart as a parabolic-shaped curve that is plotted above and below the price (Chart 23-1). This curve is often referred to as the *SAR*, which stands for "stop and reversal system." This is because the parabolic, when triggered, is often used not only to stop out a position, but to actually reverse it. Thus a parabolic would simultaneously trigger the liquidation of a long position and the entering of a short one.

The parabolic indicator is automatically calculated for us by the major charting software packages, but Fig. 23-1 shows how the dynamics of this method operate. The first step involves the establishment of a reference point. Wilder instructs us to take the extreme high or low from the previous trade. For example, if you had earlier been short and are now long, the reference point would be the extreme low for the previous (down) move.

Chart 23-1 eBay and a parabolic indicator. (Source: *pring.com*)

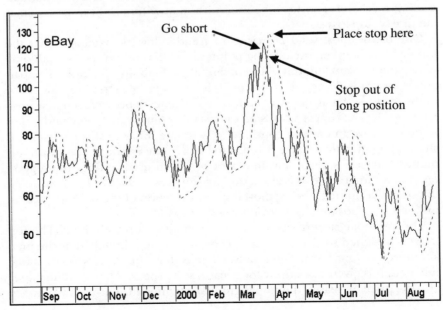

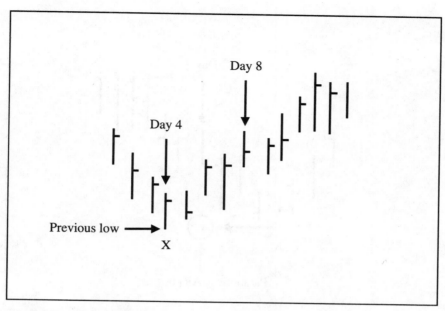

Figure 23-1 Initiating the trade.

However, every trade has to start somewhere, so if this is your first trade in this particular security, the logical point ought to be the previous minor low. In this example this would be at point X on the fourth day.

For the sake of argument, our trade is initiated on day 8. The SAR would then be placed at the previous minor low established on day 4. The SAR for the next day (meaning day 9) will be the high experienced on day 8 less the SAR multiplied by an *acceleration factor.* Wilder stated that the acceleration factor should begin at 0.2 on the first day of the trade (Fig. 23-2). This is gradually increased by 0.2 *each day that a new high from the trade is recorded* until the position is either stopped out or the maximum acceleration factor of 2.0 is reached. After that, the acceleration factor remains constant at 2.0. This means that if the price continues to make new highs, the acceleration factor rises to 0.4 on day 10 (Fig. 23-3), 0.6 on day 11 (Fig. 23-4), and finally 0.8 on day 12 (Fig. 23-5). If a new high for the trade is not recorded between, say, days 8 and 12, the acceleration factor would remain unchanged. In effect, the system is saying that if a security records a new high, this is reflective of improving momentum and that it is then appropriate to raise the stop a little more aggressively, for when momentum starts to deteriorate again, the price trend is likely to reverse quickly.

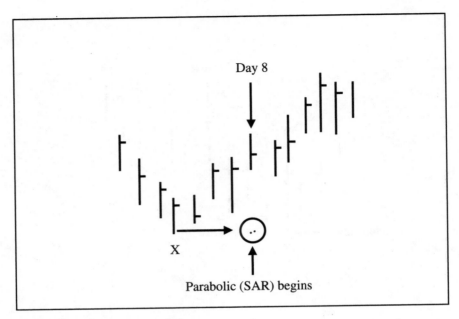

Figure 23-2   Starting the parabolic.

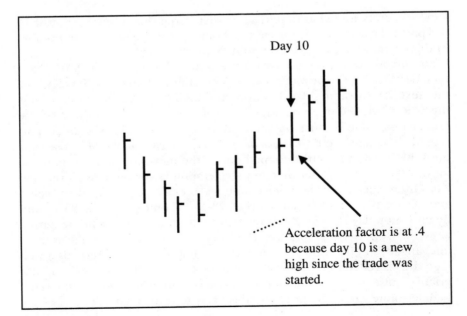

Figure 23-3   The acceleration factor kicks in.

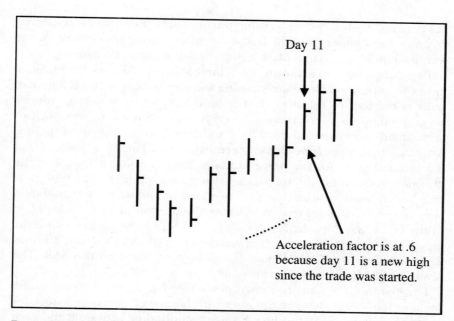

Day 11

Acceleration factor is at .6 because day 11 is a new high since the trade was started.

Figure 23-4 The acceleration factor moves to 0.6.

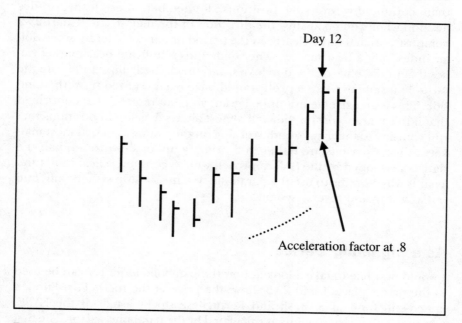

Day 12

Acceleration factor at .8

Figure 23-5 The acceleration factor moves to 0.8.

There are really two steps to using this approach. First, find and execute an entry point either from the long or short side using your favorite set of technical indicators. Then place a stop using the parabolic system.

There are really three ways in which these stops or SARs can be set. Since most of us are now able to use charting software packages, this is automatically calculated for us, so we do not have to concern ourselves with the actual methodology. For those who do not use software or who wish to understand the system more fully, I will briefly cover the three points. Actually, the first two have already been explained. The initial stop is set at the extreme point for the previous trade. Then the stop is moved in the direction of the trade with reference to the extreme price for the new trade and the acceleration factor. The final rule for positions states that you should never move the SAR for tomorrow above the previous day's or today's low. In the event that the calculation calls for the SAR to be plotted above the previous day's or today's low, then use the lower of today's or the previous day's. The next day's calculation should then be based on this SAR. The reverse would be true for short positions.

The parabolic system is sometimes termed a *stop and reverse system* because it assumes that you are always in the market. Every sell stop, for instance, is expected to produce a long position when activated, and each long stop induces a short trade. Personally, I prefer to select an entry point and use the parabolic system for the purposes of setting the stop, rather than continually reversing positions. Remember, most losing trades develop when you go against the direction of the main trend. Chart 23-2 demonstrates that quite clearly. In the period under consideration the dollar index is in a bear market. The solid ellipses indicate bear market rallies that would have resulted in losses, and the dashed ellipses indicate the two sole instances when a profit would have been realized from the long side. This is an extreme example, I grant you, but research has confirmed that if losses are to occur, they will almost always develop in positions that run contrary to the main trend. Working on the assumption that most markets in most periods are either in a primary up- or downtrend, half the signals developed by the SAR approach will be countercyclical in nature. That is why I prefer to use the parabolic system as a stop system only, and not as a stop and reverse system.

As a Signaling Device

I would now like to take a look at how the parabolic indicator can be used in the marketplace. Chart 23-3 shows the price of the Iberia First Fund, a closed-end fund of Spanish and Portuguese stocks listed on the NYSE, together with the stop points as calculated by the parabolic system. The first

Chart 23-2 U.S. dollar index and a parabolic indicator. (Source: *pring.com*)

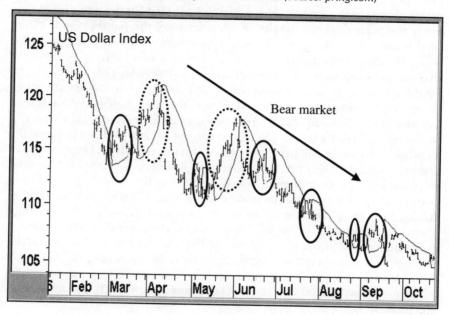

Chart 23-3 First Iberia Fund applying the parabolic. (Source: *pring.com*)

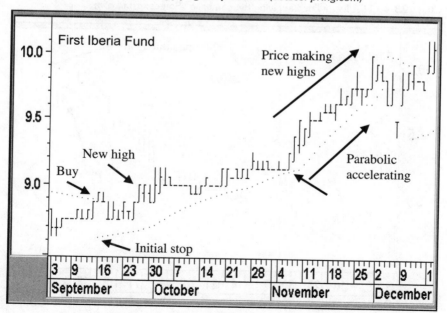

entry point would be made on day 10 of the chart (by the arrow) as the price rallies above the dotted line. The initial stop is placed at the new dotted line. Since the price declines for the first few sessions, the parabola only rallies by the amount of the initial acceleration factor, which in this case is 0.2. Then on about September 26 the price makes a new high, so you can see that the parabola starts to accelerate a bit to the upside. This is because the acceleration factor is now being increased. In early November the price nearly slips below the stop line. However, the line itself is not increased because of rule 3 stated earlier: that the stop cannot be raised above today's, or the previous day's low. In effect, you cannot get stopped out because the stop line rises above the price only when the price declines below the line. If on the next day the price had fallen, this would have represented a valid stop-loss sale. As we move on, you can see that the stop line accelerates because the price consistently makes new highs. Then in early December (Chart 23-4) the price does fall below the stop level. However, this is a countercyclical move and a new buy signal is quickly generated. Had a trader gone short at this point, the trade would have resulted in a loss, because the next buy signal occurred at a higher level than the short sale. Having established that fact, let us take a quick look at how we might go about determining the two variables, the acceleration factor and the maximum acceleration factor.

Chart 23-4 First Iberia Fund applying the parabolic. (Source: *pring.com*)

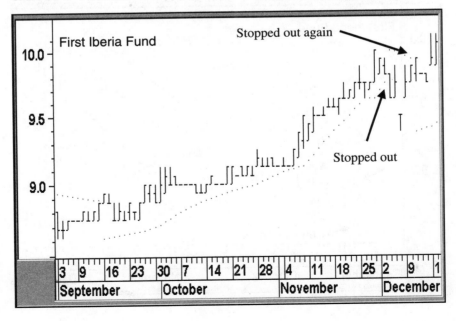

Acceleration Factors

The level of the acceleration factor is critical when setting stops. With MAs there is always a trade-off between timeliness and sensitivity. A short-term MA gives very timely signals but is so sensitive that it also generates numerous whipsaws. Alternately, a long-term term average has fewer whipsaws, but crossovers are less timely. The parabolic system works in exactly same way, but in this case, the lower the acceleration factor, the less timely the signal, and the higher the acceleration factor, the more sensitive and timely the signals. However, they result in more whipsaws. In Chart 23-5 the upper area features an acceleration factor of 0.01 with a maximum of 0.1, whereas the lower area shows a more aggressive 0.08 acceleration with a 0.8 maximum. The difference is very clear. The smaller acceleration factor featured in the top area results in far fewer whipsaws than the one featured in the lower. In this instance the smaller acceleration factor would have won hands down, but this is because of the strong-trending quality of the market. Setting levels for the accelerating factor is a trial-and-error process, just as with the process of determining the optimum span for an MA. In this case, though, we have two variables, the initial acceleration factor and the maximum.

Chart 23-5   First Iberia Fund comparing two acceleration factors. (Source: *pring.com*)

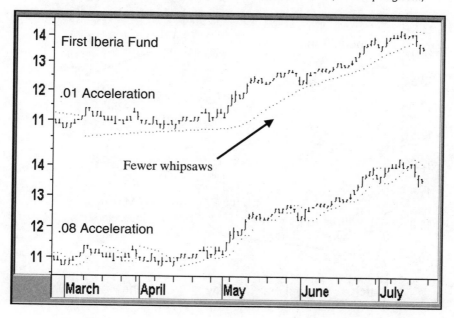

Of the two, the initial acceleration factor has by far the largest influence. Chart 23-6 shows two parabolas using the same 0.01 initial factor. The dashed line has a maximum of 0.1 and the solid line has a 0.8 maximum. As you can see, both lines are identical until the price really begins to accelerate in mid June.

Wells Wilder, the innovator of this approach, recommends a 0.02 acceleration factor with a maximum of 0.2.

Interpretation

The interpretation of the parabolic system is purely mechanical. On the whole, this approach has a lot of merit. However, one of the principal problems that I have found is that the initial stop point can often occur a long way from the entry point. In the example of the Swiss franc in Chart 23-7, there is a shorting possibility as the price violates the trendline. The first opportunity to initiate the trade was at the opening, since the price gapped down on the day and the opening was at 70.7 cents. However, the stop would have been placed above the extreme point of the rally at 73.3 cents. This is quite a huge potential loss of 2.6 cents, especially when it is considered that

Chart 23-6   First Iberia Fund comparing two maximum acceleration factors. (Source: *pring.com*)

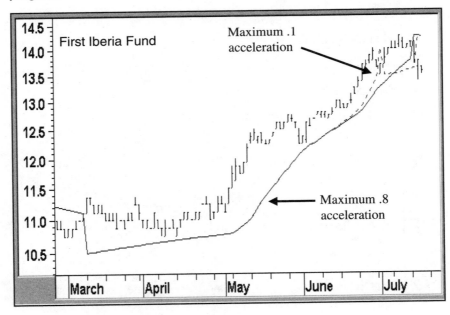

Chart 23-7 Swiss franc assessing risk using the parabolic. (Source: *pring.com*)

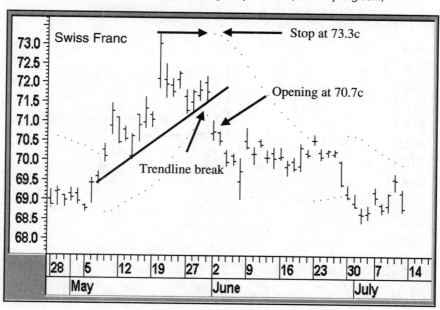

this is a highly leveraged futures market. As it turned out, the trade was stopped out for a small loss (Chart 23-8). This was a lucky outcome, but really the best thing to do under this kind of situation is not to put on the trade in the first place because the risk, relative to the reward, was just too high.

Chart 23-9 shows another example just using the parabolic signal as a basis for trading. A short signal develops around February 18 and the initial stop point offers a fairly substantial risk, since the short was made at about $53\frac{1}{2}$ and the stop is at $57. As luck would have it, the stop moved down slightly, but the price rallied up to meet it. And the short would have been covered at about $56\frac{1}{2}$ for a loss. Ironically, had a long position been initiated on the stop reversal principle, the trader would have gone home with another loss. This trade started off quite well and the price actually rallied to a new high. This meant that the stop point was progressively raised higher but not fast enough to have stopped another whipsaw resulting in a small loss. The next short trade (Chart 23-10) is a disaster, as the stop is just clipped at pretty well the high tick for the move. The long trade entails a great risk, since the stop is down at the previous low, and sure enough, the trade is once again stopped for a nasty loss. I could have shown you lots of examples wherein

Chart 23-8   Swiss franc assessing risk using the parabolic. (Source: *pring.com*)

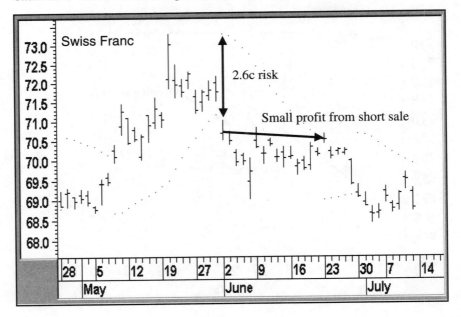

Chart 23-9   DuPont assessing risk using the parabolic. (Source: *pring.com*)

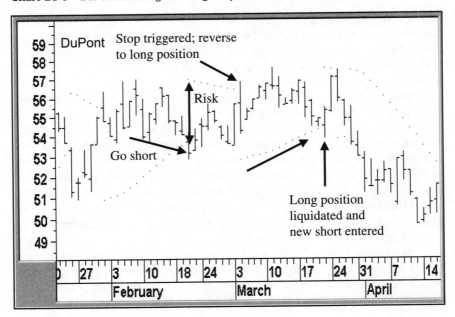

Chart 23-10   DuPont assessing risk using the parabolic. (Source: *pring.com*)

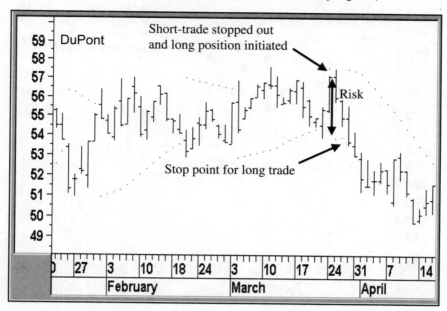

this approach would have done well in trending markets. However, I deliberately presented these examples because this type of false signal occurs far more often than we would like.

Playing Parabolic Guerilla

There are two good ways around this problem. The first is to play parabolic guerilla. In other words, do not operate on every parabolic signal, but wait until you can see a situation where the price is close to a stop and intelligent support-or-resistance point. Take the shorting signal flagged in Chart 23-11, for instance. At the time when the parabolic sell signal for International Paper was triggered, the risk was fairly high, all the way up to the top of the vertical arrow. Now, had we played guerilla and waited for the market to come to us, it would have been possible to short at the arrow just below the stop. There was even a second chance when the price rallied back to the trendline in Chart 23-12 and the parabolic line. Remember, it was only after the price had rallied back to the parabolic line 4 days earlier that

Chart 23-11   International Paper playing guerilla parabolic. (Source: *pring.com*)

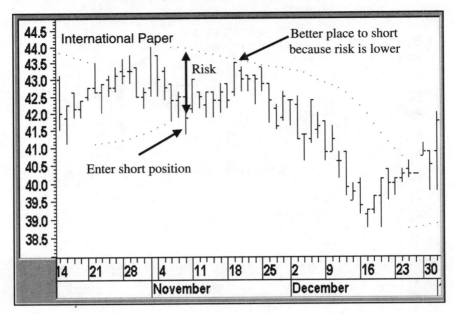

Chart 23-12   International Paper playing guerilla parabolic. (Source: *pring.com*)

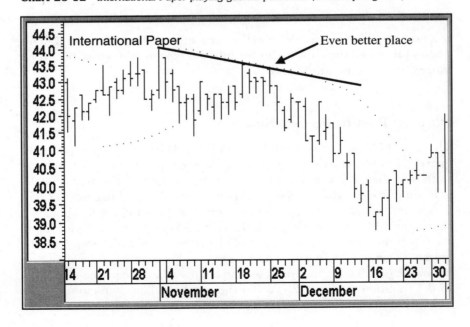

it was possible to construct the trendline, since a valid line requires two points that need to be joined. As you can see, this combination of shorting close to the stop point and close to a resistance level would have resulted in a worthwhile profit. Incidentally, this particular parabolic line was set at 0.01 with a maximum acceleration factor of 0.2. It was, therefore, less sensitive than the others that we have been studying so far.

Chart 23-13 offers a sell signal at point A. Once again the risk is pretty large since the short would be covered at the first dot. Also, the brief intraday penetration of the stop line at point A indicated a whipsaw possibility. However, had we waited for a more opportune time using patience and discipline, a far less risky trade could have been initiated. There were two possibilities. The first would be in the ellipse, for it would have been obvious at this point that the tops of these 1-day rallies represented resistance. Thus a short could have been initiated from the same parabolic signal but at a higher price. Also, the stop line was gradually declining, further reducing the margin of risk. The second possibility came at the breakdown point as the triangle was completed. Now it is certainly true that the level of risk was higher than shorting into resistance at the upper trendline of the triangle. However, the odds of a successful trade were higher at the breakdown point

Chart 23-13 International Paper playing guerilla parabolic. (Source: *pring.com*)

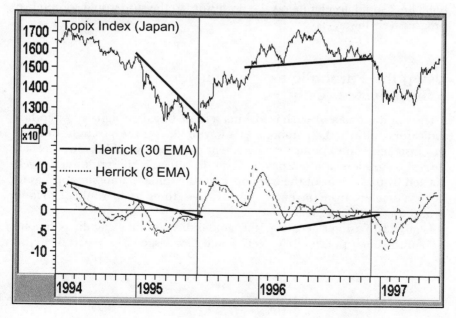

Chart 23-14   International Paper playing guerilla parabolic. (Source: *pring.com*)

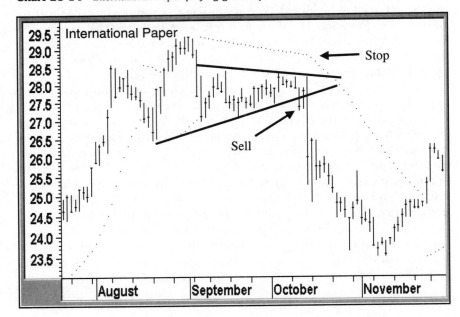

(Chart 23-14), since it indicated that the period of consolidation was over. Also, the implied decline from the break would have meant that the parabolic line would accelerate on the downside, so the stop would soon move progressively lower.

Using the Parabolic as a Stop System Only

The second useful approach is to enter a trade based on signals from other indicators and use the parabolic as a way of exiting the position. Even in this instance, sound money management principles would involve the setting of a stop loss at a reasonable level. In effect, if the trade seems well backed by the weight of the evidence, but the initial parabolic stop has to be set a long way from the entry point, the best thing to do would be to look round for another trade.

Chart 23-15 using December 1997 gold indicates that using the parabolic stop at the entry point in May 1997 would have risked $10. Apart from the

Chart 23-15 December 1997 Gold and two indicators. (Source: *pring.com*)

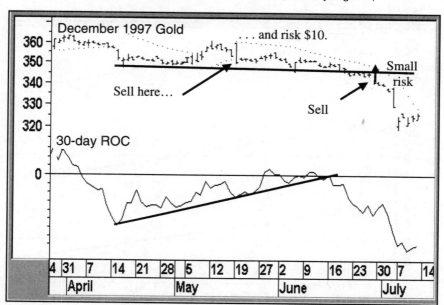

fact that this was a pretty emotional outside day, there was not much technical evidence to justify a short-term trade. After all, no trendline or serious MA breaks had taken place. Later on, we see a trendline violation in the 30-day ROC. This warned that the price could be vulnerable, but we still needed a trend signal from the price. That came on June 27, as the price crashed through the support trendline. At the time of the break, the parabolic was still in a sell mode, but now the distance between the stop point and the entry point was much less. Also, because of the break in price, the acceleration factor had begun to increase, so the stop was being progressively lowered at a faster and faster rate right from day 1. The trade ended in a profit, as the next parabolic buy developed at a lower level.

Chart 23-16 shows a classic example using JP Morgan. The parabolic had signaled a buy signal at point A. Since the price did not fall very much, the buy signal was still in force when it reversed to the upside with a breakout at point B. The breakout was well supported by the buy signal in the short-term KST and the 45-day ROC. However, the great thing was that the par-

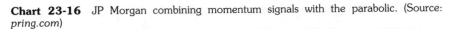

Chart 23-16 JP Morgan combining momentum signals with the parabolic. (Source: *pring.com*)

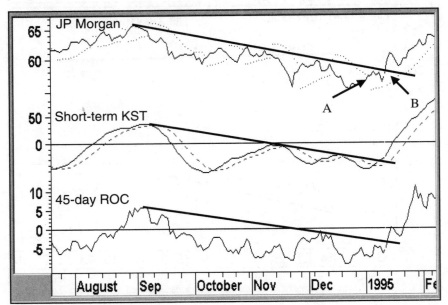

abolic stop line had already begun to move up, so the risk was not only being reduced, but continually being reduced as time progressed, and the line started to accelerate.

24

Price Projection Bands

The Concept

Price projection bands are similar in nature to envelope analysis and Bollinger bands. *These* bands also have some of the characteristics of channel lines, such as the Raff regression line. The projection band is not a momentum indicator. However, I have included a discussion of it here because it forms the basis for the calculation of the price projection oscillator, or PPO, which is our final topic.

Projection bands are calculated by finding the maximum and minimum prices over a specified timespan. The longer the time, the wider the bands, and vice versa. These extreme values are then projected forward, parallel to a linear regression line. The indicator is then displayed as two elastic bands representing the minimum and maximum price over the specified timespan. An example is shown in Chart 24-1. However, unlike the Raff regression channel and Bollinger bands, the price will always be contained by projection bands. This is because the last plot of the projection band is the high or low for the period. If the latest data are at a new high or a new low, they will, by definition, be plotted at the same level.

The bands are interpreted in much the same way as any envelope. Look for prices to find resistance at the upper band and reverse trend. The lower band should find support, and so forth.

I have noticed that in a very strong market the price will hug the band for a considerable period of time. Then when it moves away from the upper band, it indicates a dissipation of upside momentum. Chart 24-2 shows that this is either immediately followed by a price decline (such as that in December

Chart 24-1   Morgan Stanley Cyclical Index and price projection bands. (Source: *pring.com*)

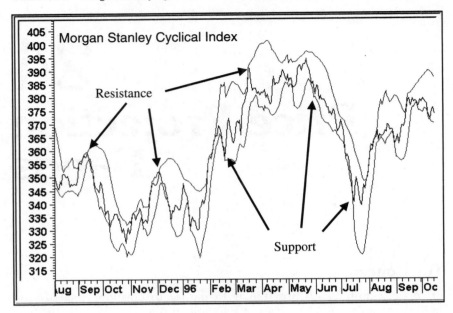

Chart 24-2   Morgan Stanley Cyclical Index and price projection bands. (Source: *pring.com*)

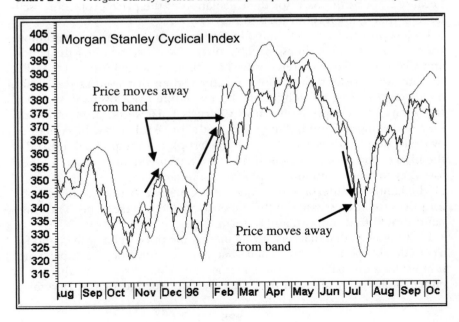

1995) or one is delayed a few periods as the price reaches a new high and then declines (such as the situation that developed in February 1996). In this instance, the price hugged the line for several sessions before moving away from it. A consolidation, rather than an actual trend reversal, followed. It really does not matter that much, because once the price moves away from the band, most of the profit from a move has usually been captured.

The same principle applies in reverse. Sometimes it is only necessary for the price to touch the line for one or two periods. The main point is that when it moves away from the band, a signal of a possible trend reversal is given. This approach is far from perfect. In late June 1996 we see an example of the price pulling away from the line (Chart 24-3), but this only proves to be temporary, as it rallies for a couple of days and then resumes its downtrend with a vengeance.

The Projection Bands and R-Square

One way of filtering these whipsaws is to combine the projection band with the r-squared indicator. Chart 24-4 features a 14-period projection band with

Chart 24-3 Morgan Stanley Cyclical Index and price projection bands. (Source: *pring.com*)

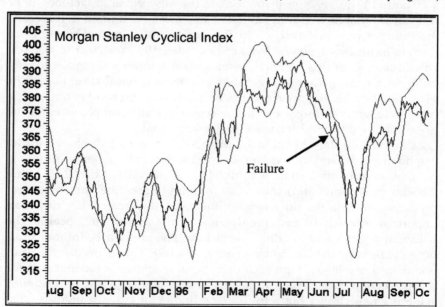

Chart 24-4   Mexico Index, price projection bands, and a 10-day r-square. (Source: *pring.com*)

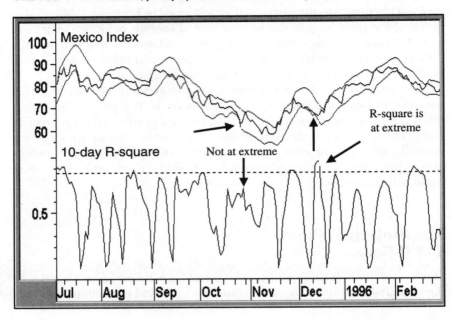

a 10-period r-square. Now if you look at the false signal in October 1995, you can see that the r-square was not at an extreme and was not, therefore, indicating a potential reversal in the downtrend. Alternately, the price starts to move away from the band in December 1995 and the r-square *is* at an extreme, so in this instance, an important bottom was registered. Not every extreme r-square reading results in a reversal, but that should not be surprising because the price may not be at a projection band extreme. The early October 1995 r-square extreme represents an example wherein the price fails to confirm with a price projection signal.

As a general rule, whenever the price touches one of the bands for an extended period and then moves sharply away from it, we get a strong signal that the prevailing trend is vulnerable. For instance, Chart 24-5 (using a 30-day projection band) shows that for a lot of the time, the more vertical the up move as the price touches the band, the greater the odds of an important reversal. An example develops at the August 1995 peak in the Nikkei at point A and another one in July 1996 at point B. In both situations the fact that the line is being continually touched means that the price is making a new 30-day high each time, because 30 days is the timespan for this projection band. When it fails to make a new high after consistently achieving new closing highs for 5, 6, or 10 days in a row, it indicates that

Chart 24-5   The Nikkei Index and a 30-day price projection band. (Source: *pring.com*)

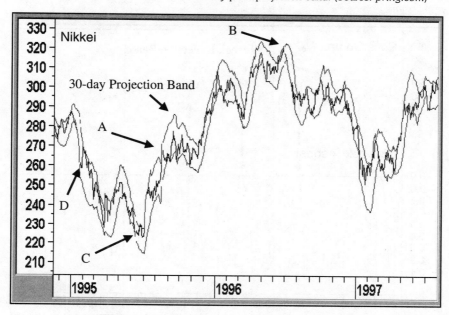

the period of urgent buying is over. The longer the period it can cling to the upper band, the greater the swing in sentiment to the bullish side (then the greater the need for a swing to the other side).

The same principle works in reverse, so in June 1995 at point C we see an example of the price hugging the band on the downside for a few days. Then the gap between the two rapidly increases.

Projection Bands with Weekly Charts

Both the projection band and r-square work quite well with weekly charts, though I have found that it is crucial to experiment with different combinations with different securities. Chart 24-6 displays a 39-week projection band together with a 13-week r-square. The vertical lines show the points where the price, having hugged or touched the outer boundary of the projection band, and then reverses away from it. At the same time, the r-square indicator reaches an overextended reading and then reverses. The late 1987 buy signal was followed by a sharp rally. The countervailing sell signal was triggered a few months later in mid February (point A), as the price touches

Chart 24-6 Price Company, price projection bands, and a 13-week r-square. (Source: *pring.com*)

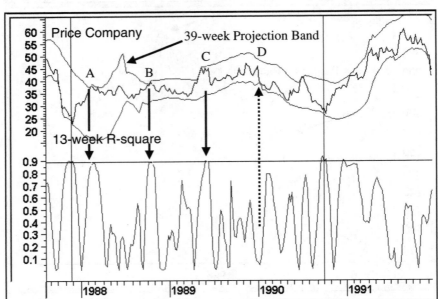

the band and quickly reverses and the r-square peaks out from its over-bought line. The trend reversal was far less dramatic, although prices did consolidate for 6 months. Do not forget that this chart covers a far greater period than the others we have been looking at. The next two sell signals in late 1988 (point B) and mid 1989 (point C) are also followed by consoli-dations. Finally, the late-1990 buy signal at the second vertical line was a clas-sic: a sharp down move in which the price touches the band, followed by a quick reversal as the projection band declines. But look at the r-square; it is also at an extreme. This combination differs from the January 1990 low (point D), when the r-square had not reached an extreme reading.

Chart 24-7 shows a weekly chart of the coffee market using the same 39-week projection band and 13-week r-square combination. There were three periods when the r-square indicator reached an extreme reading. The December 1992 signal (point A) represented a textbook sell, since the price had been hugging the projection band for a while. Later on in December 1994 (point B), all the conditions for a rally were in place, but the price con-solidated, instead. This is a reminder that a high reading in the r-square just indicates that the prevailing trend is likely to terminate, in this case, from up to sideways, not up to down. Finally, the mid-1994 peak in the r-square

Chart 24-7 Coffee, price projection bands, and a 13-week r-square. (Source: *pring.com*)

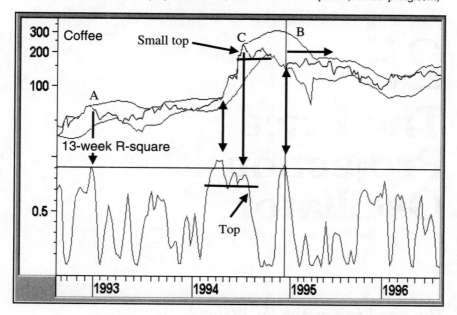

(point C) deserves closer scrutiny. This is because it occurred when the price rallied right to the upper band; the r-square then reversed direction, indicating that the price was losing its trending qualities. But it continued to rally sharply, still holding right on the band. When the final top did develop and the price moved away from the band, the r-square was overextended but below the extreme line. However, it still generated a sell indication because it completed a small top. In effect, the result was the same as if it had reversed from an extreme reading above the dashed line.

25
The Price Projection Oscillator

The Band versus the Oscillator

The *price projection oscillator* is a variation on the stochastic. The stochastic assumes that prices close at, or near to, their high during an uptrend and close to their low in a downtrend. It is when the price starts to close away from these extreme points that momentum slows and the prevailing trend starts to reverse. The calculation of the stochastic, therefore, takes this concept into consideration. The price projection oscillator, alternately, does the same thing but adjusts the maximum and minimum prices up and down by a linear regression of the price. In plain English this means that the price projection oscillator is more sensitive to short-term price swings.

Chart 25-1 shows a 45-day price projection oscillator together with a 45-day price projection band. If you look closely, you will see that there is a connection, because the price projection oscillator is really displaying the same information but in an oscillator format. See how the oscillator moves to 100 in August 1996 (point A) at the same time that the price touches the outer band. Then when the oscillator dips toward zero in October at point B, this occurs at the same time that the price moves to the lower band. In effect, we are seeing the same thing in a different way. This is similar to a comparison between a price envelope and a trend deviation oscillator based on the same timeframe.

Chart 25-1   Merrill Lynch and a 45-day PPO. (Source: *pring.com*)

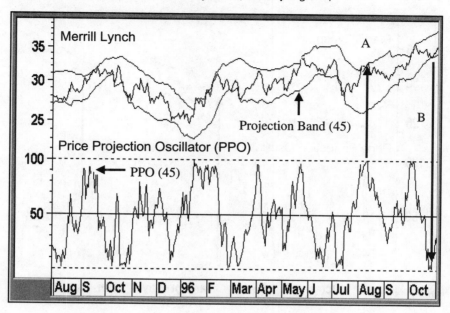

There are several methods of interpretation. The first is to spot those periods when the oscillator is at, or extremely close to, the 0 and 100 readings and use those as a filter for seeing if other indicators are pointing to a peak or trough. That would have worked quite well at the May and August 1996 highs in Chart 25-2, but not at the February low: hence the need to check out the situation with other indicators.

Another possibility is to place the overbought-or-oversold zones at less extreme numbers, say, 80 and 20 (Chart 25-3), and then wait and see when the indicator recrosses these levels on its way back toward zero. That, too, has its limitations because there are quite a few occasions when the price whipsaws above and below the lines, as it did in January 1996 and later on in the late February to early March period. Both examples are contained within the ellipses. This type of situation will leave you in doubt as to what is really going on. Again, the price projection oscillator acts as a filter, and it is necessary to refer to some other indicator based on trend to confirm these signals.

Chart 25-2 Merrill Lynch and a 45-day PPO. (Source: *pring.com*)

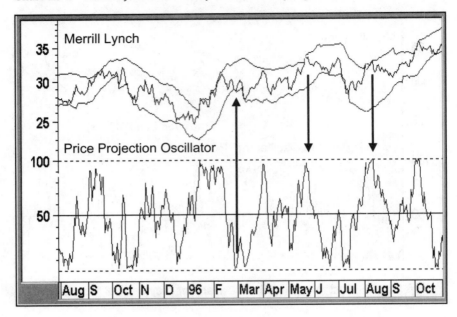

Chart 25-3 Merrill Lynch and a 45-day PPO. (Source: *pring.com*)

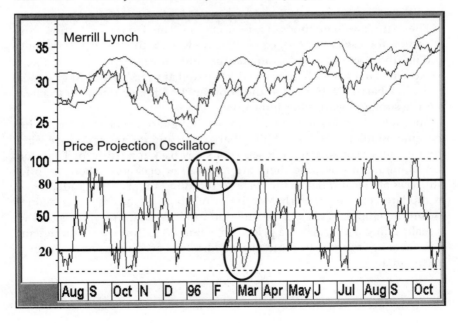

Overlaying the Two Oscillators

Another alternative is to overlay one oscillator on another, using two widely separated timespans. In Chart 25-4 I have plotted a 14-day period with a solid line and a 45-day one with a dashed line. The idea is that when both are simultaneously overbought or oversold and then start to move in the same direction, this places higher odds on the prevailing trend reversal. The reason for doing this is based on the assumption that prices at any one point are determined by the interaction of many different time cycles. Considering one oscillator only takes into consideration a limited number of cycles. However, if you look at two oscillators, the amount of cycles taken into consideration doubles.

Chart 25-4 highlights those occasions when both series are at extremes. In March 1996 (point A) both series bottom at the same time and rise in tandem. Then in April (point B) the reverse set of circumstances set in. In May (point C) both series peak again, but this was not a genuine signal because the 14-day indicator did not reach an extreme. Finally, both series did so in early July, but the price continued on its last leg down. It was not until they both rallied that a bottom was experienced (point D). For this approach to be effective, it is necessary to use timeframes that are fairly well

Chart 25-4   Merrill Lynch and two PPOs. (Source: *pring.com*)

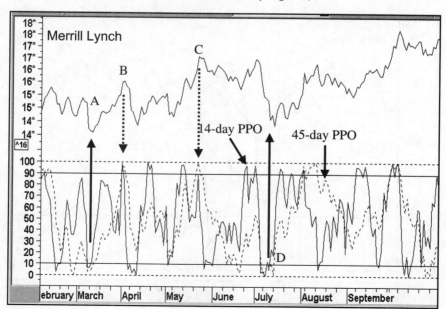

separated. A 14- and 17-day comparison would not be very helpful, but a 14- and 45-period comparison is. Generally speaking, it is best to use a combination of timespans, where the second is at least double the first.

That is why I prefer the joint trendline approach that we have discussed with other indicators. This appears to work quite well with the projection oscillator. Chart 25-5 features a 45-day oscillator on its own. You can see how we got some useful buy-or-sell signals in March 1996, December 1995, and February 1996, respectively. In February 1996 the PPO breaks down from a one-month top. This is also confirmed by a trendline break in the oscillator, followed by one in the price. Finally, a small buy signal in early March develops as a double trendline break: one for the oscillator and one for the price take place.

Chart 25-6 shows that in December 1995 the price projection oscillator violates an uptrend line just as the price is taking out its October and November lows.

Two Price Projection Oscillators

Chart 25-7 features two price projection oscillators. This arrangement again reflects the concept that price at any one particular point of time is

Chart 25-5   Merrill Lynch and a 45-day PPO. (Source: *pring.com*)

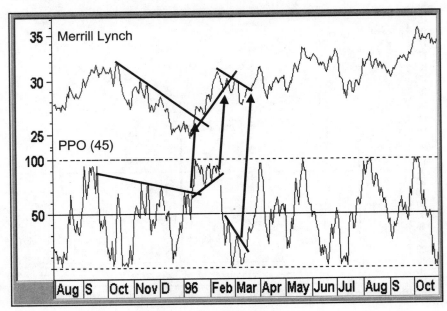

Chart 25-6 Merrill Lynch and a 45-day PPO. (Source: *pring.com*)

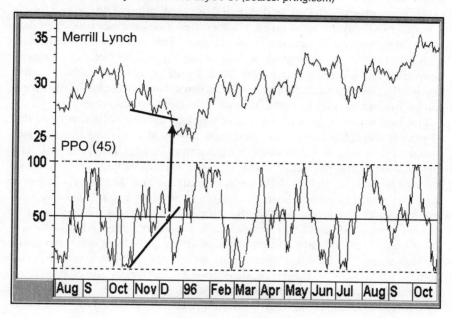

Chart 25-7 ASE Oil Index and PPO variations. (Source: *pring.com*)

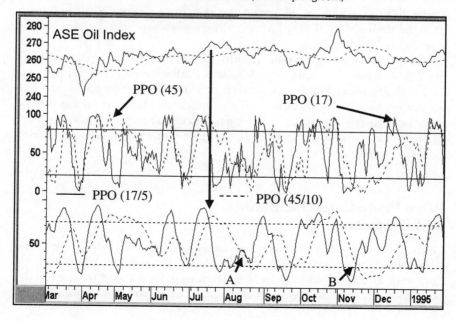

determined by the interaction of several time cycles. Here we have two indicators that reflect cycles some distance from each other. The dashed line is a 45-day PPO and the solid one a 17-day series. Look for periods when *both* price projection oscillators are at an extreme. This is because the differing cycles that these two indicators represent are topping or bottoming simultaneously and therefore the odds of a trend reversal become greater. Obviously, there are a lot more cycles at work, but by displaying two indicators, instead of one, the odds of a valid reversal are increased.

The bottom area displays an MA of the two indictors. In this case, the 17-period series has been smoothed with a 5-day MA and the 45-day series with a 10-day average. I find this arrangement to be much more useful than just looking at the raw data. There are several rules of engagement. First, look for periods when both MAs are at an extreme and then start to reverse. An example develops in Chart 25-7 in July 1994. Rule 2 is a little more reliable. It looks for crossovers of the longer-term dashed average by the shorter-term solid one. If this crossover comes at an extreme level, the signal is usually, though not always, more powerful. July 1994 offered a good sell signal. In all of these interpretations, we are really trying to establish the point at which both series reverse direction. A crossover in-and-of-itself does not guarantee this. Consider the situation in August 1994 (point A). The solid line crosses the dashed line and then starts to decline again. Only when they both bottom at the very end of the month does the price reach its low. Then in November (point B), another crossover develops. The price is clearly oversold but continues down anyway. The bottom is reached as the 45-day PPO MA bottoms. However, the rally does not really get underway until the dashed 45/10 PPO line actually crosses above its extreme oversold level in mid December.

In a really trending market, nothing in the oscillator department will work. The arrows in Chart 25-8 show that both reversals from an extreme in the 45-day series fail to signal much of a decline. I show you this example not because I have no faith in this arrangement, because I do. It is done more because it is important to offer a balanced presentation and not leave you with the opinion that this or any of the other arrangements and indicators are perfect.

Price Projection Oscillator and R-Square

Chart 25-9 features a 45-day r-square along with a 65/25 PPO. One useful technique is to look for extreme readings in the PPO and see when this indicator crosses above or below its MA. Then look for a trend reversal in the price to confirm. The inclusion of r-square offers an additional filter. In

Chart 25-8   ASE Oil Index and PPO variations. (Source: *pring.com*)

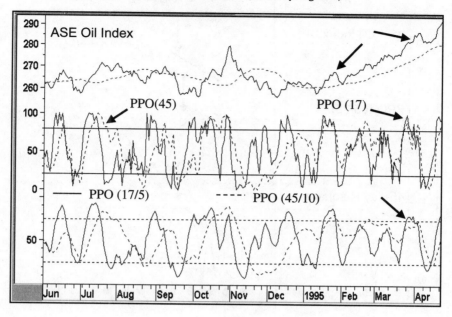

Chart 25-9   ASE Oil Index, a PPO, and r-square. (Source: *pring.com*)

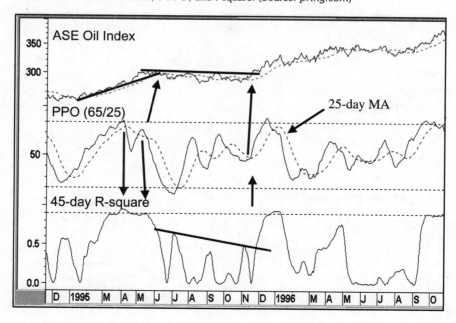

Chart 25-10   ASE Oil Index, a PPO, and r-square. (Source: *pring.com*)

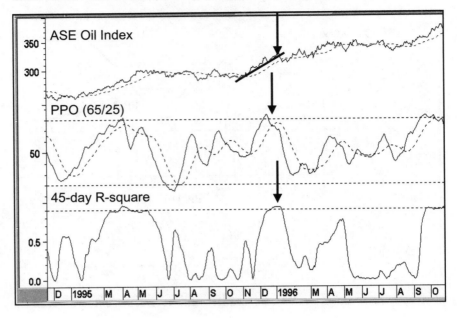

Chart 25-11   ASE Oil Index, a PPO, and r-square. (Source: *pring.com*)

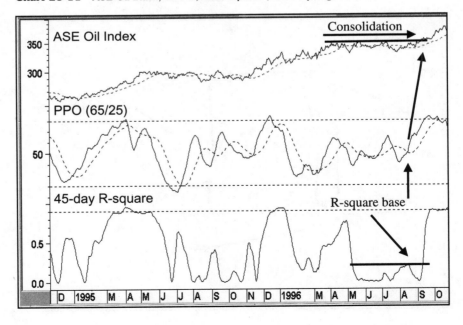

March 1995, an extreme in the r-square develops and a sell signal by the PPO is triggered. However, there was no meaningful trend reversal signaled by the price. Later on, though, the r-square touches its overbought level and starts to decline. The price subsequently violates a trendline. Since the PPO gave a bear signal by penetrating its average, there are lots of pieces of evidence indicating a trend change. In this case, the change was from up to sideways, not up to down. By late November it was possible to draw a trendline for both the r-square and price. The violation of the r-square trendline did not indicate a rally, merely that the sideways trend had probably come to an end. It was the bullish MA crossover by the PPO, combined with the price break, that indicated the trend was to be a positive one.

The rally did not last very long, and its termination in early January 1996 was signaled by the arrows in Chart 25-10, where the price breaks an uptrend line, the PPO goes negative, and the r-square crosses below the 0.9 area, indicating the probability that the uptrend was over. Actually, it ushered in a relatively long period of a slightly up-sloping consolidation. The termination of this trading range was signaled by the completion of an r-square base (Chart 25-11) combined with a PPO buy signal and price breakout to the upside.

Appendix A

Quiz Chapters 1—12

1. The linear regression indicator turns:
   (A) More quickly than a simple moving average.
   (B) More slowly than a simple moving average.

2. The linear regression slope is a direct derivative of:
   (A) A linear regression line.
   (B) A Raff regression line.
   (C) The r-square indicator.
   (D) A linear regression indicator.

3. In looking at this chart, it is:
   (A) A bull market correction.
   (B) The start of a new bear market.

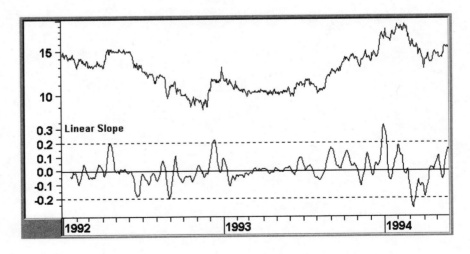

4. Looking at this chart, at the time of the vertical line, is there anything major in the linear slope that suggests that a top is at hand?
   (A) No.
   (B) Yes.

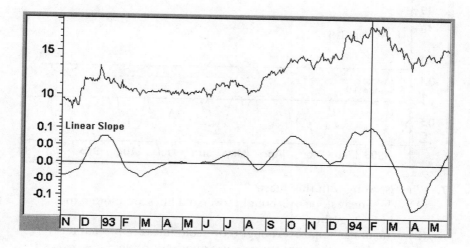

5. A high reading in the r-square indicates:
   (A) That a market has strong trending characteristics.
   (B) That a market has strong trending characteristics and is overbought.
   (C) That a market has strong trending characteristics and is oversold.
   (D) None of the above.

6. At point A, what is the r-square telling us?
   (A) That the price is in a bull market and unlikely to respond to overextended r-square readings.
   (B) That the odds favor that the strong directional movement to the upside is in the process of terminating.
   (C) That you should sell everything, but this turned out to be a false signal.

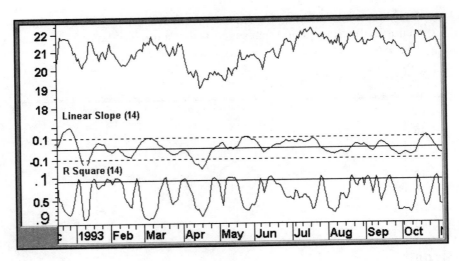

7. What is wrong with this chart?
   (A) The linear slope overbought/oversold lines are plotted too
        closely together.
   (B) The linear slope overbought/oversold lines are plotted too
        closely together, but there is also another problem not covered
        by these answers.
   (C) It is not appropriate to plot a linear slope and an r-square on the
        same chart because they are both derivatives of the same thing.

8. When the r-square reverses trend from a low level this represents:
   (A) A buy signal.
   (B) A sell signal.
   (C) That the odds favor the price starting a new trend which could be
        up or down.

9. The Chaikin formula works on the assumption that:
   (A) Market strength is derived from prices closing near the middle of
        the trading session.
   (B) Market weakness is characterized by prices closing close to the
        session low.
   (C) Market strength is characterized by prices closing near the
        session high.
   (D) Both B and C.

10. The Chaikin money flow cannot be calculated without volume.
  (A) True.
  (B) False.

11. One of the most useful interpretive characteristics of the Chaikin money flow is:
  (A) Its ability to forecast prices in the next session.
  (B) Its ability to flag strong directional price movement.
  (C) Its strong diverging characteristics.
  (D) None of the above.

12. Which letter represents the best example of a positive divergence.
  (A)
  (B)
  (C)
  (D)

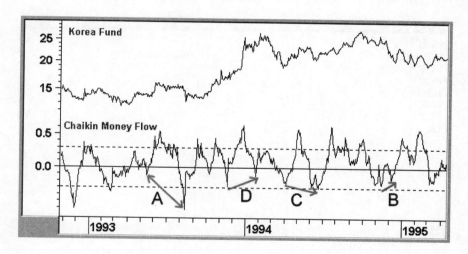

13. The principal difference between an oscillator constructed from volume and one of price is:
  (A) Volume does not reach to such extremes as price.
  (B) Price is smoother than volume.
  (C) Overbought readings in volume can come after a price decline.
  (D) All of the above.

14. Why use volume oscillators when volume displayed as a histogram is very helpful?
   - (A) Because volume oscillators can emphasize certain characteristics that cannot be easily spotted in a histogram format.
   - (B) Because volume oscillators are always at an overbought or oversold extreme.
   - (C) Because volume normally leads price.
   - (D) None of the above.

15. If the volume oscillator has peaked in this chart, what is the most likely outcome?
   - (A) The price has bottomed, at least for the time being.
   - (B) The price will continue to decline.
   - (C) None of these answers is correct because the question has been incorrectly worded.
   - (D) The price will rally and then quickly fall much further.

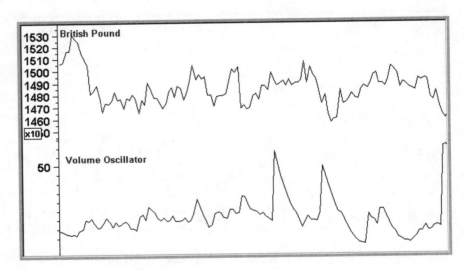

16. This is a buying opportunity because:
   - (A) The volume oscillator has shrunk to its lowest reading in years, indicating a total lack of selling pressure.
   - (B) The volume oscillator is low and the price has reached a support trendline.
   - (C) This is a kind of double bottom because the volume oscillator indicated a selling climax in June.
   - (D) B and C.

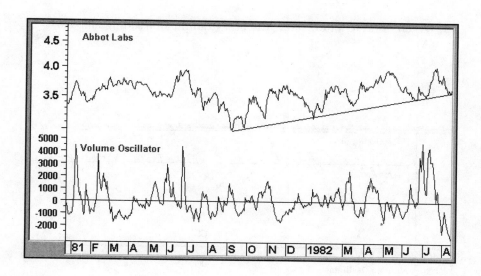

17. What factor suggests that this trendline is in danger of being violated?
  (A) The volume oscillator was declining during the late July, early August rally.
  (B) A and D.
  (C) There is nothing in the chart that warns of danger.
  (D) Volume expands as the price starts to decline in August.

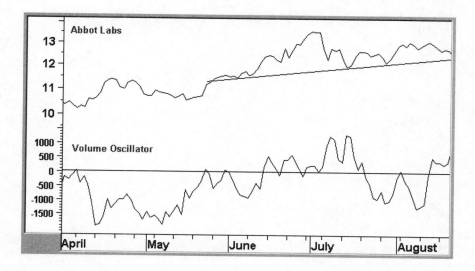

18. Which of these letters offers the best example of a selling climax?
- (A)
- (B)
- (C)
- (D)

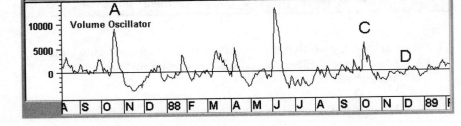

19. This situation is a:
- (A) Buy.
- (B) Sell.
- (C) Hold.

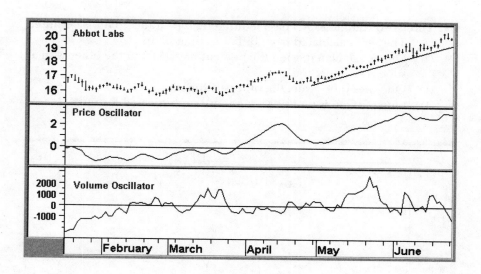

20. The price is in a trading range. In which direction is it likely to break
out according to your interpretation of the ROC of volume?

(A) Up.

(B) Down.

(C) No indication is given.

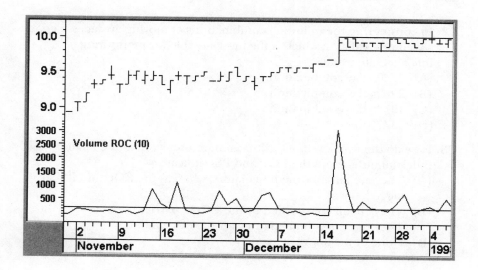

21. These two volume ROCs have a different appearance. This is because:
  (A) They are calculated from different time spans.
  (B) One is calculated using the percent method and the other with a subtraction method.
  (C) One uses ratio scale, the other arithmetic.
  (D) One of them is plotted with a more sophisticated formula.

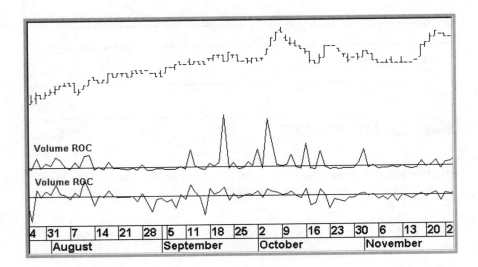

22. In considering the following combinations of moving averages used in a volume oscillator, which is the most suitable for monitoring intermediate trends?
  (A) 2/200-day combination.
  (B) 20/25-day combination.
  (C) 10/25-day combination.
  (D) 25/75-week.

23. How do the Chaikin money flow, Klinger oscillator, and demand index all differ from the ROC and RSI indicators?
  (A) They are all smoothed oscillators, whereas the ROC and RSI are jagged.
  (B) They are all constrained by the 0/100 barrier.
  (C) They require volume figures for the calculation.
  (D) None of the above.

24. Which of the following are appropriate for the interpretation of the demand index?

   (A) Divergence analysis.

   (B) Zero crossovers, trendline, and price pattern analysis.

   (C) Overbought and oversold crossovers.

   (D) All of the above.

25. Looking at this nice breakout in the demand index, this security is:

   (A) Buy.

   (B) Sell short.

   (C) Maintain a long position.

   (D) None of the above.

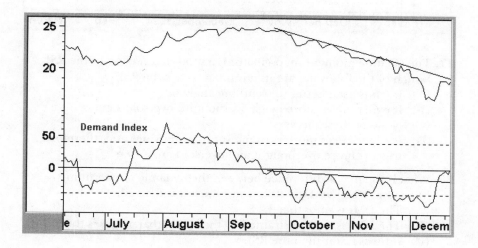

26. Which of the following methods of interpretation look as if they apply to this security and its demand index?

   (A) Overbought/oversold crossovers and trendlines.

   (B) Overbought/oversold crossovers.

   (C) Zero crossovers and overbought/oversold crossovers.

   (D) A and C.

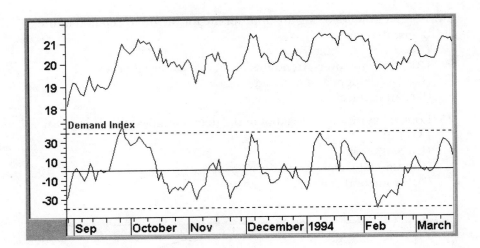

27. The Chande momentum oscillator is a modified version of the RSI.
Which of the following are its advantages over the RSI?
(A) It lends itself better to trendline analysis.
(B) It experiences more mega overbought/oversold signals.
(C) None of these answers.
(D) It experiences more extreme short-term swings and, therefore,
triggers more overbought and oversold crossovers.

28. What is the major difference between the dynamic momentum
indicator (DMI) and the RSI, from which it is derived?
(A) The DMI is smoother.
(B) The DMI is not constrained by the 0/100 barrier, as is the RSI.
(C) It turns faster than the RSI.
(D) It is more volatile than the RSI.

29. Does the period between January and March qualify for the DMI
cluster rule?
(A) Yes.
(B) No.

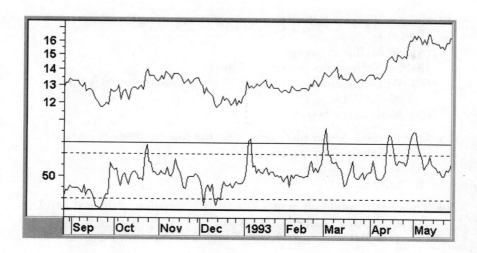

30. Does the March/May period qualify for the DMI cluster rule?
  (A) Yes.
  (B) No.

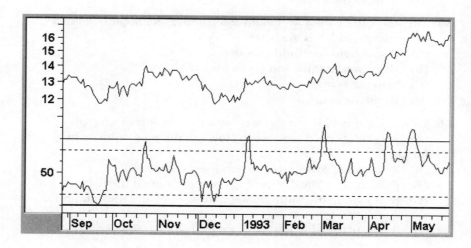

31. The Klinger oscillator incorporates volume and price.
  (A) True.
  (B) False.

32. Which is the relatively best method of interpreting the Klinger oscillator?
   (A) Signal line crossovers.
   (B) Zero crossovers of the signal line.
   (C) When the oscillator is deeply oversold and the price is close to its 89-day EMA.
   (D) None of the above.

33. One relatively better way to interpret the Klinger oscillator is to be on the lookout for divergences.
   (A) True.
   (B) False.

34. The relative momentum index (RMI) is a variation of the RSI. Which of the following characteristics is true?
   (A) The RMI is not constrained by the 0 on the downside and 100 on the upside.
   (B) They both use one parameter, the time span.
   (C) The RMI is smoother and experiences more rhythmic fluctuations.
   (D) None of the above.

35. The RMI can be used with many interpretive techniques, but in a *relative* sense, which is the best?
   (A) Overbought/oversold crossovers.
   (B) Mega overboughts and oversolds.
   (C) Extreme swings.
   (D) Trendline analysis.

36. Looking at this RMI you can see that there are lots of whipsaw overbought/oversold crossovers. How can these be reduced in number?
   (A) By applying a linear regression line.
   (B) By running a 200-day moving average through the data.
   (C) By doubling the width between these lines and the equilibrium level.
   (D) By calculating the RMI with a slightly longer timespan.

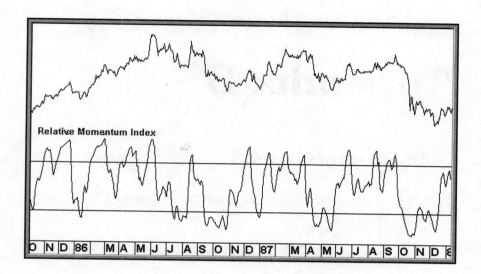

Appendix B

Quiz Chapters 13-25

1. Which securities can the Herrick payoff be calculated for?
   (A) General Motors and Microsoft
   (B) Spot gold, spot silver, and soybeans.
   (C) The S & P and the Dow.
   (D) The S & P Futures, gold futures, and bond futures.

2. Which are appropriate methods of interpretation for the payoff index?
   (A) Overbought/oversold crossovers.
   (B) Zero crossovers.
   (C) Trendline and price pattern analysis.
   (D) A, B, and C.

3. Which letter identifies a bearish extreme swing?
   (A)
   (B)
   (C)

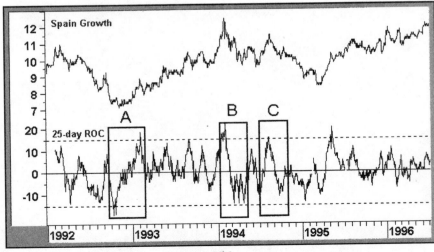

4. What is the difference between a 21-day inertia and a 21-period linear regression indicator of the RVI?
    (A) The inertia is far more volatile.
    (B) The linear regression of the RVI experiences far more whipsaws.
    (C) None whatsoever.
    (D) None of the above.

5. What assumption should be made for the future price of the following security?
    (A) It will continue to fluctuate.
    (B) It will find support and rally.
    (C) It will continue to decline.

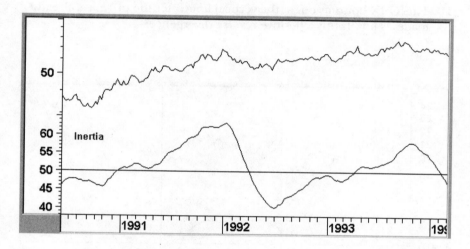

6. The Qstick indicator places special emphasis on:
    (A) The high, low, and close.
    (B) The high and low.
    (C) The open and close.
    (D) None of the above.

7. Put in a simple way, the Qstick is calculated from:
    (A) The difference between the high and low for the day.
    (B) The high, plus the low, divided by the close.
    (C) None of these answers is correct.
    (D) A simple moving average of the difference between the opening and closing prices.

8. If you were trying to plot a Qstick from a data series that contains the high, low, close, volume, and open interest, you would choose:
   (A) Any timespan because the Qstick is a very versatile indicator.
   (B) Only weekly timespans because the Qstick is better at measuring intermediate trends.
   (C) Only daily timespans because the Qstick is a short-term indicator.
   (D) None of the above.

9. Because the TRIX indicator is so smooth, it is never possible to draw meaningful trendlines.
   (A) True.
   (B) False.

10. The TRIX bottoms out at the vertical line, after the price has already made its low. Is this a positive reverse divergence?
   (A) Yes.
   (B) No.

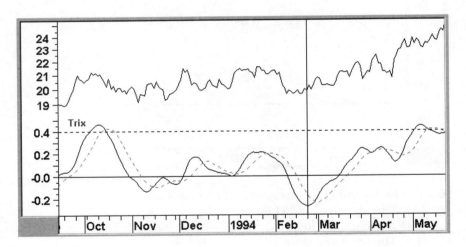

11. Directional movement is a concept that:
   (A) Tells us whether a market is oversold or overbought.
   (B) Measures the difference between yesterday's low and today's low.
   (C) Tells us whether a security price is in a trending or nontrending mode.
   (D) Requires volume figures in the calculation.

12. The ADX tells us whether a security's price is trending; the DIs tell us in which direction.
  (A) True.
  (B) False.

13. If the ADX is at an extreme high reading and trending down, you should:
  (A) Assume that the prevailing trend will continue.
  (B) Assume that the prevailing trend will reverse.
  (C) Assume that there will be a change in the prevailing trend.
  (D) Assume that the prevailing trend will continue and change much later on.

14. In this chart, the ADX starts to rally at the dashed vertical line. What is the most likely outcome for the price?
  (A) It will rally, too.
  (B) It will decline.
  (C) It will be trendless.
  (D) It will either experience a rally or a reaction.

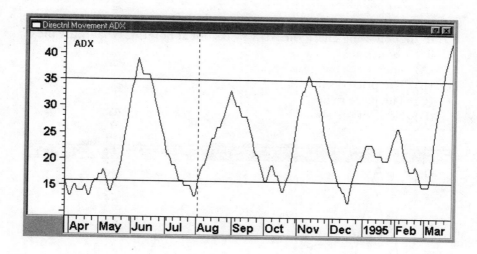

15. The DIs reflect:
  (A) Up and down directional movement over a specific timespan, which is usually 14 days.
  (B) Up and down volume over a specific timespan, which is usually 14 days.
  (C) The average directional movement over a specific timespan.

16. Looking at the following chart, which is the −DI?
   (A) The solid line.
   (B) The dashed line.

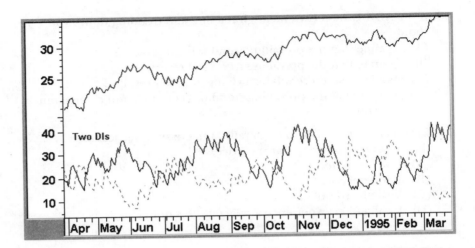

17. In the following chart, the ADX peaks out at point A. What is the most likely outcome?
   (A) The price changes trend.
   (B) The price declines.
   (C) The price rallies.
   (D) None of the above.

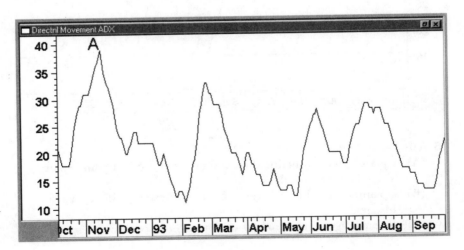

18. If the ADX reaches 150 and reverses and the previous high in the last 5 years was 85, the price is likely to:
  (A) Experience a major trend reversal.
  (B) None of these answers are correct because the question is improperly worded.
  (C) Experience a major change in trend.
  (D) There is no way of knowing how big the trend change will be.

19. Buy signals are given by the DIs when:
  (A) The +DI crosses above the −DI.
  (B) The ADX reverses from a high reading.
  (C) The ADX reverses from a low reading.
  (D) The +DI crosses above zero.

20. What is the most probable outcome given the following technical situation?
  (A) The price will rally back above the trendline.
  (B) The price will experience a trading range.
  (C) The price will decline.

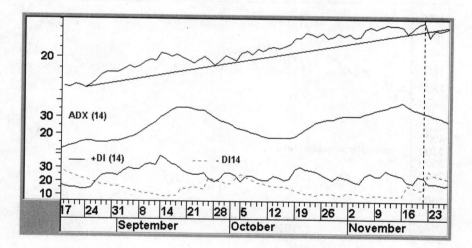

21. The CSI was originally designed to filter out the commodity that will give the trader the greatest bang for his buck, but an alternative interpretation is:
   (A) To use reversals in extreme overextended readings to signal probable trend changes.
   (B) To signal overbought and oversold conditions before they happen.
   (C) To use zero crossovers as buy and sell signals.
   (D) To use reversals in extreme overextended readings to signal probable trend reversals.

22. Looking at the following chart, what is the most probable outcome?
   (A) The price has bottomed.
   (B) The price will continue to decline.
   (C) The price will either continue to decline or experience a trading range.
   (D) None of the above.

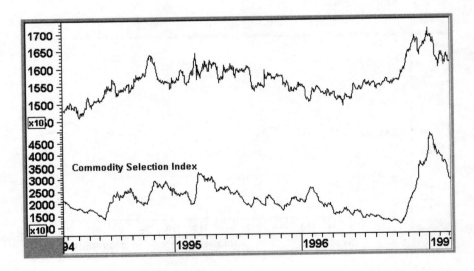

23. The parabolic system is good for:
   (A) Defining unusual overbought/oversold situations.
   (B) Setting stop points.
   (C) Calculating moving averages.
   (D) Identifying future price moves that will end in a parabola.

24. As a day trader, if you are going to go short, the best spot to place your first stop using the parabolic system is:
  (A) Above the previous strong area of minor resistance.
  (B) Below the previous strong area of minor resistance.
  (C) Below the previous strong area of minor support.
  (D) None of the above.

25. If you have a strong reason to believe that this security is in a primary uptrend, where should you place the stop for a short sale?
  (A)
  (B)
  (C)
  (D)

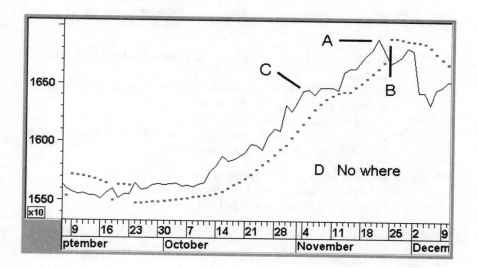

26. Which of the following parabolic lines has the largest initial acceleration factor?
  (A) The solid line.
  (B) The dashed line.
  (C) They are both the same; it is the maximum acceleration factor that causes the difference.
  (D) None of the above.

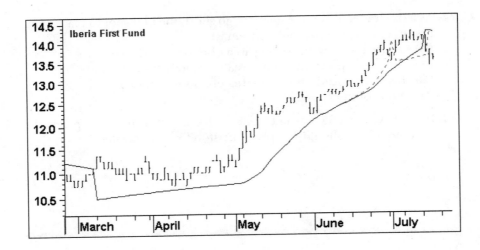

27. Where would be the best point to place a parabolic short stop, given the opportunity?
    (A) Place it immediately as the system triggers a signal, even though it is a long way from the entry point.
    (B) Wait for the price to rally to limit the risk.
    (C) Wait for the price to rally toward the parabolic line, which is also now within the vicinity of a downtrend line.

28. When does the price move outside of the price projection band?
    (A) Whenever it makes a new high for the calculated timespan.
    (B) Whenever the price rises or falls by more than 30 percent.
    (C) Never.
    (D) Soon after it crosses a moving average.

29. The price projection oscillator is:
    (A) The derivative of the stochastic indicator.
    (B) A way of displaying the price projection band, but as an oscillator.
    (C) A derivative of the RSI.
    (D) An oscillator derived from a deviation from a simple moving average.

30. What is the best way to use a price projection oscillator?
    (A) With trendline analysis, and overlaying two oscillators calculated with similar timespans.
    (B) With overbought/oversold crossovers.
    (C) With peak-and-trough analysis.
    (D) With trendline, overbought/oversold bands, and the overlaying of two oscillators calculated with widely differing timespans.

31. What benefit is derived from considering an r-squared indicator along with a price projection band?
   (A) They offer two pieces of evidence that a trend may be in the process of changing.
   (B) They offer two pieces of evidence that the trend has reversed.
   (C) Because the r-squared is an almost infallible indicator.
   (D) Because reversals in the r-squared from a high reading always result in a trend reversal, however small.

Quiz Answers

Chapters 1–12

1. (A) Yes, this is the correct answer.
    (B) No, A is the correct answer.

2. (A) No, D is the correct answer.
    (B) No, D is the correct answer.
    (C) No, D is the correct answer.
    (D) Yes, this is the correct answer.

3. (A) No, the linear slope is experiencing an extreme swing more indicative of a bear market.
    (B) Yes, the linear slope is experiencing an extreme swing indicative of a bear market.

4. (A) No, B is the correct answer.
    (B) Yes, this is the correct answer because the linear slope is very overbought and stabilizing.

5. (A) Yes, this is the correct answer.
    (B) No, A is the correct answer. The r-square only measures whether a market has directional characteristics.
    (C) No, A is the correct answer. The r-square only measures whether a market has directional characteristics.
    (D) No, A is the correct answer.

6. (A) No, this is true with the benefit of hindsight but was not known at the time.
    (B) Yes, this is the correct answer. However, because the price was in a strong linear bull trend, it did not respond to the r-square signal.
    (C) No, the signal could have been followed by a consolidation.

7. (A) Although this is true, B is the more complete answer.
    (B) Yes, this is correct because the r-square has been plotted inversely.
    (C) No, B is the correct answer because the r-square has been plotted inversely.

8. (A) No, it merely indicates that the price is likely to trend. The new trend could be down.

(B) No, it merely indicates that the price is likely to trend. The new trend could be up.

(C) Yes, this is the correct answer.

9. (A) No, it assumes that they close near the high of the session.

(B) Although this is correct, D is the more complete answer.

(C) Although this is correct, D is the more complete answer.

(D) Yes, this is the correct answer.

10. (A) Yes, this is the correct answer.

(B) No, the Chaikin relies on volume for its calculations.

11. (A) No, C is the correct answer.

(B) No, C is the correct answer.

(C) Yes, this is the correct answer.

(D) No, C is the correct answer.

12. (A) No, this is not a divergence. B is the correct answer.

(B) Yes, this is the correct answer.

(C) No, this is a not divergence because the price is higher at the second bottom. B is the correct answer.

(D) No, this is a not divergence because the price is higher at the second bottom. B is the correct answer.

13. (A) No, C is the correct answer.

(B) No, C is the correct answer.

(C) Yes, this is the correct answer.

(D) No, C is the correct answer.

14. (A) Yes, this is the correct answer.

(B) No, they are not. A is the correct answer.

(C) That is true, but it has nothing to do with the question. A is the correct answer.

(D) No, A is the correct answer.

15. (A) Yes, this is the correct answer because the oscillator is indicating a selling climax.

(B) No, A is the correct answer.

(C) No, A is the correct answer.

(D) No, A is the correct answer.

16. (A) No, although this is correct, D is the more complete answer.

(B) No, although this is correct, D is the more complete answer.

(C) No, although this is correct, D is the more complete answer.

(D) Yes, this is the correct answer.

17. (A) Although this is true, B is the more complete answer.

   (B) Yes, this is the correct answer.

   (C) No, B is the correct answer.

   (D) Although this is correct, B is the more complete answer.

18. (A) Yes, this is the correct answer because the volume oscillator is "overbought" and the price oscillator is oversold.

   (B) No, A is the correct answer because the volume oscillator reaches its extreme when the price oscillator is above zero. This indicates that this selling pressure did not result in much of a decline.

   (C) No, the price oscillator does not even come close to the type of extreme reading associated with a selling climax. A is the correct answer.

   (D) No, A is a selling climax.

19. (A) No, the trend is too extended and the volume is shrinking.

   (B) No, the situation looks weak because the price oscillator is overbought and the volume is shrinking because the volume oscillator is below zero. However, it is important to wait for the trendline in the price to break first.

   (C) Yes, the situation looks weak because the price oscillator is overbought and volume is shrinking, but the price is still above the trendline. When it is violated, that is the signal to sell.

20. (A) No, the ROC of volume is merely telling us that volume is declining as the rectangle is forming. This is perfectly natural.

   (B) No, the ROC of volume is merely telling us that volume is declining as the rectangle is forming. This is perfectly natural.

   (C) Yes, the ROC of volume is merely telling us that volume is declining as the rectangle is forming. This is perfectly natural. Therefore, the volume rate-of-change indicator is giving no indication of the direction of the breakout.

21. (A) No, the upper one is calculated using the percent method of calculation and the lower series uses the subtraction approach.

   (B) Yes, the upper one is calculated using the percent method of calculation and the lower series uses the subtraction approach.

   (C) No, the upper one is calculated using the percent method of calculation and the lower series uses the subtraction approach.

   (D) No, the upper one is calculated using the percent method of calculation and the lower series uses the subtraction approach.

22. (A) This would be far too volatile a series and would not be much different from a histogram. C is the correct answer.

(B) These averages are far too close to bring out the volume rhythms.

(C) Yes, this is the correct answer.

(D) No, these timeframes are far too long to measure most intermediate trends. C is the correct answer.

23. (A) No, C is the correct answer.

(B) No, the ROC is not. C is the correct answer.

(C) Yes, this is the correct answer.

(D) No, C is the correct answer.

24. (A) Although this is true, D is the more complete answer.

(B) Although this is true, D is the more complete answer.

(C) Although this is true, D is the more complete answer.

(D) Yes, this is the correct answer.

25. (A) No, the situation is encouraging, but the price needs to rally above the downtrend line first. D is the correct answer.

(B) No, it is too late to sell short. D is the correct answer.

(C) No, this price is a downtrend. It could go down further because the price has not yet broken above the downtrend line. D is the correct answer.

(D) Yes, this is the correct answer.

26. (A) No, B is the correct answer.

(B) Yes, they work quite well in this period, so this is the correct answer.

(C) No, there are too many zero crossover whipsaw signals. B is the correct answer.

(D) No, B is the correct answer.

27. (A) No, D is the correct answer.

(B) No, both series are constrained by the calculation, the RSI by 0 to 100 and Chande by ± 50.

(C) No, D is the correct answer.

(D) Yes, this is the correct answer.

28. (A) No, D is the correct answer.

(B) No, this is not true. D is the correct answer.

(C) This is normally true, but it is not the major difference. D is the correct answer.

(D) Yes, this is the correct answer.

29. (A) No, the cluster rule requires the DMI to move above the 80 level three times in 3 months and to retreat below 70 after each peak.
(B) Yes, this is correct because the cluster rule requires the DMI to move above the 80 level three times in 3 months and to retreat below 70 after each peak.

30. (A) Yes, this is correct because the cluster rule requires the DMI to move above the 80 level three times in 3 months and to retreat below 70 after each peak.
(B) This is incorrect because the cluster rule requires the DMI to move above the 80 level three times in 3 months and to retreat below 70 after each peak.

31. (A) Yes, this is the correct answer.
(B) No, A is the correct answer.

32. (A) No, there are too many whipsaws. C is the correct answer.
(B) No, there are too many signals. C is the correct answer.
(C) Yes, this is the correct answer.
(D) No, C is the correct answer.

33. (A) Yes, this is the correct answer.
(B) No, A is the correct answer.

34. (A) No, they both have the same constraints. C is the correct answer.
(B) No, the RMI also requires a momentum factor. C is the correct answer.
(C) Yes, this is the correct answer.
(D) No, C is the correct answer.

35. (A) Yes, this is the correct answer.
(B) No, this indicator is constrained by the 0/100 combination and so cannot experience such conditions. A is the correct answer.

36. (A) No, D is the correct answer.
(B) No, D is the correct answer.
(C) No, this would eliminate all of the signals. D is the correct answer.
(D) Yes, this is the correct answer. The longer timespan will have the effect of smoothing the appearance of this specific indicator.

Chapters 13–25

1. (A) No, the payoff index requires open interest in its calculation and this is not available for individual stocks.
   (B) No, the payoff index requires open interest in its calculation and this is not available for commodities that trade on a spot basis.
   (C) No, the payoff index requires open interest in its calculation and this is not available for market averages.
   (D) Yes, this is the correct answer.

2. (A) Although this is true, D is the more complete answer.
   (B) Although this is true, D is the more complete answer.
   (C) Although this is true, D is the more complete answer.
   (D) Yes, this is the correct answer.

3. (A) No, B is the correct answer.
   (B) Yes, this is the correct answer.
   (C) No, B is the correct answer.

4. (A) No, C is the correct answer.
   (B) No, C is the correct answer.
   (C) Yes, this is the correct answer.
   (D) No, C is the correct answer.

5. (A) True, but C is the more complete answer.
   (B) No, C is the correct answer.
   (C) Yes, this is the correct answer because the inertia has just given a sell signal by crossing below the 50 level. Also, it is possible to construct a small head-and-shoulders top for the price.

6. (A) No, C is the correct answer.
   (B) No, C is the correct answer.
   (C) Yes, this is the correct answer.
   (D) No, C is the correct answer.

7. (A) No, D is the correct answer.
   (B) No, D is the correct answer.
   (C) No, D is the correct answer.
   (D) Yes, this is the correct answer.

8. (A) No, the Qstick requires the opening price and cannot be plotted with this data series, which does not record the opening price.
   (B) No, the Qstick requires the opening price and cannot be plotted with this data series, which does not record the opening price.
   (C) No, the Qstick requires the opening price and cannot be plotted with this data series, which does not record the opening price.
   (D) Yes, this is the correct answer because the Qstick requires the opening price in its calculation.

9. (A) No, it will be difficult to find periods when you can construct a
meaningful trendline, but *never* is too strong a word.

(B) It will be difficult to find periods when you can construct a
meaningful trendline, but *never* is too strong a word. This is,
therefore, the correct answer.

10. (A) No, because a reverse divergence involves two peaks or troughs in
the oscillator and price. In this case, the smoothing in the TRIX
calculation is delaying the reversal to the upside, a perfectly
normal phenomenon.

(B) Yes, this is correct because the lag in the TRIX is due to the
smoothing that merely delays its reversal point.

11. (A) No, C is the correct answer.

(B) No, C is the correct answer.

(C) Yes, this is the correct answer.

(D) No, C is the correct answer.

12. (A) Yes, this is the correct answer.

(B) No, this is a true statement.

13. (A) No, C is the correct answer.

(B) No, C is the correct answer because the trend could change to
sideways.

(C) Yes, this is the correct answer.

(D) No, C is the correct answer.

14. (A) Not necessarily. The rising ADX merely indicates that the price
will experience some directional movement, which could be
down, too.

(B) Not necessarily. The rising ADX merely indicates that the price
will experience some directional movement, which could be up,
too.

(C) No, D is the correct answer.

(D) Yes, this is the correct answer. The one thing we can rule out is a
sideways trading range.

15. (A) Yes, this is the correct answer.

(B) No, A is the correct answer.

(C) No, A is the correct answer.

16. (A) No, B is the correct answer.

(B) Yes, this is the correct answer.

17. (A) Yes, this is the correct answer.
   (B) No, all that is being signaled is a probable trend change.
   (C) No, all that is being signaled is a probable trend change. A is the correct answer.
   (D) No, A is the correct answer.

18. (A) No, B is the correct answer because the ADX can never go above 100.
   (B) Yes, this is the correct answer because the ADX can never experience a reading above 100.
   (C) No, B is the correct answer because the ADX can never go above 100.
   (D) No, B is the correct answer because the ADX can never go above 100.

19. (A) Yes, this is the correct answer.
   (B) No, A is the correct answer.
   (C) No, A is the correct answer.
   (D) No, the +DI never goes below zero. A is the correct answer.

20. (A) No, because the ADX had reversed direction and the −DI has crossed above the +DI.
   (B) No, because the −DI has crossed above the +DI.
   (C) Yes, this is the correct answer.

21. (A) Yes, this is the correct answer.
   (B) No, A is the correct answer.
   (C) No, A is the correct answer.
   (D) No, A is the correct answer because sometimes a trend change, as opposed to a trend reversal, is signaled.

22. (A) No, C is the correct answer.
   (B) No, C is the correct answer.
   (C) Yes, this is the correct answer because the CSI has peaked from an extreme level, thereby indicating a change in trend. In this case, it happened to be from up to sideways.
   (D) No, C is the correct answer.

23. (A) No, B is the correct answer.
   (B) Yes, this is the correct answer.
   (C) No, B is the correct answer.
   (D) No, B is the correct answer.

24. (A) Yes, this is the correct answer.
   (B) No, A is the correct answer.
   (C) No, A is the correct answer.
   (D) No, A is the correct answer.

25. (A) No, if you firmly believe the direction of the main trend is up, you
should not be shorting, since the near-term price movements that
go against the direction of the main trend usually end up in
unprofitable situations. D is the correct answer.

(B) No, if you firmly believe the direction of the main trend is up, you
should not be shorting, since the near-term price movements that
go against the direction of the main trend usually end up in
unprofitable situations. D is the correct answer.

(C) No, if you firmly believe the direction of the main trend is up, you
should not be shorting, since the near-term price movements that
go against the direction of the main trend usually end up in
unprofitable situations. D is the correct answer.

(D) Yes, this is the correct answer.

26. (A) Yes, this is the correct answer.

(B) No, A is the correct answer.

(C) No, A is the correct answer.

(D) No, A is the correct answer.

27. (A) No, unless you are acting on every signal.

(B) No, C is the correct answer.

(C) Yes, this is the correct answer. If such a situation develops, it gives
you the best of both worlds, since the parabolic line and trendline
reinforce each other as resistance points.

28. (A) No, C is the correct answer.

(B) No, C is the correct answer.

(C) Yes, this is the correct answer.

(D) No, C is the correct answer.

29. (A) No, B is the correct answer.

(B) Yes, this is the correct answer.

(C) No, B is the correct answer.

(D) No, B is the correct answer.

30. (A) No, D is the correct answer.

(B) No, D is the correct answer.

(C) No, D is the correct answer.

(D) Yes, this is the correct answer.

31. (A) Yes, this is the correct answer.

(B) No, this is not definite. Also, the trend may have changed from up
or down to sideways. It does not necessarily have to reverse. A is
the correct answer.

(C) No, it is good, but certainly not infallible. A is the correct answer.

(D) That is not correct. A is the correct answer.

Index

A

Acceleration factor, 209, 215–216
ADX, 178–180
    ADX and the DI's, 186–190
    extreme ADX readings,
      195–199
    high and low readings, 181–184
    low readings, 199–202
    overlaying the ADX on the DI's,
      191–192
Aroon, 151–156
    concept of, 151
    interpretation of, 151–154
    and moving averages, 154–157

B

Bollinger bands, 224
Business cycle (four-year), 26

C

Chaikin money flow indicator
  (CMF), 56–69
    concept of, 56
    divergences in, 56–62
    and trading ranges, 62–70

Chaunde,Tushar, 87, 151
Chaunde momentum
  oscillator(CMO), 86–96
    double Chaunde, 97
    vs. the ROC, 89
    vs. the RSI, 86–87
    smoothing and, 93–96
    and trendlines, 91–92
Churning, 52
Commodity Selection Index (CSI),
  204–206
Crash, 1987, 26

D

Demand Index, 71–85
    divergences in, 71–73
    and fluctuations around zero, 75
    interpretation of, 70–71
    and overbought/oversold
      crossovers, 77–78
    and price patterns and
      trendlines, 78–85
    and zero crossovers, 74
Directional Movement System:
    ADX, 178–180
    ADX and the DI's, 186–190

ADX high and low readings,
  181–184
ADX low readings, 199–202
and directional indicators
    (DI's), 177, 184–186
and directional movement
    defined, 172–176
extreme ADX readings,
    195–199
and extreme point rule, 190–191
overlaying the ADX on the DI's,
    191–192
and plus and minus DM, 173
and smoothing the DI's, 193–195
and true range, 176–177
Dorsey, Donald, 167
Dynamic Momentum Index
  (DMI), 110–120
    and cluster rule, 113–116
    and smoothing, 117–118
    vs. the RSI, 110–113
    and ten-day MA, 118–121
    and trendlines, 120
Double whammy, 52

F–I

False breakouts, 103

Herrick, John, 131
Herrick Payoff Index, 127–140
    concept of, 127–129
    divergences in, 133–134
    extreme swings in, 134–138
    and moving averages, 138–140
    and overbought/oversold,
        crossovers, 131–133

and trendlines, 133–134
and zero crossovers, 129–131

Inertia Indicator, 167

K

Klinger oscillator, 121–126
    basic concepts of, 121
    divergences in, 125–126
    vs. 89-period EMA, 124–125
    and smoothing, 126–7
Klinger, Stephen, 122

L

Linear downtrend, 100
Linear uptrend, 100
Linear regression, 1–3
Linear regression indicator, 4–9,
  18, 167
Linear regression line, 1–3
Linear regression slope, 10
    and long-term momentum,
        24–27
    and r-squared, 20–25

M–O

MACD, 121
Maximum acceleration factor, 213
Moving averages, 1, 4, 6, 8, 12, 25,
  27, 28, 34, 39, 42, 93, 118, 119,
  125, 238
    and Aroon, 154–156
    and Qstick, 159–162
    and Herrick Payoff, 138–140

Open interest, 127
Outside day, 71

P

Parabolic Indicator, 207–224
    and acceleration factor,
        209, 215–216
    advantages of, 207–208
    and guerilla trading with the
        parabolic, 219–222
    and how it works, 208–214
    and maximum acceleration
        factor, 214
    and stop and reverse system
        (SAR), 208, 209, 212
    and stop system only, 222–224
Peak-and-trough analysis, 156
Perpetual contract, 128–129
Price projection Bands, 225–231
    and r-squared, 227–229
    vs. price projection oscillators,
        232–233
    and weekly charts, 229–231
Price Projection Oscillator (PPO),
    232–241
    and arrangements, 236–238
    and overlaying, 235–236
    and r-squared, 238–241

Q

Qstick, 157–162
    concept of, 157–159
    price patterns of, 159–162
    and moving averages, 159–162

R

Raff regression channel, 225
Relative Momentum Index (RMI),
    97–109
    and arrangements, 105–108
    differing characteristics in
        bull and bear markets with,
        100–103
    vs. the RSI, 97–100,103–105
Relative Volatility Indicator (RVI),
    163–166,167
    concept of, 163–166
R-squared, 10–17
    and CMO, 94
    and linear slope indicator,
        20–25
    and price projection bands,
        227–229
    reversals from high
        readings, 10
    reversals from low
        readings, 11–12
    and trading ranges, 14–17,
        19–28
Rise over run, 18
ROC vs. Chaunde momentum
    oscillator, 89
RSI, 91,181,199
    vs. Chaunde momentum
        oscillator, 86–7
    vs. the dynamic momentum
        index, 110–112
    vs. relative momentum index,
        97–100, 103–105

S

Selling climax, 29, 32, 39, 45, 51, 55
Sibbet, Jim, 70
Stop and reverse system (SAR), 208, 209, 211

T

Trend deviation, 42
TRIX Index, 141–150
    calculation of, 141–145
    divergences in, 145–148
    and overboughts and oversolds, 145–148
    and weekly and monthly charts, 148–150
True range, 176–177

V–W

Volume leads price, 121
Volume oscillator, 42–56
    advantage of vs. volume ROC, 44
    calculation in, 42–45
    and combining with a price oscillator, 51–55
    and setting parameters, 46
Volume rate of change, 29–41
    and divergences, 31
    and smoothing, 33–36
    and subtraction method, 37–38

Wilder, Welles, 172, 194, 204, 207, 208, 216

About the Author

Martin J. Pring is the highly respected president of Pring Research (**www.pring.com**), editor of the newsletter *The Intermarket Review,* and one of today's most influential thought leaders in the world of technical analysis. Pring has written more than a dozen trading books and has contributed to *Barron's* and other national publications. He was awarded the Jack Frost Memorial Award from the Canadian Technical Analysts Society.

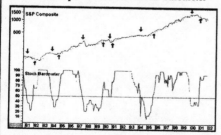

Installation
Instructions

This CD has an Autorun feature. Insert the CD into the CD-ROM drive and it will start automatically. Please allow sufficient time for loading.

If the Autorun feature does not work, insert the CD, open your CD-ROM drive and double-click on the Setup.exe icon. Then, access the program by clicking on Start, Programs, Pring and locate the icon for the tutorial title you are playing in the flyout.

1. We recommend not changing the default installation settings.
2. This program is best viewed using small fonts.
3. This CD is best viewed in 800 × 600 pixels and 256 colors.
4. For additional support, please go to Support at **www.pring.com**.

Advanced Technical Analysis CD Tutorials:

Learning the KST
Intro to Candlestick Charting
Tech's Guide to Day Trading
Breaking the Black Box
How to Select Stocks

MetaStock CD Tutorials:

Exploring MS Basic
Exploring MS Advanced
Super CD Companion
Indicator Companion
Market Analysis Companion
Selecting Stocks Using MetaStock

*Visit **http://www.pring.com** for info on these and other products.*

Pring Research, Inc.

1539 S. Orange Avenue, Sarasota, FL 34239
800-221-7514 • 941-364-5850
Internet: www.pring.com • E-mail: info@pring.com

SOFTWARE AND INFORMATION LICENSE

The software and information on this diskette (collectively referred to as the "Product") are the property of The McGraw-Hill Companies, Inc. ("McGraw-Hill") and are protected by both United States copyright law and international copyright treaty provision. You must treat this Product just like a book, except that you may copy it into a computer to be used and you may make archival copies of the Products for the sole purpose of backing up our software and protecting your investment from loss.

By saying "just like a book," McGraw-Hill means, for example, that the Product may be used by any number of people and may be freely moved from one computer location to another, so long as there is no possibility of the Product (or any part of the Product) being used at one location or on one computer while it is being used at another. Just as a book cannot be read by two different people in two different places at the same time, neither can the Product be used by two different people in two different places at the same time (unless, of course, McGraw-Hill's rights are being violated).

McGraw-Hill reserves the right to alter or modify the contents of the Product at any time.

This agreement is effective until terminated. The Agreement will terminate automatically without notice if you fail to comply with any provisions of this Agreement. In the event of termination by reason of your breach, you will destroy or erase all copies of the Product installed on any computer system or made for backup purposes and shall expunge the Product from your data storage facilities.

LIMITED WARRANTY

McGraw-Hill warrants the physical diskette(s) enclosed herein to be free of defects in materials and workmanship for a period of sixty days from the purchase date. If McGraw-Hill receives written notification within the warranty period of defects in materials or workmanship, and such notification is determined by McGraw-Hill to be correct, McGraw-Hill will replace the defective diskette(s). Send request to:

Customer Service
McGraw-Hill
Gahanna Industrial Park
860 Taylor Station Road
Blacklick, OH 43004-9615

The entire and exclusive liability and remedy for breach of this Limited Warranty shall be limited to replacement of defective diskette(s) and shall not include or extend any claim for or right to cover any other damages, including but not limited to, loss of profit, data, or use of the software, or special, incidental, or consequential damages or other similar claims, even if McGraw-Hill has been specifically advised as to the possibility of such damages. In no event will McGraw-Hill's liability for any damages to you or any other person ever exceed the lower of suggested list price or actual price paid for the license to use the Product, regardless of any form of the claim.

THE McGRAW-HILL COMPANIES, INC. SPECIFICALLY DISCLAIMS ALL OTHER WARRANTIES, EXPRESS OR IMPLIED, INCLUDING BUT NOT LIMITED TO, ANY IMPLIED WARRANTY OF MERCHANTABILITY OR FITNESS FOR A PARTICULAR PURPOSE. Specifically, McGraw-Hill makes no representation or warranty that the Product is fit for any particular purpose and any implied warranty of merchantability is limited to the sixty day duration of the Limited Warranty covering the physical diskette(s) only (and not the software or information) and is otherwise expressly and specifically disclaimed.

This Limited Warranty gives you specific legal rights; you may have others which may vary from state to state. Some states do not allow the exclusion of incidental or consequential damages, or the limitation on how long an implied warranty lasts, so some of the above may not apply to you.

This Agreement constitutes the entire agreement between the parties relating to use of the Product. The terms of any purchase order shall have no effect on the terms of this Agreement. Failure of McGraw-Hill to insist at any time on strict compliance with this Agreement shall not constitute a waiver of any rights under this Agreement. This Agreement shall be construed and governed in accordance with the laws of New York. If any provision of this Agreement is held to be contrary to law, that provision will be enforced to the maximum extent permissible and the remaining provisions will remain in force and effect.